Michael Whiting

Michael Whiting is an Anglican priest and an Archdeacon Emeritus in the Diocese of Adelaide. Prior to retiring in 2012, he was chaplain to the archbishop of Adelaide and archdeacon for education and formation. For over thirty years he led Roman Catholic and Anglican schools, his final appointment being as deputy headmaster and chaplain of St Peter's College, Adelaide. Since 2014, Michael has been a Visiting Research Fellow in History at the University of Adelaide.

The study of Bishop Augustus Short has been a special interest for many years. This volume was preceded by *Augustus Short and the Founding of the University of Adelaide*, commissioned and published by the University of Adelaide Press in 2014.

This book is available as a free fully searchable ebook from
www.adelaide.edu.au/press

AUGUSTUS SHORT

The early years of a modern educator

1802-1847

by

Michael Whiting

with a Foreword by

The Very Reverend Professor Martyn Percy

BARR SMITH PRESS
An imprint of
The University of Adelaide Press

Published in Adelaide by
University of Adelaide Press
Barr Smith Library
The University of Adelaide
South Australia 5005
press@adelaide.edu.au
www.adelaide.edu.au/press

The Barr Smith Press is an imprint of the University of Adelaide Press, under which titles about the history of the University are published. The University of Adelaide Press publishes peer reviewed scholarly books. It aims to maximise access to the best research by publishing works through the internet as free downloads and for sale as high quality printed volumes.

© 2018 Michael Whiting

This work is licenced under the Creative Commons Attribution-NonCommercial-NoDerivatives 4.0 International (CC BY-NC-ND 4.0) License. To view a copy of this licence, visit http://creativecommons.org/licenses/by-nc-nd/4.0 or send a letter to Creative Commons, 444 Castro Street, Suite 900, Mountain View, California, 94041, USA. This licence allows for the copying, distribution, display and performance of this work for non-commercial purposes providing the work is clearly attributed to the copyright holders. Address all inquiries to the Director at the above address.

For the full Cataloguing-in-Publication data please contact the National Library of Australia: cip@nla.gov.au

ISBN (paperback) 978-1-925261-69-1
ISBN (ebook: pdf) 978-1-925261-70-7
DOI: http://dx.doi.org/10.20851/short-educator

Book and cover design: Zoë Stokes

*Dedicated to Janine
for her ever loving-kindness (ḥesed' Heb.),
inspiration and encouragement.*

Contents

Foreword		XI
The Very Reverend Professor Martyn Percy		
Preface		XIII
1	**Westminster School 1807-20**	1
	Education in England	1
	Westminster School	2
	Life in the classroom	6
	Life outside the classroom	12
	Religious faith and practice	12
	King's Scholar	14
	Westminster and Short	17
2	**Student of Christ Church: Undergraduate 1820-23**	21
	Oxford University and Christ Church	23
	Social and religious life in Christ Church	27
	Academic life in Christ Church	30
	The tutor	33
	Thomas Vowler Short's influence and example	34
	The proctor	39
	The learning experience	40
	Collections	42
	Whither a new curriculum?	42
	Christ Church and Short	44

3	**Holy orders and teaching at Christ Church 1824-35**	47
	The path to ordination	49
	Charles Lloyd's influence and example	52
	The ordained life: A curacy 1827-28	60
	The ordained life: Teaching student 1828-35	62
4	**Reform and revival in Church and society 1800-50**	71
	Reform in England	73
	'No Peel'	74
	The 1830s	77
	English Christianity: Revivals and reforms	78
	Methodism and the Evangelicals	81
	Pamphleteering for Church reform	83
	The *Church Temporalities Act 1833*	86
	'The religious movement of 1833' begun in Oxford	88
5	**Rural vicar and Oxford matters 1835-47**	95
	Vicar of Ravensthorpe	95
	Select Preacher 1838	100
	The professor of poetry 1841	102
	Tract 90 (1841)	105
	WG Ward and the Convocation of 1845	108
	The Bampton lectures 1846	111
6	**A bishop of the colonial Church 1847**	115
	The other turning point of 1840-41	116
	Bishop Charles Blomfield's initiatives and influence	117
	Bishop Broughton and the Reverend Edward Coleridge	120
	A diocese for South Australia?	124
	Miss Angela Burdett Coutts and a benefaction	125

A diocese of Adelaide and an invitation to Augustus Short	131
The consecration in Westminster Abbey	142
Departing for South Australia	145
Postscript	151
The view and vision from Christ Church Meadow	
Appendix A	155
Biographical excerpts from *The Westminster School Register*	
Appendix B	157
Augustus Short and Henry Bull	
Appendix C	161
Excerpts from the *Colonial Church Chronicle*	
References	169
Index of selected terms	181
Acknowledgements	185

Foreword

Christ Church, Oxford, has a proud history of founding higher education establishments. Halford Mackinder founded an extension college of Christ Church at Reading in 1892, and this has now grown into a truly global university. Two decades before, and on the other side of the world, Augustus Short, first Anglican Bishop of Adelaide, was the pivotal intellectual and strategic founder, and became the first vice-chancellor, of the University of Adelaide in 1874. That university, Australia's third, was founded by a spirit of benevolent, altruistic and entrepreneurial educational vision, inclusive of equal education for women and of the granting of science degrees. This crucial role of Augustus Short was well documented in Michael Whiting's companion volume, *Augustus Short and the Founding of the University of Adelaide* (2014).

Short's spirit of adventurous innovation and creativity in education owed much to his experiences at Christ Church, first as an undergraduate and then as a teacher between 1820-35. This volume, *Augustus Short: the early years of a modern educator 1802-1847*, details how Short's wisdom, and enterprise in education, arose from his early education at Westminster School, and then his university life at Christ Church. Here he came under the influence of some stirring intellectuals of his day, especially Professor Charles Lloyd, Thomas Vowler Short, WE Gladstone, and the initial leaders of the Oxford Movement, John Henry Newman and Edward Bouverie Pusey. During these formative years, Short found himself a participant in some of the events of the most intense period (1820-50) of social, political, cultural and religious reforms experienced in England for generations. Christ Church and Oxford were central to these vibrant and challenging times.

This volume brings to life how Augustus Short was maturing into an impressive churchman, especially devoted to education, in the years prior to his arrival in South Australia in 1847, at age forty-five. It documents for the first time the early Short story, and it is equally an Oxford — and Christ Church story. Short believed that education was character forming and provided the satisfaction of curiosity, as well as the means of social and cultural advancement for all — his own scholarships at school and university enabled him to realise education's enduring gifts and he was to amply repay those benefits in his later years in South Australia. I thoroughly commend Michael Whiting's outstanding book. It represents a very real contribution, not just to the history of Christ Church and one of its distinguished alumni, but also to the history of a modern educator in colonial South Australia.

The Very Reverend Professor Martyn Percy
The Dean, Christ Church, Oxford

Preface

The focus of this study, intended for the general reader interested in Australian religious history, is the early life of Augustus Short before he arrived in South Australia on 28 December 1847 as the first bishop of Adelaide in the United Church of England and Ireland. Born on 11 June 1802 at Bickham House near Exeter, Devon, he was forty-five years old at the time he embarked for South Australia on 1 September 1847.

Two previous biographies of Short have been written. In 1887, FT Whitington published *Augustus Short, First Bishop of Adelaide: A Chapter of Colonial Church History*. In 1974, Judith Brown published *Augustus Short, D.D. Bishop of Adelaide*. Short's early years, however, are relatively unexplored in these biographies. Recounted in this volume are many key experiences and influences, people and events, which shaped Short before 1847.

Most biographies take an approach similar to portraiture in art; this volume errs towards that of the landscape. Ever-changing foregrounds, middle- and backgrounds are delineated; figures come into view and fade; the atmosphere is at once rich in drama, and then appears tranquil. All the while, we view Short coming to maturity amidst the embracing presence of the established United Church of England and Ireland.

Christ Church, Oxford, featured prominently in Short's life from the age of eighteen to forty-five and thus it is a recurring presence in this study. Its impact on Short (and later through him on the society of South Australia) is recounted here — at times a dominant presence, then an understated background, but always there. Short cherished his learning, at both Westminster School and Christ Church, and became expert in using the intricacies of words in English and the Classical languages to express his thoughts and understandings. Even in adolescence, his learning soon led into careful and prudent actions. His habits of behaviour and belonging matured in early adulthood to focus on his religious beliefs. All the time, his character — his beliefs maturing at the core — concerned him as he came to believe that it was the foundation of his destiny. In his way — orthodox, traditional, conservative — he grew to believe that his destiny revolved around obedience to God, trust in His Providence, and assurance of His love. Ordained and consecrated a bishop of the established Church a brief two months before embarkation, he thrilled to the challenge of his calling. His first forty-five years had prepared him well.

1

Westminster School 1807-20

Education in England

At the beginning of the nineteenth century, throughout England, there existed a well-established approach to educating some young boys beyond elementary education, a network of schools often called Public Schools. These schools were all independent, privately endowed and self-governing, and tended to be the preserve of the landed aristocracy and the socially prominent of the cities. Schools such as Eton, Winchester and Westminster enjoyed centuries of history and were often distinctive in having boarding facilities, a reliance upon the Classics in their curriculum, some delegation of school government to senior boys, a practice of corporal punishment, fagging as a tradition, and close ties to the Universities of Oxford and Cambridge. All of these public schools had a religious foundation, usually linked with the established United Church of England and Ireland, and their social intention was to prepare boys for the life of a gentleman, and to help them master, during their adolescent years, skills of social adaptability and self-reliance (Chandos 1984, p. 28).

However, such schools were not immune from the rapid changes within England of the first half of the nineteenth century. The pressure from religious quarters for reformation in education built as the century progressed. In 1802, Dr Thomas Rennell, Master of the Temple, criticised the incompatibility of a concentration on pagan literature in the Classics with the Christian doctrine espoused in the chapels of such schools. At Westminster School, before 1820, there was an annual performance of a play by Terence; often, *The Eunuchus* was the chosen text and it was sometimes criticised on moral grounds. Nevertheless, the annual production continued well into the 1840s.

In the *Edinburgh Review* of 1810, Sydney Smith published an article, 'Remarks on the System of Education in Public Schools', which took up the theme of reformation of such schools and government intervention. On another level, in 1816, newly elected MP in the House of Commons Henry Brougham, a colleague of Sydney Smith, succeeded in having appointed a select committee to inquire into the education of the lower orders and the 'abuses of charities connected with education of the poor'. The intention was clear, as under the terms of reference the committee's warrant could be taken to include the public schools, for these were, technically, endowed grammar schools, expressly established by the will of the founder in some cases, 'to serve what were called "*pauperes et indigentes*" [poor and indigent scholars]' (Burgess 1958, pp. 36-8).

Most long-established Public Schools maintained a belief that the classical curriculum in fact provided a completeness to the education of the young scholar and gentleman. Latin, Greek and mathematics were the heart of the Public Schools' curriculum, training the mental faculties, and more importantly, forming character. Many reformers still maintained, as Richard Lovell Edgeworth had in 1809, writing in essays on 'Professional Education' in the *Edinburgh Review* that

> [t]he principal defect in the present system of our great schools, is that they devote too large a portion of time to Latin and Greek. It is true, that the attainment of a classical literature is highly desirable; but it should not, or rather need not, be the exclusive object of boys during eight or nine years. (In Vaughan & Archer 1971, p. 47)

The questions of what constituted appropriate knowledge and how the curriculum ought to be organised in both elementary and secondary education became strongly disputed. In an atmosphere of political tensions and social reform, the pendulum of debate swung from considering education as a way of ensuring stability in society to considering education as a means of social reform. The former view was held largely by the governing class, which sought to enhance the hierarchical class structure of the English nation.

Westminster School

> Westminster School, the College of St Peter at Westminster, bears its character upon its face; it nestles under the wing of the famous abbey, it was founded by pious men centuries ago, and it retains a multitude of traditions and not a few old-world customs that perpetuate an atmosphere of mediaevalism mingled with modernism. (Shore 1910, p. 1)

When Westminster School began, and who founded it, is unknown. However, it evolved from a school integral to the Benedictine Monastery of Westminster, the Abbey of St Peter. This monastery was dissolved by Henry VIII in 1540, and the school was mentioned in the *Booke of the Erection of the King's Newe College* at the time of the surrender, hence the beginnings of the royal designation for the founding members, who were known as 'King's Scholars' (Carleton 1965, p. 2). Westminster School was described in books of the time as 'a publique schoole for Grammar, Rhethorick, Poetrie, and for the Latin and Greek Languages' (Thornbury 1878, p. 463). From 1560 the school, following the directions of Queen Elizabeth, had been under the responsibility, and financed from the revenues, of the dean and chapter of Westminster Abbey.[1] The foundation put in place by Queen Elizabeth thus comprised an ecclesiastical and an academic partnership, with the dean and select clergy controlling both entities, as at Eton and Winchester (Carleton 1965, p. 5). This situation still prevailed during Augustus Short's time and the collegiate school was officially termed The Royal College of St Peter in Westminster.

The location of the school as a part of the abbey buildings lent a connection of social standing to the school which even older foundations, such as Eton and Winchester, could only envy (Staunton 1865, p. 116). Likewise, the proximity to the Houses of Parliament brought privileges: in Short's time the speaker of the house, Mr Speaker Abbott (1802-17), an old Westminster boy, reserved seats in the House of Commons for pupils from the school so they might attend debates.

The buildings of Westminster School, in Augustus Short's day, were to the south of the abbey, grouped around the Dean's Yard and the School Yard (Little Dean's Yard). The imposing dormitory of the monks became the school where pupils were taught; the Abbot's Dining Hall became the College Hall; and the Abbey Church the School Chapel:

> Excluding the dingy-looking boarding-houses, the school buildings are quite worthy of the Abbey to which they belong. First and foremost is the School. There is no nobler Hall in England, save its neighbour, Westminster Hall. For nearly three hundred years (1591-1883) all classes were held there. It is nearly one hundred feet in length, and was found large enough for the teaching of 400 boys. It was divided into the Upper and the Under School by a curtain. (Minchin 1901, p. 200)

One can only speculate what a seven-year-old boy made of Westminster School when he first saw it in 1809. Augustus was born on 11 June 1802, the third son of Charles Short, a London barrister, who intended that his son would enter the legal profession. (At the age of fourteen, Charles Short had entered Augustus for a future legal life in the Middle Temple; see his reminiscences, SLSA, PRG 160/32.) In choosing Westminster for Augustus, Charles was influenced by a tradition within the extended Short family. The brother of Charles was William Short (the Archdeacon of Cornwall in April 1813 — a significant post within the Diocese of Exeter); William's son, Thomas

---

1   As a 'collegiate church', Westminster Abbey was endowed with a governing chapter, but unlike cathedrals, which also had chapters, it was not a bishop's see but came directly under the monarch's authority, as a 'royal peculiar'.

Figure 1.1 Little Dean's Yard — the central open space of the school, with the dormitories to the right.
Source: 'Little Dean's Yard', Westminster School, illustration by GR Sarjent, 1837. Reproduced from a postcard in the author's possession.

Figure 1.2 The room at Westminster School referred to as 'School', built in the 1090s as the monks' dormitory. Students would go 'up School' to attend lessons in this room.
Source: 'School c.1840', watercolour by GR Sarjent. Reproduced from a postcard in the author's possession.

Vowler (1790-1872), had preceded his younger cousins, Mayow and Augustus, to Westminster School in 1803. Mayow, a brother two years older than Augustus, had also been admitted in 1809. His father noted in his reminiscences: '[P]laced at Westminster at the same time with Mayow, July 1809, but finding him too young I sent Augustus in February 1810 to Mr Adkins, Langley Broom School' (SLSA, PRG160/32).[2]

The parents had made a premature move in 1809 by enrolling Augustus as a boarder and probably hoping the older brother would comfort and protect the younger one. Augustus was withdrawn and readmitted to the school in 1811. The headmaster at the time was William Carey (1769-1846 — he was later bishop of Exeter, and then bishop of St Asaph). John Sargeaunt (1898, pp. 214-5) wrote:

> The School had never rejected very young boys, but in Carey's time the number of them was perhaps larger than before ... Infantile games flourished among them. A contemporary declamation names the top, the hoop, and the marble, to which Lord John Russell adds the pea-shooter. It might be thought that the tender children, who could delight in such sports, would receive some protection from their Masters. Carey took a different view of education, and the infants had to fight their own battles. Nor were the battles merely metaphorical. Carey encouraged fighting, and a 'mill' in 'fighting green' was accounted an adequate reason for adjourning school. 'When I was a boy at Westminster,' wrote the Bishop of Adelaide, 'the boys fought one another, they fought the Masters, the Masters fought them, they fought outsiders; in fact, we were ready to fight everybody'. Short himself, as a child of seven, was compelled to do battle with a chimney-sweep, and to fight the only friend he had in the School.[3]

Short's own words were:

> [I]t shows the rough discipline to which in those days the simplicity of childhood was exposed when I recount how, as a point of honor, I was urged to fight an offending chimney-sweep, and in order to prove my courage, to engage another little fellow of my own size and age — my only acquaintance and friend in the school. In both cases I came off victor; but in the latter instance, I am happy to say, the battle only cemented a friendship which endured through the rest of my school days and in to college life at Christ Church, Oxford. (Short 1882 in Whitington 1887, p. 5)[4]

---

2 Mayow attended Christ Church and then was called to the Bar at the Middle Temple on 13 June 1833, eventually serving as a magistrate in Jamaica. He died in 1868.

3 John Sargeaunt was classics teacher at Westminster 1890-1922. He was born in 1857 and died in 1922.

4 It is reasonable to believe that Short is referring here to John Edward Jeffreys, eldest son of Rev. John Jeffreys. John Edward was at Westminster with Short and admitted as a King's Scholar in 1815 at the age of fourteen. He was elected to a studentship at Christ Church, Oxford, in May 1820, alongside Short. They both excelled in the Classics and Jeffreys obtained a second-class degree in 1823 when Short was given a first-class. Jeffreys died suddenly on 22 June 1824.

Flashes of indiscipline abounded: Tanner refers to students resorting to 'the prize ring, the cockpit, and the rat-catchers' den', and states that Lord de Ros — admitted the same year as Short, in 1809 — kept fighting cocks 'in the space between the floor of the Dormitory of his boarding-house and the ceiling of the room below' (1934, p. 37).

A central element of the school culture was fagging. Sargeaunt records:

> Fagging was a no less onerous duty, but never obtained from the authorities the recognition accorded to the art of self-defence. Lord Albemarle relates how he had to brush the clothes, clean the boots, and fill the basin of his fag-master — a kinsman who was less than kind. Even with a gentle master a fag lived a slave's life. [Recollecting later, when he was bishop of Adelaide], Short admits that his misery found some alleviation from the kindness of Charles Longley, afterwards archbishop of Canterbury whose 'breakfast fag' he was; but in his old age avowed that his first year at School was the most wretched in his life. When, in the early days of the colony, carpet-curates in South Australia complained to their bishop of the hardness of their work, 'You ought,' he said, 'to have been a fag at Westminster'. (1898, p. 223)

Many years later, in 1882, when in retirement and visiting a refuge for homeless boys in London, Short recalled: 'Why, those boys' beds are much more comfortable than mine was in my old Westminster school days, for they have bolsters and I had a log of wood' (in Whitington 1887, p. 267). Short was here referring to the fact that duties for the fag included carrying a log to the dormitory for use as firewood when cooking breakfast the following morning; overnight, the fag used this log, wrapped in his clothes, as a pillow (p. 267).

Once a boy became a King's Scholar, however, fagging sometimes took on a different tone. Short reminisced in 1882 that fagging then became a

> euphemism assimilated to that of patron and client under the old Roman law … [I]t often was the basis of lasting goodfellowship. At the Pan-Anglican Conference of 1878 my friend the Primus of Scotland [Robert Eden, 1804-86; Bishop of Moray, Ross and Caithness, 1851-86; Primus, 1862-86] reminded me that he had been my 'junior' in St. Peter's College, Westminster, whereupon I immediately 'fagged' him to get me some luncheon, with which order he very good-humouredly complied. (In Whitington 1887, p. 4)

Life in the classroom

Short's time at the school coincided with a peak in enrolment, not exceeded again in the nineteenth century: 317 students in 1812 and 324 students by 1818 (Shore 1910, p. 43). Pupils at Westminster were divided into set groups: there were forty King's/Queen's Scholars (educated free); four boys on a Foundation (scholarship) created by Bishop Williams; Town boys, who were either full boarders or half boarders; and Home boarders. The greatest honour was to be elected as a King's/Queen's Scholar, all of whom were to be under fifteen years of age on the 1 January in the year of election, and to have been at least a year previously at the school. Such election meant entrance to the college, a distinct part of the school. The King's Scholars lived together in the college, and were distinguished by a cap, a gown 'made of thick black cloth', 'a double-breasted waistcoat', a white neckcloth and 'drab knee-breeches and white stockings and buckled shoes' (Tanner 1934, p. 72). In the abbey they wore white surplices, as being part of the foundation of the collegiate church.

The ambition of Short's parents in returning him to the school when they did was to secure the distinguished prize of a King's Scholar. As Augustus's father, Charles Short, reminisced later: 'At Westminster 1816, Augustus got 4th into College, not then 14 years old' (SLSA, PRG 160/32). Applications for King's Scholar were examined by the electors — the dean of Westminster Abbey, the dean of Christ Church, Oxford, and the master of Trinity College, Cambridge, and assisting them were two other examiners, called posers, with the headmaster. Generally there were twenty to thirty candidates, with the mutual competition, called the 'challenge', extending over seven or eight weeks (Staunton 1865, pp. 119, 135):

Figure 1.3 Short's King's Scholar dress, 1816-20.
Source: Reproduced with permission from Schools and colleges of England, R Ackermann, 1816.

> The Challenge ... an oral examination for admission to College protracted over many weeks between February and May. In the presence of the Head Master as judge, the 'Minor Candidates' challenged each other on translation and grammatical rules based on the set texts, Ovid and the Greek Epigrams, so that each day their rank order changed according to the dexterity of questions and answers. The candidates employed 'helps', boys already in College, who took on the task of preparing the

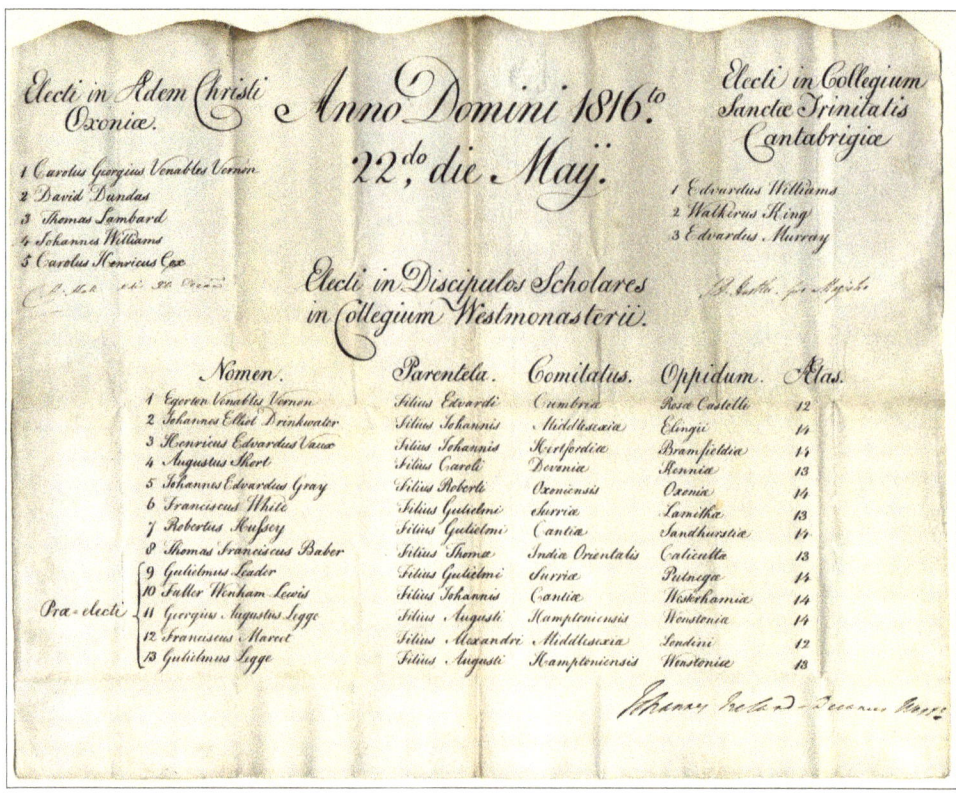

Figure 1.4   Original record of Augustus Short's election as a King's Scholar 1816.
Source: Reproduced by kind assistance of the Governing Body of Westminster School.

> challengers for their long ordeal, in return for a reward of about 15 pounds when the exam was complete. The helps were present, rather like counsel, to argue niceties of interpretation before the Head Master, and to seek the favourable arbitration for their own candidate. (Field 1987, p. 69)

Short recalled in 1882:

> The challenge … began from the bottom. In the morning a Greek, and the afternoon a Latin passage, selected by the head-master and prepared beforehand, was to be construed and parsed by the lowest candidate but one, and whose place could be taken by the lowest if the former was corrected by him three times, and he himself could pass in turn the like ordeal of questioning without similar failure … after eight weeks competition I got in fourth. (In Whitington 1887, p. 4)

It was just as well Short was fourth on the list of successful King's Scholars: if he had been first, and 'elected head into College', he would have been carried around the precincts of the school in triumph and recorded as 'the Liberty Boy' (Tanner 1934, p. 66).

A former headmaster, Henry Liddell, gave evidence to the Public Schools Commission in 1860 on his opinion of the value of 'the challenge':

> [I]t brought the younger boys together and introduced relations between the Seniors and the Juniors in a very praiseworthy character. The Seniors from being teachers (they coached entrants) often became protectors of the Juniors, a connexion was initiated which often continued through life, and was of great benefit to the parties concerned. Another advantage was that it made the older boys keep up their grammar and gave them habits of teaching and organisation which were most valuable. (In Forshall 1884, p. 51)

This rigour of examination remained an influence on Short, as did the advantage to him of a generous scholarship to complete his schooling. Both aspects in his own schooling were to reappear in his planning in Adelaide of the Collegiate School of St Peter, and of the schools in Pulteney Street, and indeed in his leadership as the initial vice-chancellor, then the second chancellor, of the University of Adelaide after 1874.

> The Queen's — King's — Scholars are part of Queen Elizabeth I's Royal Foundation of the College of St Peter which encompasses both Westminster School and Westminster Abbey. They are required by statutes to attend certain Abbey services, and have other ceremonial duties to perform in connection with the Abbey and the Crown. There are 40 Queen's Scholars and it is usual for eight Scholars to be elected every year. Since Elizabethan times the Scholars have resided in a boarding house known as College — the present building dates back to the early 18th century … Since at least the 17th century the Westminster Scholarship Examination has been known as the Challenge. For centuries it was an oral grammatical contest … (Westminster School 2016b, p. 8)

Following election as a King's Scholar in 1816, Short was educated with the other King's Scholars in the one large room simply referred to as 'School', built in the 1090s as the monks' dormitory. Passing through the Burlington Gate and climbing stairs to go 'up School', Short was made aware of his school's antiquity as names of past students, dating back several centuries, were engraved on the stonework. In School, every day, Latin prayers would be conducted. All pupils were taught in School, with Upper and Lower Schools separated by a curtain.[5] There were no private rooms for study, and often it was an unpleasant environment. In School there were broken windows and no heating until water pipes were introduced in 1837; and in 1814 various stone walls collapsed, leaving the roof in a precarious situation (Field 1987, p. 118).[6]

Pupils dined in the hall (Staunton 1898, p. 136); the College Hall previously was the Abbot's dining hall, built in the 1370s and was, and remains, an integral part of

---

5   The very large pig iron bar, from which the curtain hung, remains in place today.
6   The extensive undercroft beneath the school is today used by both Westminster Abbey and Westminster School. The abbey's museum was once there.

Figure 1.5 Augustus Short's dormitory at Westminster School.
Source: Reproduced with permission from Schools and colleges of England, R Ackermann, 1816.

Figure 1.6 Hall of Westminster School, considered the most historic space in Westminster. Note the open fire.
Source: Reproduced with permission from Schools and colleges of England, R Ackermann, 1816.

the abbey buildings, abutting the southwestern tower. It is one of the oldest and finest examples of a mediaeval refectory in existence, and in continuous use. It is immediately behind today's Abbey Shop, well known to all visitors to Westminster Abbey. In Short's time the hall had an open fire on a raised octagonal hearth in the centre, with smoke escaping through the louvre (which remains in the roof to this day). Short would have been reminded in this venue of the school's royal association: it was in this hall that Queen Elizabeth Woodville, wife of Edward IV, took sanctuary in 1483 with her son Prince Richard, soon to be one of the murdered Princes in the Tower; and Queen Elizabeth I visited on several occasions to view school plays. Short also would have seen, three times a day, the painted heraldry on the wall behind the high table: the arms of Westminster, of Christ Church Oxford, and of Trinity College Cambridge — constant reminders of the higher education he aspired to.

In 1818, John Bassett Campbell was about to retire from his position as resident Usher [the senior schoolmaster] living in Miss Best's residence; she conducted a boarding house at No 1 Little Dean's Yard, within Westminster School precincts. He wrote to his successor, Henry Bull (see Appendix B) and revealed aspects of the daily life of an usher in the school in Short's time:

> The management of the boys forms no difficulty now, as it did 9 years ago ... [I]f a man has a Studentship [at Christ Church Oxford] and is fixed on the Church, he cannot probably do better than by coming here ... [Y]ou may easily have 40 or even 50 pupils ... [Y]ou must be under master in due time[7] — when you would have a good house — about 900 pounds a year — could marry — and hold a living as well ... I did not allow football nor fives against the wall near Miss B's windows ... I allowed cricket — the wicket being at the bottom — only single wicket, of course ... (Letters in the possession of the headmaster 1818 in Carleton 1965, pp. 176-8)[8]

Thomas Vowler Short's record of learning was still relevant in Augustus' time:

> The 'school lessons', those which were done in class, were not well managed, but our 'private studies' were invaluable ... Every Saturday, in the two senior forms, [the student] brought the book to the master, and it was marked with the date of the day at the point which he had reached ... in this way I had read through before I left school Homer's *Iliad* and *Odyssey*, Xenophon's *Anabasis* and *Cyropedia*, Sophocles, several plays of Euripides, Cicero's *Offices* and *Tusculan Disputations*. Each book was read through *as a whole*. It made me look at the meaning and contents of the book, and not merely at the construing of it. It created a habit of quiet study carried on in private, and formed the best basis for academical study. I am convinced that this system was the source of that success which attended Westminster men of my standing, and which was very remarkable. (TV Short 1875, p. xlvii, emphasis in the original)

---

7 Bull did indeed become the under master in 1821.
8 Note that a studentship at Christ Church was the equivalent to a university fellow in other colleges.

Life outside the classroom

For recreation, pupils of Westminster were fortunate in Short's time, for they had reasonable open areas nearby, as Lord Albermarle described in around 1810 (in Shore 1910, pp. 62-3):

> Tothill Fields, now the site of a large and populous town, was the Westminster playground in my time. In one part of the field was a large pond called the 'duck'. Here we skated in the winter and hunted ducks in the summer. Near the duck lived Mother Hubbard, who used to let out guns to the boys. At Mother Hubbard's you might have fowling-pieces of all sorts and sizes, from the golden touch-hole down to one which, from a deep dent in the barrel, was called the gun which shoots round the corner. Which guns were used for shooting at the snipe that then frequented the neighbourhood, and even at the tame ducks upon the duck-pond that occupied a corner of the fields. In 1810 a ditch was dug around the ground, of which the surface was levelled; in 1814 a fence was erected.

A contemporary of Short's, Edward Barrett Curtis (admitted 1815, left 1821) recounted how he had shot snipe in the osier beds close to the Willow Walk (now called Warwick Street) and at the Chelsea Waterworks at Battersea, and how he had kept a pack of beagles in the kitchen of No 1 Vincent Square, hunting with them regularly in what is now Battersea Park (Carleton 1965, p. 138).

However, even during Short's final years at the school, the playing fields at Tothill Fields were under siege. The growth of London was rapid in the first quarter of the nineteenth century, especially after 1815 and the end of the Napoleonic wars. With the enclosure of Tothill, beginning in 1808, and the opening of Vauxhall Bridge in 1816, there was a rapid growth of building in the abbey's vicinity. The last reserve of open space, when Short's time came to an end, was Vincent Square, a 10-acre space [4.5 hectares] reserved for the school thanks to the foresight of Dr W Vincent, headmaster (1788-1802) then dean of Westminster (1802-15). The Fields presented the adolescent boys with much adventure, from shooting to skating to mud-larking in the ponds and ditches, and even to some of the earliest cricket matches ever recorded (Field 1987, p. 128).

Religious faith and practice

Given Short's future as a clergyman, what possible influence did Westminster School have on his maturing religious faith? In 1802, the headmaster, Dr Vincent, published a *Defence of Public Education*, and gave an account of the religious teaching in the school which still prevailed a decade later:

> In the Under School the boys translated the Psalms almost daily; they then proceeded to the gospels; then to a collection of 'Sacred Exercises', appropriate to the school, and finally produced a composition in verse from the Psalms, every Monday. The Catechism, or Archbishop's Wake's exposition was regularly repeated on Monday morning. In the Upper School the 'Sacred Exercises' were used for compositions in verse. Greek Testament, Grotius, and the Hebrew Psalms, and throughout the year, a history or other portion out of the Scriptures was appointed for a Bible exercise in verse. (In Forshall 1884, p. 35)

The ritual of school common prayer, and the physical presence of the abbey —The Cloisters formed part of the school buildings and pupils walked through, and played in them, every day — shaped many young men's views of faith and life:

> [In School] old customs have been, and still are, kept up in the school. For instance, Latin prayers, including the 'Pater Noster' and the 'Gratia Domini Nostri', are still said at the beginning and end of school, both in the morning and afternoon. The prayers are said by the captain of the school and three monitors in turn, each taking a week. The monitor of the week kneels in the centre of the school, with his face turned to the east; the head-master, the usher, and the other masters kneeling in file behind him. There can be little doubt that these customs were derived, and have been handed down unchanged, from the old days before the Reformation. (Thornbury 1878, p. 467)

Furthermore:

> [t]he school preserves many splendid and interesting privileges, greatest of all perhaps, not only in its direct, but in its influence upon Westminsters, the right to use the Abbey as its chapel. It would be difficult to over-estimate the influence exerted upon many a thoughtful and sensitive lad by the Abbey and its connection with the school and its history. One, at any rate, as an O.W., I know, looks back upon his friendship — the word is curious but adequate — for the Abbey in his boyhood days with fond recollection; so must many another. (Shore 1910, p. 77)

The abbey gave an unmistakable ecclesiastical tone to Short's schooling. All pupils attended the abbey worship twice on Sunday and once on Saturday. On Saints' Days they attended either at the ordinary service at 10 am, or at a special (non-choral) service held in the abbey at 8 am, at which the masters officiated, and the headmaster or under master preached. On these occasions, the headmaster, the master of the King's Scholars, and the King's Scholars attended services as part of the Collegiate body, entering in procession and occupying places in the choir. There was an annual Confirmation either at the end of June, or in early July, and candidates were always prepared by the headmaster (Staunton 1898, p. 146). Certain ancient customs persisted in Short's time. For example, at Coronations the King's Scholars formed part of the Procession of the Regalia, from the Jerusalem Chamber to the High Altar which preceded the service, because they were part of the collegiate body, and, by tradition the King's Scholars retained the ancient right to be the first to greet the new Sovereign.

In terms of an intellectual and emotional understanding of the Christian faith, therefore, Short had an education that was integrated with the liturgical life and the rituals of an ancient religious institution. The setting of the school within the abbey precincts simply underlined the uniqueness of having the monarch, as Visitor, presiding over the destinies of both the school and the abbey. The abbey was considered a 'Royal Peculiar' — an ecclesiastical body outside any diocesan structure and directly under the monarch's rule. Thus pupils were introduced to a world where the Christian faith, in particular the established Church, and English society were assumed to coexist without question. In Short's retirement, Whitington records he visited the abbey on St Peter's Day, 29 June 1883, being the thirty-sixth anniversary of his consecration by Archbishop Howley:

> there was nothing of which he was fonder than the grand old Abbey. He would stroll about in the cloisters and in and out of the building itself ... [T]he place had a peculiar charm for him, and no wonder. Under its wing he had been educated, within its walls he had received his commission to act in his Master's Name, and had assisted in imparting that commission to his successor, and in its honour he had named his own cathedral church and collegiate school in Adelaide with the same dedication. (1887, p. 280)

King's Scholar

During the first year, King's Scholars were called Juniors, during the next, Second Election, during the third, Third Election, and Seniors in the last (Forshall 1884, p. 5). Dacres Adams, who was a Junior in 1820 — the year Short left for Oxford — recorded in 1840 a woeful view of a less-than-privileged life, although it was considerably advantaged when compared to other young men of his age:

> In winter I get up at half-past seven, excepting every fourth day, when I get up at six. At eight I carry my master's books into school. I am in school till nine, excepting the times I am sent about messages ... from half-past nine to ten I go to breakfast, and at ten I go into school to lesson ... I am obliged, every time I go into school, to bring three pens, three quarterns, and a dip, and a knife. At twelve I go into the green and play at hockey. I may be sent away from play if anyone chuses. At one I go to dinner, where I have to mash some potatoes for my master, and brown them before the fire, and to toast his meat. After I have done that I may sit down to dinner if there is time, for I have only half an hour to do everything ... every fourth day I have things to do for the Third Election — to clean their (ten) candlesticks, to get candles for them, to put them on their desks. I make their ten beds, which takes a great while, for I

must do all my master's things just the same. I have to brush clothes for ten fellows, fill eight pitchers, and clean eight basins, to wash up their (ten) sets of tea things. (In Carleton 1965, p. 51)

Short proved an academically able student, as he revealed in his reminiscences in 1882:

[D]uring the succeeding four years I went through the usual course of lessons, and by means of 'private studies', as they were called, enlarged my reading and taste for the classics. Under the personal direction of the head-master [then William Carey] I thus read the *Odyssey, Hesiod, Anabasis*, and *Cyropaedia* ... Under [Dr Edward Goodenough, headmaster from 1819] I won two prizes for Latin verse. (In Whitington 1887, p. 4)

Yet, still reminiscing (1882), he could see the limitations of his Westminster school days. He may have excelled in the Classics but

in other respects [I] went, after election to Christ Church, Oxford, ill-grounded in scholarship as well as deficient in general education and knowledge ... I left Westminster on May 9, 1820 ... but cannot say that in Scriptural knowledge, or religious instruction, or moral discipline the purpose of Queen Elizabeth's foundation had been well or adequately carried out in regards myself or the other king's scholars during my sojourn in St Peter's College and dormitory. (In Whitington 1887, p. 4)

His cousin, Thomas Vowler Short, concurred in the general reaction to education at the school:

There was a great deal that was good at the school when I was there, but a great deal, too, that was evil. Forty boys were shut up for the night in a large room (the college dormitory) by themselves, and the master never came in except for prayers, after notice given. There was much tyranny, much self-indulgence in eating and drinking and in jesting which were 'not convenient'. Few boys went through the trial unharmed, but our characters were strongly formed, and we acquired a great knowledge of human nature. (TV Short 1875, p. xlvii)

The reputation of the Westminster School was enhanced, nevertheless, by its connections with the Universities of Oxford and Cambridge. For those who were King's Scholars, there were three studentships available at Christ Church, Oxford, tenable for seven years, and three scholarships at Trinity College, Cambridge, tenable until the holder graduated with a BA (Staunton 1898, pp. 143-4). King's Scholars remained confident of securing one or the other of these generous opportunities. For Short, this was the only way a university education might be possible. The reputation of studentships at Christ Church and scholarships at Trinity College gave much social status as well as educational opportunity (Forshall 1884, p. 45).

The examination was before the deans of Westminster and Christ Church, and the master of Trinity College, Cambridge, and was conducted verbally using Latin or Greek authors, although some papers were written. Standard expectations were twelve

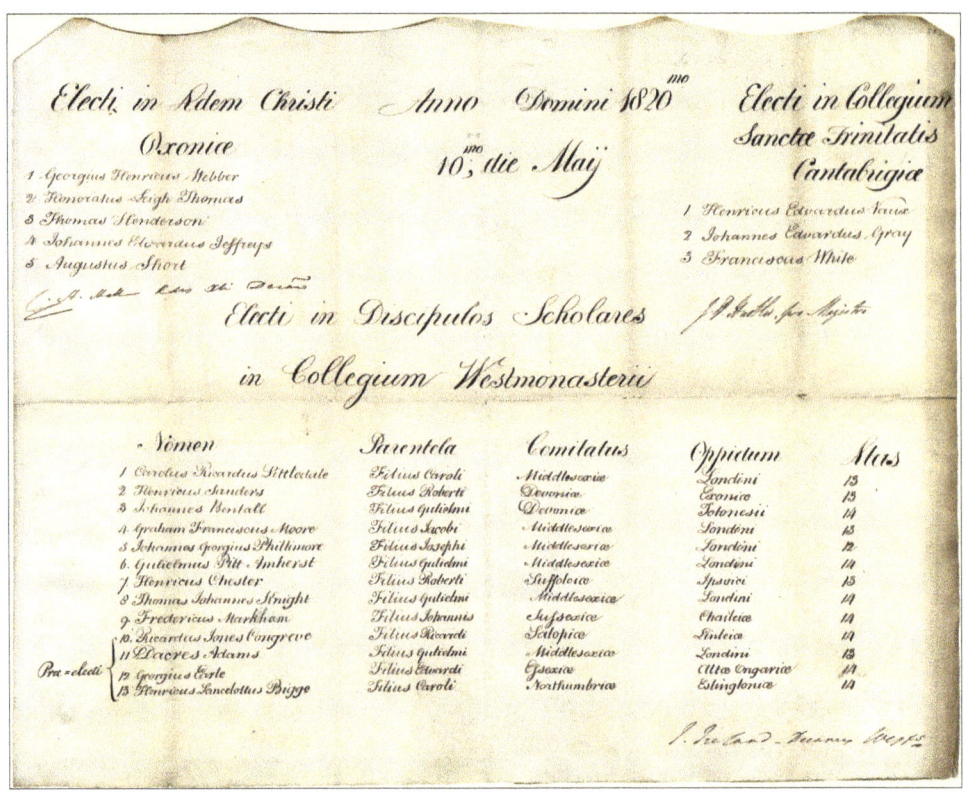

Figure 1.7 Original record of Augustus Short's election as a Student to Christ Church Oxford 1820.
Source: Reproduced by kind assistance of the Governing Body of Westminster School.

books of Homer's *Iliad*, Virgil's *Aeneid*, chapters of *Genesis* in Hebrew, four books of Euclid, and some algebra and arithmetic. The candidates began the examination on the Monday reading Latin letters requesting admission to the universities; the following day the headmaster and under master oversaw the major valedictory speeches of candidates. At precisely 11 am on the Wednesday, the headmaster entered the college hall and read out the names of the successful candidates (Forshall 1884, pp. 56-7).

Augustus Short's father recounted some of his son's achievements in his reminiscences: '1819 3rd December acted in the Adelphi, with considerable applause … 1820 gained two prizes in verse' (SLSA, PRG 160/32). On 9 May 1820, Augustus was elected to Christ Church, Oxford, on a studentship, as he reminisced in 1882:

> In my own case no interest was required, and no application made for a Christ Church studentship. Indeed, my father not having been at the university, had neither connection with nor knowledge of the classical authorities, who might perhaps have

been able to assist me. Whatever advancement, therefore, in life I obtained I owe, under God, to Queen Elizabeth and my own efforts. (In Whitington 1887, p. 10)

When it came to election to a studentship at Christ Church, Short knew that Thomas Vowler Short, his cousin by twelve years, was already, in 1820, a tutor and a censor at Christ Church; whether he influenced the election can only be speculated. The dean and canons of Christ Church retained discretionary rights to elect pupils to studentships and often nepotism prevailed as the sons of canons or other relations were elected, regardless of merit, with few commoners included. Open competition for the valuable studentship was unheard of (Thompson 1899, p. 15; Bill 1973, p. 12).

Short remarked in 1882 to his biographer:

I now more fully realised than ever before the great advantage offered by the royal foundation of St Peter's College, Westminster, to the sons of professional men who have to make their own way in the world. By successful personal competition when 'standing out' for college, I had gained the first rung of the ladder of life, and following up the career then opened to me I found myself in an honourable and profitable position as a Christ Church tutor within four years after I had taken my degree. (In Whitington 1887, p. 10)

There is little doubt that Short deserved a studentship on academic merit. However, he was certainly helped by the extended family pattern of schooling, and the connections with Christ Church. Such links were cemented in 1820 when Thomas Vowler Short became the tutor for his young cousin.

Westminster and Short

When Augustus Short left Westminster School in 1820 he departed from an institution that was about to experience rapid and unexpected decline, in both enrolment and prestige. Following Vincent's departure in 1803, there was continuing mismanagement by the successive headmasters. With some neglect by the dean and chapter of Westminster, along with the rapid transformation of London and environmental decay of the Westminster neighbourhood, combined with an institution dominated by adolescent authority and brutality, enrolments declined sharply. From an enrolment of 332 in 1818 the school had only sixty-seven boys by 1841 (Field 1987, p. 61).

When the seventeen-year-old Short matriculated to Christ Church, Oxford, on 20 May 1820, his nine years at Westminster School had profoundly shaped him. Tenacity, resilience and independence were habits he had acquired; and the virtues of self-help, advancing by one's personal abilities, efforts and merit, had been instilled. The rigours of masculine competition, and its rewards for success, not least in academic study, were impressed on him. He had learned to consider the Classics as a natural

Figure 1.8 'The Royal College of St Peter at Westminster' today, with the School and Abbey as one foundation. Westminster School comprises the buildings to the right, adjoining the Abbey.
Source: Google Earth, © 2015.

study, not for their content so much as for the boast that a student's abilities at logic, clear thinking, fluent expression and even the attainment of higher moral standing were inherent in a study of such literature. He had no illusions as a young adult, however, of the limiting effect an isolating and self-regarding educational institution could have on its members.

Short had experienced church and school as one institution. The Royal College of St Peter at Westminster, as a joint ecclesiastical and academic body, left the young Short perhaps convinced that this collegiality was perhaps an ideal institutional arrangement. When he entered Christ Church he discovered a similar type of collegiality — cathedral and college as one. His vision for Adelaide, after 1847, initially embraced a collegiate school, with theological training, in a joint foundation with a university.

As a tutor and a censor at Christ Church, Thomas Vowler Short had an influence of a kind in electing students from Westminster School. The extended family expectations would have been keenly felt by the adolescent Short, and must have been their own spur to academic endeavour. Short was old enough in May 1820 to be asking and pondering several questions regarding his education: what worth was it to him; what worth did his society assign to his learning; and what advantages for his future life did his pursuit of higher learning mean? The privileges of being a King's Scholar at school, and now a student at Christ Church, removed the struggle in education which some of his contemporaries experienced. What now would the young Short make of his opportunities in adulthood?

2

Student of Christ Church: Undergraduate 1820-23

The cool spring sunlight in May 1820 lit the Tom Quad as Augustus Short, now almost eighteen years old, gazed upon his new place of learning. He marvelled at his good fortune in having formally matriculated to Christ Church, Oxford. This had been the university home of contemporary political greats such as Lord Liverpool, then Prime Minister, and George Canning, Foreign Secretary. The Member of Parliament for Oxford was another alumnus, Robert Peel, considered a future national leader. Augustus had entered what was recognised as a seat of learning for people who were making a difference to society. He understood enough to know that the reforms of an earlier dean, Cyril Jackson, had made Christ Church attractive as a nursery for conservative reformers.

What was more extraordinary to the young scholar was that the college ('the House') and cathedral were one: a single foundation where the dean was master of both institutions. No other university college had such an intimate relationship with the United Church of England and Ireland; it reminded Augustus of the joint foundation of school and abbey at St Peter's College, Westminster, from where he had come. Underlining this reality, the rooms looking over the quadrangles of Christ Church housed many clergy; this was an established hub of the scholastic Church of England. Now, Augustus made his way to the rooms of his ordained cousin, twelve years his senior, who held the positions of tutor and censor in Christ Church. Thomas Vowler Short was delighted that his young cousin had been elected on a studentship from Westminster School; he expected to be a vital friend and influence during Augustus's years as a student.

Figure 2.1 (left) Short first entered Christ Church through this gate under the Tom Tower.

Source: 'The "Fayre-Gate" or entrance to the Great Quadrangle, commonly called Tom-Gate', engraving by John Le Keux. Reproduced from Memorials of Oxford, James Ingram, vol. 1, 1837.

Figure 2.2 (below) The entrance to Christ Church, under the Tom Tower.

Source: 'The West Front', engraving by John Le Keux. Reproduced from Memorials of Oxford, James Ingram, vol. 1, 1837.

So much would happen to shape and educate Augustus Short, and important choices for his future would arise.

Oxford University and Christ Church

Augustus Short matriculated as a Commoner (that is, an ordinary citizen, not of aristocratic or royal background) to Christ Church in May 1820, a fact which was recorded in the dean's Admission Book.

Short, in 1882, in his eightieth year, briefly recollected his years as an undergraduate at Christ Church (PRG 160/7; see also Whitington 1887). Frederick Oakeley, a fellow matriculant (spring to summer 1820), wrote more lengthy reminiscences when he was in his sixties. From a titled family and privately tutored, Oakeley, in an account of those first days in *The Months* (1865-6), recalled some of the sensations he felt in attending Christ Church:

> My available knowledge of Oxford dates from the summer of 1820 when I went up from my private tutor's to be matriculated at Christ Church. It happened to be the time of the Commemoration[9] and I was taken by my graduate friend to witness the imposing spectacle ... To a youth educated mainly in the country, and never at any school, no sight could be more impressively brilliant than that which this annual gathering presents ... There is the sweeping semicircle of Doctors of Divinity and Law, in their robes of scarlet and pink, backed by the rising tiers of particoloured ladies, beaming with bright and jubilant countenances, the whole surmounted by a crown of undergraduates, with their summer costume, contrasting so curiously with that ugliest of professional badges — the undergraduate gown. (In Quiller-Couch 1892, p. 304)

Short was entering an established and complex educational world. By the 1820s, the wider Oxford community comprised nineteen colleges and five halls; the latter were not corporate bodies and were generally without endowments. The colleges, all being residential, were independent in their teaching and in determining their curriculum; the university organisation was focused on final examinations and the granting of degrees. College life had many distinctive and original features. Tuckwell, in his *Reminiscences of Oxford* (1908), gently lampooned the teaching fellows of the university, known as Dons, and their academic world:

> For of Dons there were four kinds. There was the *cosmopolitan* Don; with a home in Oxford, but conversant with select humanity elsewhere ... there was the *learned* Don,

---

9   Oakeley is here referring to ceremonies commemorating the benefactors of the university, held at the end of the academic year. Frederick Oakeley (1802-80) was ordained in the Church of England in 1828 but followed JH Newman to Roman Catholicism in 1845. He then had a distinguished ministry as canon of Westminster and is famed as the translator from Latin of John Wade's hymn of 1743, *O Come all Ye Faithful*.

amassing a library, editing Latin authors and Greek plays, till his useful career was extinguished under an ill-placed, ill-fitting mitre … there was the *mere* Don … Head of a House commonly as a result of a squabble amongst the electing Fellows … lastly, the *ornamental* Don, chosen as Proctor or Vice-Chancellor. (p. 19, emphases in the original)

Debate and conversation filled the air, in common rooms and during the obligatory afternoon stroll; each person knew of the other and collegial friendships were the norm. The intellectual speculations were as great at Christ Church, 'the House', as elsewhere.[10]

Formally called 'The Dean, Chapter and Students of the Cathedral Church of Christ in Oxford of the Foundation of King Henry the Eighth', Christ Church was unique in the academic world because its foundation encompassed both cathedral and college. The Visitor of Christ Church was the reigning monarch and the bishop of Oxford was alone among English bishops in not being the Visitor of his own cathedral. It was the grandest, richest and most aristocratic college in the University of Oxford, and held the lead intellectually after promoting reform of the examination system in the early decades of the nineteenth century (Bill 1973, p. 12). Among its undergraduates and graduates were 101 studentships, comprising those, such as Short, elected from Westminster as well as others nominated by the ruling dean and chapter.

Founded in 1546, Christ Church had been a place of learning from 1525, originally known as the Cardinal's College, after its founder Cardinal Wolsey. Prior to the monasteries being dissolved under Henry VIII (King of England from 1509 until his death in 1547), there had been on the site a priory dedicated to St Frideswide (the patron saint of both the university and the city of Oxford) who had died about 737 and was canonised in 1480. A contemporary of Short wrote in 1837 of the Diocese of Oxford:

> After the bishop's see had remained at Oseney from 1542 to 1546, the king by letters patent of 4th Nov. in that year transferred it to his college at Oxford, which he once more re-established under the mixed form of a cathedral and an academic college, styling it in his foundation charter, ECCELSIA CHRISTI CATHEDRALIS OXON. EX FUNDATIONE REGIS HENRICI OCTAVI. This foundation consisted of a bishop, a dean, eight canons, eight petty canons (chaplains) a gospeller, a *postiller* (answering to Bible-clerks), eight clerks (singing-men), a master of the choristers, an organist, eight choristers, sixty scholars or students, a schoolmaster, an usher, and *forty* children. The latter part of this plan, however, does not seem to have been adopted. But in place of the scholars, schoolmaster, and children, one hundred students were appointed. (Ingram 1837, pp. 46-7, emphasis in the original)

---

10 Christ Church was, and still is, referred to as 'the House', from its Latin title, *Aedis Christi* — House of God.

The dean and canons (the chapter), from Henry's time, governed the site, its precincts, estates and all other property on condition that Regius Professors of Divinity, Hebrew and Greek continued to be endowed.

Christ Church in 1820 comprised a remarkable set of buildings. The oldest was the twelfth-century collegiate cathedral, originally the Priory Church. On its southern side was the chapter house, primarily built in the thirteenth century but with a striking Romanesque doorway built in 1150. The chapter house was sited on the eastern side of a small cloister, the heart of the former monastic buildings. On the south side was the former priory refectory, which was until the eighteenth century the library; it had become residential quarters by 1820.

The first of the college buildings had been the kitchen, followed by the hall:

> This magnificent and well-proportioned room is of itself sufficient evidence of Wolsey's vast conceptions and architectural taste. Its dimensions are about 115 feet by 40, and 50 feet in height, having a richly carved roof of oak, profusely decorated with armorial bearings of the King and Cardinal, and exhibiting the date of 1529 … The lobby, staircase, and approach to the Hall are not of the same period, but were added by Dr Samuel Fell, about the year 1640 … [T]he vaulted stone roof of this part, of exquisite fan-work, supported by a single light pillar, has been generally and justly admired. (Ingram 1837, p. 51)

Approaching the hall,

> one passes through the archway at the south-east corner of the Quadrangle, and ascends a wide staircase notable for the wonderful fanwork tracery of the ceiling … The Hall itself has no rival in Oxford and no superior in England, Westminster Hall only excepted. The window above the dais contains full-length stained-glass representations of Wolsey, More, Erasmus, Colet, and other great men of the Reformation era; and the walls are hung with a very fine collection of portraits, including those of Henry VIII and Wolsey (by Holbein). (Peel & Minchin 1906, p. 111)

The most striking architectural feature to first greet the young matriculant in 1820 was a great bell tower dominating the skyline, the Tom Tower. Designed by Christopher Wren, the tower was completed in 1684 and in May of that year, '[a]s soon as the Tower was ready for its tenant, "Great Tom" was hoisted up and hung in its new home, and from thence it rang out for the first time on the anniversary of the Restoration, May 29, 1684' (Thompson 1900, p. 98). There began a tradition of ringing the bell every night, 101 times, commemorating the original scholars of 'the House'.[11]

The dean, being both head of 'the House' and the cathedral dean, was, and remains, a direct appointment of the monarch. The position was one of power and prestige, and

---

11   Great Tom is still rung at 9.05 pm every night — Oxford is five minutes west of Greenwich Mean Time.

Figure 2.3 Christ Church Hall in 1814.
Source: 'Hall of Christ Church'. Reproduced with permission from Ackermann's Oxford: A selection of plates from Rudolph Ackermann's 'A history of the University of Oxford, its colleges, halls, and public buildings', 1814 — and James Ingram's 'Memorials of Oxford', 1837, with notes by HM Colvin, 1954.

with the chapter, the dean administered extensive estates throughout England. This governing body not only controlled a vast income, but held considerable ecclesiastical patronage within and without Christ Church. The dean was the authority in academic matters — admitting undergraduates, appointing the tutors — and it was the dean's reputation upon which Christ Church most depended (Bill & Mason 1970, p. 6).

The 101 students, and other undergraduates and graduates, were distinctive by their academic standing: those reading for their BAs were *discipuli*; those completing BAs and taking MAs were *philosophiae*; and the most senior were the *theologiae*. Every elected student received a stipend from the Christ Church endowments, and this increased with seniority; yet there were conditions: degrees were to be completed within a reasonable time, and the student was to remain unmarried (although dean and canons could be married). Most students took holy orders in the established Church. As men married, entered into careers or returned to life on their country estates as members of the landed aristocracy, so vacancies arose. A studentship of Christ Church was awarded for life and was intended not only to enable the student to take his degree but also to assist him to prepare himself for a career in the Church or other profession, or to become a tutor in 'the House'. One Christ Church man defined a studentship as an honour 'peculiar to Christ Church; something between a scholarship and a fellowship at other colleges' (Baker 1981, pp. 23-4).

Studentships, however, were not necessarily awarded on merit, or as a result of open competition; in fact, Christ Church held a reputation as assisting poorer scholars and not regarding studentships simply as prizes (Bill 1973, p. 14). While not sinecures, studentships did confer some advantages not to be lightly disregarded. The most pivotal for Short was that tutors were chosen from students; Short himself had the good fortune to be chosen as a tutor in 1828. Those entering holy orders were offered the choice of ninety livings, or benefices. These were posts as vicar or rector in charge of parishes; the dean and chapter nominated the incumbent. Short himself also had that good fortune in 1835. He was later to remark in 1882:

> By successful personal competition when 'standing out' for college, I had gained the first rung of the ladder of life, and following up the career then opened to me I found myself in an honourable and profitable position as a Christ Church tutor within four years after I had taken my degree. (In Whitington 1887, p. 10)

Social and religious life in Christ Church

Generally the eighteenth century had been regarded as a time of laxity in Oxford academic life, and the grandeur of Christ Church's buildings and environment encouraged some to believe that only the wealthy and landed aristocracy were associated with the institution. Christ Church academic records tend to refute this view (especially records of Collections, as outlined below). Undergraduate life, however, was anything but studious for some: there were those who were attending purely for the social scene, filling in time before inheriting the estate, title or family fortune, and in the meantime living an indulged and wasteful life. The 'gentlemen commoners' were examples of this: 'the body of gentlemen commoners is small in Christ Church, and a considerable portion of them does not care to graduate at all, but merely spends an idle year or two in Oxford, and sets a bad example to others' (Rogers 1861, p. 109).

Oakeley, writing in 1865-6, noted that he found it difficult to adjust to the community life of Christ Church:

> I do really think that Christ Church, the college at which I entered, as it was the highest in repute for the advantages of this world, was also, in my time, the most degraded in respect of all that relates to the true end of our existence … I cannot

recollect any set of men, however regular in ordinary college duties, and however given to reading, of whom I do not feel sure that whatever possible exceptions in the case of individuals, they were, as a set, addicted to vice and loose conversation. (In Quiller-Couch 1892, p. 302)

Mark Pattison (a future vice-chancellor of the university), in his *Memoirs* (1885), lamented that 'the vulgar estimate of people by income and position ... as the only standard of merit' seemed universal at Oxford because 'the most permanent stamp of college reputation is the social stamp' (p. 17). He recollected that when he was seeking to enter Oxford in 1830 he was counselled by Mr Paddon, who had been the private tutor in the early 1820s of Lord Conyers, a childhood friend of Pattison's and a resident of Christ Church:

> Lord Conyers' capacity and attainments were such, that his tutor had at one time indulged a hope of his reading successfully for honours. But any such hope was early dissipated by the demoralising atmosphere of Christ Church; and at the time we arrived in Oxford I found Lord Conyers entirely possessed by the opinion of his set, that it was unworthy of a man of his position to 'sap'. Mr Paddon sorrowfully resigned himself to see his pupil follow the ordinary course of a 'nobleman' at the University, i.e. misspend his time, and acquire nothing. (pp. 20-1)

The aristocracy preferred Christ Church, and generally a life of indolence and indulgence, wine parties and hunting, to the studious life. The social set was all-important, wine parties dominating: such parties lasted 'for several hours', according to Oakeley (1865-66 in Quiller-Couch 1892, p. 302), with people 'drinking glasses of wine, eating a few almonds and raisins and preserved vinegar'.

Short recollected later, in 1882, in his reminiscences:

> The discipline however of the College had been lax, and the efforts of the new censors (Bull and [Augustus's own cousin] Short) to restore good order were of course met with considerable opposition from those young men of independent fortunes, who resented all restrictions upon their hunting arrangements or going to Ascot races ... and they gave practical proof of their displeasure. I recollect bonfires being started in Peckwater 'quad' on more than one occasion; again, all the doors of the dean's and the canons houses were one morning found painted red ... [T]hese were the follies of the aristocratic youths furnished with ample fortunes, having exuberant spirits, and allowed (in some degree) a privileged idleness with little College or moral restraint! (SLSA, PRG 160/7)

Frederick Oakeley confirmed Short's opinion of the 'wrong set':

> A freshman who does not at once drop into a respectable set is in imminent danger of finding himself in a bad one. This was soon my case ... I got into the habit of card-playing and attending late suppers ... [M]y name went up every morning to

the senior censor with those which were of no good odour. I also grew irregular at morning chapel, and was constantly visited by a scout bearing in his hand a folded slip of paper, in which were inscribed the words, 'One hundred lines of Virgil, Wednesday, [Morning Chapel]'. (1865-66 quoted in Quiller-Couch 1892, p. 317)

Short appears to have dropped into a respectable set and been more resilient than his contemporary. The determination and single-mindedness he had achieved at Westminster School obviously remained with him at Christ Church, as he recounted in 1882:

> with my classical reading I associated, by way of amusement, boating, and became one of the Christ Church racing crew — rowing being an exercise familiar to Westminster boys from their daily practice on the Thames. This demanded a stricter habit of life than was at that time fostered by the convivial parties in college. And so both in study and amusement I was saved from many temptations and follies. (In Whitington 1887, pp. 7-8)

Being in the racing crew, he reminisced in 1882, 'necessitated a habit of life and denial of excess. This proved very beneficial' (SLSA, PRG 160/7). Rowing had commenced at Christ Church, on the Isis in 1815, and in the 1820s when Short rowed, the house crew competed for Head of the River three times against Brasenose and Jesus Colleges (Butler 2006, p. 127).

Short knew, as Westminster had instilled in him, that there would probably be only the one opportunity to advance socially and intellectually. This would be through careful study and making wise choices with regards to friends — under the eye of his experienced cousin. At the same time, however, Short was never allowed to forget his social status. Cox (1870) records how, on the eve of Short matriculating, a moment of silliness underlined the place of a Westminster pupil elected on a studentship:

> An attempt was said to have been made at Christ Church to get permission for the Students to wear a silver tassel to their caps! It was also said to have been met by a reproof from one in high authority, who answered the application at once: 'O yes, certainly; but on condition that you wear on your sleeve a silver badge, marked W.C.B.' i.e. Westminster Charity Boys. (p. 83)

Many formative events and incidents characterised Short's time. For instance, in August 1823, Short's final year as an undergraduate, the senior student of Christ Church, the Rev. C Atterbury, riding on the box of the Costar's coach[12], was crushed to death when the Birmingham coach turned over. The preceding Sunday he had preached at St Mary Magdalen parish church in Oxford, where he was the vicar, on the text *Set thy house in order for thou shalt die and not live* (Ingram 1837, p. 108). It was a salutary lesson for all in the house, especially one like Short who at the time was contemplating what path his life should take after graduation.

---

12 Mr Costar conducted an extensive coach service in Oxfordshire and surrounds.

As all students were residents, their daily lives revolved around Christ Church's ancient buildings, the accommodation, and the house procedures. Community life centred on the hall, which was lighted with wax candles in brass candlesticks and where meals were served on pewter plates. At the bottom of the social scale were servitors, the lowest order of undergraduates, who were often the sons of poor clergymen, and received free board for performing menial tasks and serving the masters, especially at meals. However, top of the social scale were the noblemen, dining at the head table, and the gentlemen commoners, who were seated with the graduates. On the north side of the hall sat the senior masters, on the south the junior masters; nearby were the chaplains and the bachelors of arts. All sat on benches except the dean, who graced the solitary chair. Dining was in the hands of manciple, cook and butler who managed handsome profits from the food and wine supplied (Thompson 1900, p. 217).

While dinner was always at 5 pm, the times for chapel were just as set. Attendance for prayers was strictly enforced; Latin prayers every morning at 8 am and every evening at 9.15 pm, except Sunday when evening chapel was at 4 pm. Holy communion occurred on the first Sunday of the month following choral matins, which began at 8 am. This at least surpassed other colleges where holy communion was once a term (p. 217).

Academic life in Christ Church

The unique role of dean of Christ Church had seen an inspired choice in 1783 when Cyril Jackson (1746-1819) was appointed, remaining in office until 1809. A leading mathematician, noted botanist and fellow of the Royal Society, Jackson did much to raise the social and academic standing of Christ Church. Short passed often, in the north transept of the cathedral, Francis Chantrey's statue of Jackson (Thompson 1900, p. 182).[13] Jackson's two great contributions were a reformed examination system and an enhancement of tutorial teaching. In 1800 (with the heads of Oriel and Balliol Colleges) he instigated significant reforms to the university's examinations with a system of honours examinations, conducted orally. Classics and mathematics were initially included together but in 1807 became separate examinations, both necessary for the degree. Graduates were either first or second class but a third class had been introduced in 1809, and a fourth class was subsequently introduced in 1830. The *Literae Humaniores* Final Examination included Greek and Roman literature, elements of mathematics and physics, moral philosophy, logic and doctrinal articles, and elements of religion. Ancient history, rhetoric, poetry and moral and political philosophy were later additions (Dowland 1997, p. 181).

---

13   This statue is now in the foyer of the hall.

This need for colleges to prepare men for an independent and competitive university examination meant renewed emphasis on the relationship between undergraduate and tutor, and this had a dramatic effect on the standards of college tuition. Jackson had relished this and set about enhancing the role of tutors in Christ Church, persuading outstanding scholars to accept these positions. The tutor as the kernel of teaching and learning in the house attained its height in the 1820s; this is vital in understanding the influences on Short as he matured in his learning, ideas and beliefs, and became a tutor himself in due course. As well as all tutorial teaching, the colleges of Oxford retained control of admissions and student accommodation.

For centuries, Oxford had been a cradle of the Church of England, sharing this distinction with the colleges of Cambridge. Generally, because the clergy governed them, the colleges maintained the doctrines and teachings of the established Church. Until 1830, conservative politicians dominated in England, with significant numbers either educated at Oxford or Cambridge. To ensure the support of the university for the established order, a requirement of an undergraduate matriculating to Oxford (until 1854) was to declare his adherence to the established Church by subscribing to its statement of doctrine, the Thirty-Nine Articles of Religion, printed as an addition to the *Book of Common Prayer*. In fact, no-one in Short's time could qualify for the BA degree without an examination of the gospels in Greek, knowledge of the Thirty-Nine Articles of Religion, and a study of Joseph Butler's *Analogy of Religion*.

Teaching and learning was thus in the hands of the clergy and much of the continuity and strength of Christ Church's character came from the dominant clerical element. The emphasis was distinctly on a training of the intellect in judgement, beliefs and morality, through a traditional education centred on the Classics and mathematics. There was a reluctance to advance the cause of learning by attention to vocational studies or new areas of academic interest such as the sciences, modern languages, history and law.

The dean in 1820 was Charles Hall (1809-24). Frederick Oakeley, writing in 1865-66, paints a somewhat florid picture of him, while maintaining that the tone of Christ Church was low during Hall's time:

> I must say a few words of the college-authorities who presided over the education at Christ Church in my time. At the head of them when I first went and for two or three years later, was Dean Hall — a very handsome and gentlemanlike old man, who was said to have got himself into great difficulties by profuse expenditure and who at length exchanged his deanery of Christ Church for the more valuable one of Durham … I can see him now marching up and down Christ Church Hall at Collections, with the senior censor by his side, his hand planted in the belt of his cassock, and his cap almost perched upon the bridge of his nose. His manner, at least to me, was always haughty and overbearing, and I have no pleasant recollections about him. (In Quiller-Couch 1892, p. 311)

Figure 2.4 A rare view of the cathedral — the Latin Chapel is foremost on the right.
Source: 'The Cathedral from the N.W.', engraving by John Le Keux. Reproduced with permission from Memorials of Oxford, James Ingram, vol. 1, 1837.

Dean Hall was very irregular in chapel attendance, being so unpunctual that many undergraduates waited in the nave till his arrival and then, following in his wake through the opened door, went safely to their seats in the choir, as Oakeley (1865-66) related:

> [The dean] generally sailed in just before the ' Prayer of St. Chrysostom', to the great relief of a host of undergraduates, who took advantage of this …
>
> At Christ Church the only way in which religion, as such, was put before us was in the public prayers at the college, than which nothing could well have been more adverse to its proper influence … [L]ittle or no care was taken to secure even the decent behaviour of those who attended chapel as a general rule … [T]he names of those present used, when I was at Christ Church, to be noted by the registering student during the time of the service itself; and the period chosen was especially. (In Quiller-Couch 1892, p. 330)

Despite such unsatisfactory atmospheres of a social and religious kind in Christ Church, Short seems to have developed a modest and conforming manner as an undergraduate;

by his actions his main concern, increasingly, was to nurture his character in particular ways. He does not appear to have involved himself in the more wayward elements of college life, and the influence of his cousin was more than likely the key influence.

The tutor

Thomas Vowler Short had preceded Augustus by just over a decade from Westminster School to Christ Church. In his eighties, writing his reminiscences, Augustus Short recalled:

> Leaving Westminster on May 9th 1820, as elected Student of Christ Church, I was placed as pupil under my cousin the Rev. T Vowler Short, subsequently the Bishop of St Asaph. I soon learned to value his sterling honesty and truthfulness, as he was sincerely religious, and the sincerity of his character and religious honesty of purpose, gave him influence with the undergraduates. My taste for reading, which had been strengthened at Westminster by what were called 'Private Studies'[14] and by two prizes I had won for Latin Verse, found me among my Cousin's pupils who were reading for Classical Honours … As a reading man I had been thrown among the steadier portion of the undergraduates of 1820 — The venerable E Pusey, and Lord Ashley (now Lord Shaftesbury) were then among the senior pupils of my cousin, and afforded a high example to their fellow students of good conduct and intellectual culture. (SLSA, PRG 160/7, emphases in the original)

Thomas Vowler's experiences of 1809 still largely prevailed in 1820.

> Every undergraduate was placed under the care of a tutor, who superintended his education, and taught him all that he was taught, except what he had learnt from College or University lectures, which generally was little or nothing. The tutor saw his pupils each by themselves. They brought the book they were reading to his rooms when summoned to do so. This, in my own case, as a hardworking youth, was very rarely. I do not think that on an average I construed to my tutor one hour during a term. (TV Short 1875, p. xlviii)

Thus teaching and learning centred on the tutors and their relationships with undergraduates; and assistance came from private tutors and not university professors. Christ Church led the way at Oxford with usually five or six tutors in the house, when other colleges struggled to find at least two. This often meant, at Christ Church, smaller classes with more tutorial attention, leading to more success under the new system of examinations. By Short's time, Jackson's legacy was well established with an oligarchy of tutors such as Frederick Barnes, Thomas Vowler Short, John Bull, John Cramer and Charles Longley. All, except Barnes, had been students at Westminster — it was a small

---

14 That is, some Classics approved by the headmaster, and studied apart from the school lesson.

world (Curthoys 2012, p. 201). During Dean Hall's time, Christ Church received ninety-four firsts in twenty-nine honours examinations — the highest academic standard in the university.

Tutors, nevertheless, had a difficult and demanding role in the 1820s. Subjects were not subdivided, so the tutor was responsible for the guidance and supervision of a student's entire studies. This required the tutor to be familiar with, and read with their students, the authors and their works being studied. Yet Thomas Vowler reflected on the failings and shortcomings of an Oxford education as practised in the house:

> As the advantages and disadvantages of the tutorial system are little understood in the world, the opinion of an old college tutor may be of some value. The *theory* of the Oxford system, as discoverable in the statutes, is that every undergraduate should have a tutor, or guardian, assigned to him by the head of his college, who should superintend his education, watch over his conduct, and guide him in his studies pursued under various professors. The *practice* in my time was, that the tutor had usurped the office of the professor, and was the only person, except the college lecturer, who taught the young men anything. (TV Short 1875, p. viii, emphases in the original)

Two tutors during Augustus Short's time stood out. One was Thomas Vowler, and the other John Bull, Henry Bull's brother (see Appendix B). Frederick Oakeley reminisced in 1865-66: '[G]ood work done there by Tutors like Thomas Vowler Short and Dr Bull. Short, "the Old Growler", Pusey's friend and teacher, destined for a bishopric later, was a strong educational influence in the College til 1829' (in Mallett 1924, p. 219). Others concurred with this assessment of Bull and TV Short, with the latter being described as a prelate of exceptional integrity and benevolence' (Thompson 1900, p. 180) after his elevation to the episcopacy. For Augustus Short these men represented something of the rewards for diligence and consistency in studies.

Thomas Vowler Short's influence and example

Thomas Vowler Short was born on 16 September 1790 at Dawlish, Devon, where his father, the Reverend William Short, was curate. Thomas's father had been educated at Eton and Christ Church and, after his initial curacy, became rector of King's Worthy in Hampshire. He was later a prebendary of Westminster, chaplain to the bishop of Exeter, archdeacon of Cornwall, and preceptor and chaplain to the Princess Charlotte, the daughter of King George IV, then Prince of Wales, whose early death deprived her of the throne (Brown 2014). Educated initially by his father, Thomas Vowler had entered, at thirteen, Westminster School, where his headmaster was Dr Carey, later his predecessor as bishop of St Asaph. Carey became his patron and Charles Longley, who appears to have been his fag whilst at Westminster and was later archbishop of Canterbury, became a lifelong friend. Having been elected a Westminster scholar to Christ Church in May 1809 as a student, he obtained a double first three years later, in Classics and mathematics. In 1816, by which time he was a tutor in the house, he was offered one of the ninety livings in the hands of the dean and chapter, the curacy of Cowley. At first Thomas Vowler demurred, but then he changed his mind, accepting the parochial challenge as a serious calling to the merely academic life of the tutor (Brown 2014, n.p.). This example was not lost over a decade later when Augustus Short had to consider the same challenge, and resolved it in a similar way to Thomas Vowler.

While a teaching student and a tutor of the house, 1819-29, Thomas Vowler was working on a history of the Church of England, obviously sharing his ideas and conclusions with his undergraduates and colleagues, Augustus included. Augustus Short recollected in his reminiscences that, by permission of the dean, he resided

Figure 2.5   Bishop Thomas Vowler Short.
Source: 'Thomas Vowler Short, Bishop of St Asaph', painting by MA Shee. Reproduced from Wikimedia Commons.

> in College under the Rev T Vowler Short during the Long Vacation, preceding the Michaelmas examination in the Classical School. While thus 'staying up' I was favoured by riding with my Cousin to different places in the neighbourhood of Oxford; the scenes of battles, or events during the great Civil War. He was then writing that portion of his History of the Church of England. I look back with much real pleasure on that Vacation spent in College with 3 other students under the Rev T V Short's kind supervision. Altogether this was the most profitable portion of my undergraduate life. (SLSA, PRG 160/7, emphases in the original)

When the book, *A Sketch of the History of the Church of England: To the Revolution, 1688* (TV Short 1832), was published, the concerns of the book had been well traversed by himself, as well as by others in Christ Church, not least Charles Lloyd, whose thoughts are covered in Chapter Three. Yet Thomas Vowler was pioneering fresh paths.

> I am just going to publish a sketch of the 'History of the Church of England', in two volumes octavo, which is to give the world, particularly my own profession, a new view of ecclesiastical history. So says vanity ... I have tried to be fair and to avoid all party views, a line of writing which is not likely to suit the taste or prejudices of either party. (TV Short 1832, p. liv)

He had written in the Preface of the 'sketch':

> The author of the present sketch discovered after he had been admitted into orders, that the knowledge of English ecclesiastical history which he possessed was very deficient. It was a point concerning which, information was not to be readily obtained, but in which he felt that he ought to have made diligent search during the professional preparation of himself, on which every educated man, who is engaged in the instruction of others, is peculiarly bound to enter; he was distressed that his knowledge of the sects among the philosophers of Athens was greater than his information on questions which affect the Church of England; and he determined to devote a considerable portion of those few hours, which a laborious employment left at his disposal, to the study of the history of his own church. (p. v)

An extensive history, Thomas Vowler's work included several important Appendices scattered throughout. These were intended to recall his students and colleagues to the roots of English Christianity, with titles such as 'On the Dissolution of the Monasteries'; 'Doctrines Prevalent at the End of the Reign of Henry VIII'; 'History of the Thirty-Nine Articles of Religion'; 'History of the Translation of the Bible'; 'History of the Compilation of the Common Prayer Book'. He conceived of English Christianity as being characterised by having an independent Church, having a distinctive English liturgical history, and practising a faithfulness to scripture. In this he shared with the Regius Professor of Divinity, Charles Lloyd, the same concerns highlighted in Lloyd's lectures and private classes during the 1820s (TV Short 1832, p. 24).

The discussions about the themes and details of this book obviously featured strongly in Augustus's relationship with his cousin, and influenced Augustus with its appeal to the early Church for patterns of worship and behaviour to refute Roman Catholic practices and doctrines. Proclaiming it as 'unknown in the early church' (p. 24), Thomas Vowler dismissed transubstantiation, abuses of pilgrimages, worship of relics, and private or solitary masses. He affirmed that in confession and penance, 'the rule of our church corresponds with the practice of the primitive Christians during the first four centuries' (p. 24). On the centrality of the episcopate he asserted that

> the elements of the argument [for episcopacy] will be that at a certain time it was found existing in the church; that history states not when it began; and that the supposition of it having existed from the time of the apostles is not contradicted, but rather supported by the apostolic history. (p. 305)

He reminded his younger cousin frequently of his view: 'the more I have studied the doctrines of the Church of England, the more convinced I am of their accordance with the spirit of primitive Christianity, and the directions given in the Bible' (TV Short 1847, p. 9). Thus Short heard from his most significant personal influence material relevant to the independence, continuity and integrity of the established

Church. Eventually, taking holy orders in 1826, Short was to follow closely in the patterns of understanding and beliefs of his cousin.

Thomas Vowler's influence on Short was not just ecclesiological, but also educational. From 1819, for a decade, Thomas Vowler was given key positions of responsibility: censor, public examiner and proctor. During this period he was clearly developing reformist ideas regarding the role of the university, and especially about the public examinations he prepared his undergraduates for. He argued strongly that ways should be found for a university education to be made available to more young men. The residential requirement for all undergraduates of the University of Oxford drew Thomas Vowler's ire because of its discrimination:

> [B]elieving, as I do, that Oxford still offers the most beneficial system of education for ordinary students, belonging to the professional branches of society, or to the higher orders, I cannot help deploring the necessity under which this University labours, of rejecting annually a considerable number, because her walls cannot contain them. (TV Short 1822, pp. 37-8)

Alarming was the way he regarded the standard of matriculants:

> Young men enter the University at a much later period of life than they used to do; yet their ignorance on most topics which have not been immediately placed before their eyes is excessive. Of Christianity they frequently know little or nothing; on mathematical subjects they have so long delayed the study, that they often find some difficulty in acquiring that which would have been an easy task to them three or four years before ... and arithmetic is remembered as a species of knowledge in which they had once made some proficiency. (pp. 37-8)

The tutor's academic responsibility was paralleled with an expected pastoral concern for each student; after all, most tutors, being in holy orders, saw this as a genuine ministry (Thompson 1899, p. 28). Thomas Vowler became highly respected for his pastoral care of undergraduates, his catechising among pupils at the university's school, and for pastoral ministry with college servants and their families. According to a resident of Oxford forty years after TV Short left:

> His interest in and kindness to the poor of Oxford, especially the families of college servants, though I fancy almost unknown to his contemporaries, are remembered and appreciated now by those at the time who were almost children'. (Preface to TV Short 1832, p. 1)

In 1820 he had become a censor of the house. The censors (senior and junior) were the key administrative and academic colleagues for the dean, and were responsible for tuition and discipline within the house. The senior censor was regarded as 'a most important, dignified, and lucrative position' (Baker 1981, p. 23) and often led to significant preferment in the Church. These examples were not lost on Augustus Short, a call to ministry transcending privilege and power. Oakeley, in 1865-66, recorded this vignette of the two censors:

> They [Dr Bull and TV Short] used to run their chance of such interruptions [when teaching], under the conviction that they were fully equal to the encounter. Thus it sometimes happened that when Short was engaged in illustrating the Fifth Book of Ethics by the laws of political economy, or while Bull was in a *furore* of classical enthusiasm over an ode of Pindar or a chorus of Sophocles, there would enter the manciple — a pale, placid official connected with the culinary department — who came to Bull as the senior censor, or, in his absence, to Short as the junior, to take their pleasure as to the dinner at the master's table for the day … [T]o the manciple's interrogative Short would reply, with a slight manifestation of impatience at the interruption, 'Oh, anything you've got, — a boiled leg of mutton and a pudding'. (In Quiller-Couch 1892, p. 327, emphasis in the original)

In Short's fourth year, 1823, Thomas Vowler's importance to the house was recognised when he was 'elected' (that is, appointed) librarian in the house, public examiner, and one of two proctors within the university. Here is Oakeley in 1865-66 again:

> [T]hose who are acquainted with the present Bishop of St Asaph [TV Short] and who know that a character so simple, so truthful, and so up-right is not the creation of a day, will not be surprised to hear that the well-known Thomas Vowler Short, of forty-five years ago, was the precise counterpart of the honest Welsh prelate, minus the wrinkles, gray hair, apron and lawn sleeves. Among the many sorrowful recollections connected with my undergraduate days, not one of the least is that I did not fall more directly under the practical influence of that truly good man. As it was I knew only enough of him to be cowed and replied by his blunt and somewhat uncouth manner, especially after a withering examination which he once gave me at Collections in the fifth book of Ethics. (In Quiller-Couch 1892, p. 314)

An apocryphal story about Short was that on learning of his double first class in 1812, he immediately sat down to study St Paul's Epistle to the Romans.

As a public examiner, Thomas Vowler continued his promotion of reforms for the examination system in the university; he was conscious that mathematics and arithmetic particularly were 'apt to be neglected' in many of the feeder schools, most clearly Westminster, where standards during the 1820s seemed to be slipping (Curthoys 2012, p. 206). In 1822, during his third year of tutoring his young cousin, Thomas Vowler gave vent to his criticisms of the 'new' public examination system, and proposed thoughtful reforms to both enhance the learning experience for the undergraduate and raise the educational standards at the same time. He expounded his views in *A Letter addressed to the Very Reverend The Dean of Christ Church on the state of the Public Examinations in the University of Oxford*, focusing on the length and monotony of the drawn-out six-week process of the public examinations (TV Short 1822, pp. 7-8).

During 1823, when holding the position of proctor on the governing body of the university for twelve months, Thomas Vowler recalled:

> [W]hen in my capacity of proctor I had in the year 1823 a seat at the board of heads of houses, through which all statutes must pass, and in which from the practice of the University they always originate, the question of the examination statute was brought forward, yet such was the terror of any fundamental alteration, that a statute was prepared which did not meet with the approbation of convocation. (TV Short 1822, p. 29)

Thomas Vowler did not succeed with his reformist ideas while Augustus was his student, yet, when Dean Charles Hall was succeeded by the rather lacklustre Samuel Smith (1765-1841) from 1824, it was said that Thomas Vowler's influence as censor was a prime reason for the improvement in tone and appearance of Christ Church during the remainder of the decade (Curthoys 2012, p. 205).

The proctor

The post of proctor was of substantial significance, being the first line in maintaining the discipline and behaviour of undergraduates, and thus the tone and appearance of the university as a whole (Rogers 1861, p. 27). It was essentially a policing role. The two university proctors joined the vice-chancellor and the heads of colleges on the governing body of the university, the Hebdomadal Board. Proctors were therefore statutory officials in the university government, retaining the right of veto over decisions of the Convocation — the assembled graduates of the university.

Cox (1870) records how proctors were 'expected to be ubiquitous and omnipresent':

> Some of the duties of the office were formerly more trying, and to quiet, refined men more disagreeable than they have become since the institution [about 1829] of an enlarged and effective 'University Police'. The night-walking (at least the worst part of it); the searching of ill-famed houses ... the being called out, sometimes *called up*, to put a stop to a row resulting from protracted wine parties: — such duties as these often deterred quiet, nervous men from undertaking the office when it came to them ... [B]y way of compensation for the 'disagreeables' above mentioned, the proctorship was wisely surrounded with honour, invested with patronage, and endowed with a liberal income. (p. 221, emphasis in the original)

Oakeley, when recalling in 1865-66 the Commemoration of 1820, which Augustus Short also attended, was astounded at the reception Dr John Bull received from some of the undergraduates:

> The first of these was the extraordinary unpopularity of the Senior Proctor of that year — my kind friend and sometime tutor, Mr [afterwards Dr] Bull, of Christ Church ... [T]his really kind-hearted man had contrived to earn for himself the unpopular

characters of a tyrant and a tuft-hunter; and the under-graduate world poured forth upon him, at the annual saturnalia, the pent up fury of the preceding two terms … [T]hey hissed, they yelled, they roared like a bull, with a manifest allusion to the proctor's ill-starred name. (In Quiller-Couch 1892, p. 304)

It is unlikely that, after his Westminster experiences, Augustus Short was as shocked by this display as the more naïve Oakeley was. When Thomas Vowler held the post of proctor the significance for Short of being related to, and in the company of, such a commanding figure more than likely had an impact on him. The notion of the ordained serving in a worthwhile and varied fashion in the academic world was an example for him, and, while he did not say so, this may have been an influence on the decisions he was making about his future career or vocation.

Through his cousin, Short became acquainted, either personally or by conversation and debate, with some of the significant and emerging scholars of the university. Thomas Vowler was intimate with John Keble, fellow of Oriel College, before Keble left for a rural ministry in 1823[15]; he tutored Edward Bouverie Pusey, and they formed a mutual lifelong regard for each other; he tutored William Ewart Gladstone, as Augustus Short was to do; and he was a public examiner of John Henry Newman when he presented for his degree. Some of these figures dominated the early days of the Oxford or Tractarian Movement from 1833.

His cousin was renowned for maintaining a notebook, *History of My Pupils*, in which he expressed candid opinions about some of those who were tutored by him. However, in relation to Augustus, Thomas Vowler was circumspect and simply factual.

The learning experience

What constituted the substance of Short's formal tutorial education? When the university examination statute was adopted in 1800 it encompassed a wide range of subjects. Mathematics and physics were separated out at a later date, and the remaining subjects grouped under the title *Literae Humaniores*. Law and Hebrew disappeared, as did metaphysics and history, with *Literae Humaniores* left with moral philosophy, logic, divinity, Greek and Latin. Thomas Vowler recalled that

> about two years and a half of an academical life are spent in a course of study, which, as far I can judge, is nearly as good as it can be. It generally commences with the Greek historians and Latin poets, and ends with the historians of Rome and the poets of Greece, while mathematics, logic, rhetoric, and moral philosophy are pursued according to the abilities and wishes of the pupil; divinity forms a necessary part of every examination for the degree, as well of the course of instruction. (TV Short 1822, p. 21)

---

15 JH Newman recounts how Thomas Vowler was present on 30 July 1839 for the consecration of Keble's church at Hursley; see Tracey 1995, p. 117.

The examinations, into the 1820s, were oral, highlighting a student's skill in construing Greek and Latin. Logic held a prime place because it trained the mental faculties in how to discriminate in argument, and to state questions distinctly (Bill 1988, p. 267). The focus on deductive thinking suited matters of law, morals and religion; centring on words and ideas rather than on the observation of facts or of nature. Mathematics held sway as an introductory study of logic and of astronomy. The classical authors, the literature of ancient Greece and Rome, were seen as superior for the development of mental acuity, and moral and social relationships. For example, Copleston, writing in 1809, advocated the study of Thucydides as much for contemporary as for classical reasons: '[F]rom no study can an Englishman acquire a better insight into the mechanism and temper of civil government; from none can he draw more instructive lessons, both of the danger of turbulent faction, and of corrupt oligarchy' (in Bill 1988, p. 275).

This was to be echoed by Augustus Short, over forty years later, when he wrote a letter from Adelaide to his former student, WE Gladstone, on matters of Church organisation:

> [S]ome Central Authority should exist in England ... asserted ... by a Reformed Convocation containing its proper Lay Element. Even then, if the Central Authority should go wrong, it would still be open for the Diocesan Churches to take, in the last resort, their own view ... When we read Thucydides together, I flatter myself I pointed out this principle, stated in the Speech of the Corcyreans against Athenian 'Imperial' oppressiveness (SLSA, PRG 160/81, emphases in the original)

A Royal Commission regarding university education, reporting in 1852, observed:

> From the year 1807 to 1825, the students were encouraged to study many works which have now almost entirely disappeared from the university course, such as Homer, Demosthenes, Cicero, Lucretius, Terence, Plutarch, Longinus, Quintilian. A list of twenty classical authors was not infrequent even as late as 1827. (In Bill 1988, p. 296)

Thomas Vowler had himself criticised the course of study as early as 1822 and looked for examinations which were written and more analytical (TV Short 1822, p. 21).

Religion and ethics were intertwined: the former permitting the latter, the latter providing rational thought to religious principles. The classical authors were often read for their portrayals of problems of evil and good. In order to gain a degree, as well as being examined in these studies (in the early years of the nineteenth century) a student was examined closely in the doctrines of the Christian religion, and specifically in the foundations of the established Church. The expectations were that by construing a passage of the Greek testament, a student would demonstrate his understanding of sacred history and Christian doctrine. The evidences of Christianity and the Thirty-Nine Articles of Religion became paramount (Bill 1988, p. 301). The curriculum, therefore, was overwhelmingly a classical and literary one; it developed, skills such as logical thinking, and fluency and clarity, with attention to brevity (Curthoys 2012, p. 172). Where were the young men in debate and argument regarding politics, history, morals and religion? What were the clergy of Oxford trying to safeguard with such a curriculum?

Collections

The culmination of most teaching and learning every term at Christ Church was an event for each undergraduate called Collections, an informal system of examining designed to test academic progress. This oral examination was presided over by the dean and censors, and a list of all the reading presented by the student from the term was recorded in the Collection Books, as well as the comments of the examiners. This emphasis on accountability and recording had set Christ Church apart from other colleges since at least the seventeenth century. For the undergraduate, it provided both an incentive for, and genuine test of, progress in learning.

An undergraduate's record accounted for his reading in Herodotus, Thucydides, Livy, Polybius, Homer, Virgil, a good deal of Cicero, Xenophon, some Plato, and the plays of Euripides, Aeschylus, Sophocles, and Terence, and the inevitable Euclid and Aristotle. He also read a course of logic and theology, which included Butler's *Analogy of Religion* (Bill 1973, p. 15). The impact of Collections was to raise the academic standard at Christ Church so much so that the university honours system actually appeared diminished in comparison; surpassing the university examinations in quality and intention (Bill 1988, p. 223). Tutors and their small intimate classes were the centrepiece, and not university professors in lecture halls.

Whither a new curriculum?

In later life, Short developed a keen fascination and curiosity for the sciences. It is interesting to note where the sciences, as studies in their own right, stood in the early nineteenth century at Oxford. It would be erroneous to think that because of the prevailing curriculum there was no interest in scientific discoveries. In fact, it appears that precisely because of the conservative bias in the curriculum, many of Oxford's professors and tutors, graduates and undergraduates, were drawn to the gathering revolution in scientific understanding. In 1818 the university created the position of Reader in Geology, appointing William Buckland, whose lectures were popular. During the 1820s attendances at mineralogy classes averaged thirty-four, and sixty-one for geology. This from an average 400 new matriculated students each year (Brock & Curthoys 1997, p. 546). Buckland was regarded as a pioneer in historical geology, especially the study of fossils. There is a delightful lithograph of Buckland (a canon of Christ Church from 1825) lecturing on 15 February 1823. Present were many of the leading lights of Christ

Church, some of them acquaintances of Augustus Short — Thomas Vowler Short, Charles Longley, John Bull, Josias Conybeare, and other luminaries such as Thomas Arnold (later Regius Professor of Modern History), Charles Lloyd (Regius Professor of Divinity) and Richard Whateley (later Professor of Political Economy) (Brock & Curthoys 1997, p. xix). Buckland (1820) asserted that the new scientific world was complementary to a classical education and wrote of the 'ingrafting (if I may so call it) of the study of the new and curious sciences of Geology and Mineralogy, on that ancient and venerable stock of classical literature from which the English system has imparted to its followers a refinement of taste peculiarly their own' (pp. 2-5).

At Christ Church the creation of an anatomy school in 1768 had been pioneering and by Short's time the school held extensive collections of specimens illustrative of both human and comparative anatomy. The Anatomy School, accessed behind the hall, conducted a range of studies with animal and human remains, some bodies even acquired from prisons for dissection. In 1822 John Kidd (Westminster pupil and Christ Church student), already the Lee Reader in Anatomy, was appointed the Regius Professor of Medicine and made an immediate impact on undergraduates and graduates alike. He secured the first two microscopes to appear at the university and became renowned for his promotion of science education. His influence contributed to the house, accounting for one-fifth of medical graduates at the university in the first decades of the century, many completing *Literae Humaniores* prior to a medical degree.

Typical of many of his contemporary science proponents, Kidd believed the teaching of science to be complementary and ancillary to the traditional curriculum, writing in 1818: '[T]hese branches of science, in this place at least, may be considered with reference to Divinity, Classics, and Mathematics in the same light as the supernumerary war-horses of Homer's chariots; which were destined to assist, but not to regulate, the progress of their nobler fellow-coursers' (in Brock & Curthoys 1997, p. 560).

Short became an enthusiast for science in education. Many years later, this interest was apparent when he wrote to the *South Australian Register* on 11 March 1869 on the subject of a museum in Adelaide:

> Sir — I understand that on the completion of the new Lunatic Asylum the present building adjacent to the Botanical Gardens will be available for other purposes ... I venture to suggest to those who will have the disposal of the present abode for lunatics whether it might not usefully be occupied as a museum of natural history, comparative anatomy, geology, and mineralogy. There the fossil relics of prehistoric nature, together with the forms of existing species, might be collected and arranged for the study of our intelligent youth, and the acquisition of enlarged ideas of the magnificence of creation to all observers.

> The colony has outgrown its Institute as a Museum — it is simply contemptible. The library it contains affords no help to the scientific enquirer in astronomy, anatomy, mineralogy, and engineering, and other departments of practical science. There can therefore be no school in Adelaide of medicine and surgery; no instruction given in mineralogy and geology; though the province abounds in metallic ores and valuable stones; no scientific information to be obtained even as to the best mode of forming a dam across the Torrens; no research encouraged into the stratification; water supply; comparative use of fossil flora and fauna of this both ancient and modern portion of the globe…..
>
> Cricket and croquet, rowing and athletic sports, bad elocution and worse acting, Mutual Improvement and Literary Societies are now in fashion; but the conceit engendered by little knowledge and the narrowness of sectarian associations need the correction which an enlarged study of nature and of the world could probably impart. At present it is scarcely possible to lay the foundation even of a scientific professional life within the colony, much less to complete the education of the surgeon or physician, the civil engineer or mineralogist, the astronomer or mechanician, the architect, sculptor, or painter. ('Letter to the Editor', p. 3)

Christ Church and Short

Short graduated as a Bachelor of Arts in 1823 with a first class in Classics, the highest general distinction the university could give. Then followed a period of two years as a private tutor outside Christ Church. Christ Church had been for four years an environment of books and conversation, of collegiality and affection from a few, of the spaciousness of the Meadow and its easy walks, and above all, the charm and calm joy of cathedral worship. What was the context then for Short making decisions about his future?

His reluctance to live the high life while in the house, and his studious approach to undergraduate life, reflected his character of seriousness and single-mindedness. In his reminiscences he reflected on this:

> My aim of Classical distinction in the 'Schools' and the necessity of <u>hard</u> reading threw me into quieter companionships: at length with Michaelmas Term of 1823, after the 'Long Vacation' passed as I have described, at the final examination I obtained First Class Honours in Classics — this distinction opened a successful University career to me. At that time Dec 22nd 1823[16], the unexpected death of a beloved sister at our home in Great George Street Westminster, *exercised I believe a strong influence for good on my character*. I remember well the <u>terrible</u> shock her unforseen death gave one on the letter reaching one in Christ Church and the miserable night I passed in the Mail

---

16 Short's recollection is in error here: his sister Augusta died on 22 January 1823.

> Coach going up to London, I was alone inside, the Cold was severe, the Cheswell was frozen over <u>that</u> night, and I had great difficulty in keeping myself warm in the Coach. (SLSA, PRG 160/7, emphasis in the original)

Understandably, the grief of his father, Charles, recorded in Charles's own reminiscences, was even more poignant:

> I am constantly thinking of her. She was very handsome and accomplished, without one spark of vanity or affectation, she was truly religious & with the utmost sweetness of temper towards all around her — her loss I consider the heaviest blow I have received … [She was] buried in North Cloister of Westminster Abbey by Dean Ireland. (SLSA PRG 160/32)

At the same time, in all these undergraduate years, the influence, example and presence of his cousin was marked; the relationship became close and for several decades after, TV Short was to continue to encourage and support Augustus Short in his vocation, his learning, and his family life.

The 1820s were actually at the end of a long era of a particular style of school and university education. Change was building in society and in the universities, and there were insistent new ideas regarding what should constitute learning in the professorial lecture or the tutorial. Universities elsewhere (in Germany and Scotland, for example) were pioneering new directions in teaching, centred more on a university-wide professorial model. The certainties of the links between a classical and mathematical education with social conformity and progress were seriously being challenged. The groundswell of social and political changes demanded in the wake of the Napoleonic Wars, and in an increasingly industrialised and commercialised society, encouraged talk of reform in both the provision and the content of education. Short was aware of this changing landscape.

In later years, as a key founder of the University of Adelaide in 1874 (Whiting 2014), Short was to promote views about academic education obviously influenced by his years at Christ Church. He was to favour professorial teaching over the tutorial, and this may have been in the light of Christ Church possessing the most professorships in the university: the university chairs of Divinity, Hebrew, and Greek, along with the Reader in Anatomy. After his own experience as a Christ Church tutor outlined in the following chapter, he probably concurred with JH Newman's comments of 1839: 'College Tutors are over worked — and Professors could take from them advantageously many departments of general education — and then the Tutors would be more strictly guardians and formers of their Pupils' minds' (Tracey 1995, p. xvi).

Likewise, Short was to favour university government being in the hands of the professors rather than controlled by independent colleges. The example of Christ Church's governing body, appointed by the Crown, having a significant number of professors left a lasting impression on Short. He witnessed first-hand the advantages of linking the endowment of chairs with fellowships (or, as they were known at Christ Church, studentships); for example, Dean Gaisford (dean 1831-55) had held his studentship while being professor of Greek for many years.

Short, like so many of his contemporaries, was fascinated with the challenges of the scientific and industrial revolutions, and with political and social change; he knew education would have to change, and needed to be made available to the wider population. He was developing a keenness regarding education, especially its utilitarian and scientific aspects, and its place in the moral purposes of religion. Yet the largely old-fashioned education that Short had experienced, which had prevailed in England for many decades, had served him well in many ways. He now began to test that learning in relation to another seemingly settled way of life, that of the ordained in the established Church.

Little did he comprehend the manner and magnitude in which both education and English Christianity would be engulfed by change during his coming adult years, and the key role he would play in both, eventually, on the other side of the world.

3

Holy orders and teaching at Christ Church 1824-35

Just as Westminster School was unique in being part of one foundation with the abbey, its school chapel, so Christ Church had the cathedral of the Diocese of Oxford as its chapel. As he worshipped in Christ Church Cathedral, this most public union of Church and education felt not only familiar but natural to the young scholar.

Time and again during term, Short, on entering the cathedral (built in the second half of the twelfth century) with its very truncated nave, found his gaze riveted on the chancel at the east end with its striking late-fifteenth-century stone vaulted ceiling. Twelve stone lanterns hung in the air, completing the extraordinary ribbed ceiling. To the left, along the north aisle beyond the Lady Chapel, lay the Divinity or Latin Chapel. Here, at the beginning of each term, Latin prayers were said before all the students of the house. Lying in an arch to the south side of this chapel was the tomb of Lady Elizabeth de Montacute, who died 'on Tuesday after the feast of the Blessed Virgin, 1355' (Britton 1821, p. 42). She is said to have endowed a chantry in this location for two priests, 'to celebrate divine service daily, for the soul of Lady Elizabeth de Montacute, and for the souls of John Bokingham, Bishop of Lincoln, and all her parents and friends' (p. 42).[17]

The story was well told that Catherine of Aragon, Henry VIII's first wife, prayed in this chapel in 1518 near the shrine of St Frideswide, for the birth of a male heir. Short was to understand that these unanswered prayers ultimately led to the separation from the Roman Church and the beginnings of the English Reformation. Short often

---
17 Britton's book became available to students in May of 1821, Short's second year.

Figure 3.1   Short, at a service in the cathedral. Short is one of the staff seated to the right.
Source: 'Service in Christ Church Cathedral, 1830s', coloured lithograph. Reproduced by permission of the Dean and Governing Body.

Figure 3.2   The Latin Chapel, Christ Church.
Source: 'Latin Chapel, Christ Church Cathedral, Oxford'. Reproduced from a postcard in the author's possession.

noted the decorated vaulting, with the bosses detailing the waterlilies that are so much a part of the rivers of Oxford, the Cherwell and Isis. The fine woodwork of the stalls boasted prominent carvings: a crown of thorns, a cardinal's hat supported by angels (after Cardinal Wolsey), the emblems of the Evangelists, and the sacred monogram, IHS. The splendid windows shone, especially in the summer: one was of St Catherine, the Madonna and holy child, and the patron saint of Oxford, St Frideswide; another depicted an archbishop with a cross merging into his crooked pastoral staff; and yet another centred on St Frideswide, with St Margaret and St Catherine on either side of her. So much history and so many prayers.

Augustus had heard the Latin Chapel sometimes referred to as St Catherine's, the patroness regarded as the patron saint of students in theology. So it was to this chapel that all preparing for ordination came to hear the lectures of the Regius Professor of Divinity, who spoke from the pulpit, itself an outstanding example of seventeenth-century woodwork, the canopy seemingly suspended in the air like a halo.[18]

A clergyman, recalling his time in the chapel as it was in Short's day, enthused:

> It is that supremely excellent thing, a church within a church, without which no cathedral can be what its builders intended it to be; nor any religious building fulfil that instinctive desire of men for an inner place, where they can find their way to the inner places of their own hearts. In such a home of recollectedness, doubly guarded against the dogging world without, is 'rest without languor and recreation without excitement'; in such a place one is 'never less alone than when alone'; and the fine sympathy with the needs of workaday humanity, which led mediaeval architects to build such sanctuaries as this chapel here ... had led men in far earlier ages to find room even within the travelling tabernacle of a wandering tribe for a holy place and a holy of holies. (Deamer 1897, p. 103)

The path to ordination

When Short graduated with first-class honours in Classics, his life changed profoundly, as he described in 1882: 'My father had intended me for the Chancery Bar, but now wished me to follow a scholastic career, which seemed opening before me' (in Whitington 1887, p. 9). This was no simple choice; such a future meant a role and function in the university, hopefully Christ Church, requiring the taking of holy orders. For Short this was not a formality.

Short's response to a personal call to the ordained ministry reveals much about his maturing character, nurtured at Westminster and deeply influenced by colleagues

---

18 This pulpit now stands in the nave opposite the main pulpit of the cathedral. The Latin Chapel meanwhile houses the reconstructed shrine of St Frideswide and the altar has been removed, yet every day Morning Prayer is said here by the clergy.

at Christ Church. His understanding of the ordained life was vital in his commitment and leadership during his future thirty-four years in South Australia. For him, becoming ordained clearly introduced a pattern of stability and reliability into his life, which developed and deepened in the face of the multitude of challenges a colonial episcopate was to bring.

Short was not much interested in a functional view of the ordained ministry, which emphasised preaching and evangelism. For Short there was a priestly character to embrace and understand; the attainment of this character had nothing to do with accident of birth or social status or even educational opportunity, but was a result of prayer, entering into the sacramental life of the Church, and living in the Christian community. Given his background, this liberated Short considerably. He had experienced the varied religious community of Christ Church, both the house and cathedral, for four years, on an intimate and personal level. Short wrote later, in his reminiscences, of his final undertaking at the end of 1823 to become a tutor while his call to take holy orders was reaching the point of commitment:

> [A]t this time in Christ Church, my position was good either in Private or College tuition. My career as a Tutor thus seemed marked out accordingly and in compliance with my father's wish I adopted it. In the following years I successively travelled with a young Christ Church pupil as his private tutor ... In 1826 at the Long Vacation I became private tutor to William and John Forbes: the prime heirs to the estate of Callander, Scotland, and the latter afterwards in the Coldstream Guards. (SLSA, PRG 160/7, emphasis in the original)

Short also stated:

> In the next summer, with two other pupils, I visited the lakes in Cumberland, as well as York and some other cathedral towns. Afterwards I became domesticated in the family as a private tutor of these pupils, and I consider it a providential event in my early life to have lived with this excellent and religious household. (1882 in Whitington 1887, p. 9)

By late 1825, Short had a growing sense of the providence of God, and was feeling an all-consuming purpose or direction taking over his life. Likewise, as he felt the call to ordination — that is, the kind of person it would require him to be, and the need to let his character be formed around a focus of serving God's kingdom — he also began to understand the renunciations this might mean. These were to become more obvious to him during his time teaching at Christ Church.

The practical reality of being prepared for ordination was surprisingly uninspiring. All undergraduates at the University of Oxford were required to study the evidences for the Christian religion, to possess some knowledge of the Old and New Testaments and the history of their compositions, and to understand and subscribe to the Thirty-Nine

Articles of Religion as proved by Scripture. To then proceed as a graduate to the ordained ministry in the Diocese of Oxford required only acceptance by the diocesan bishop and attendance at a short course of twelve lectures given by the Regius Professor of Divinity — lectures always delivered in the refined atmosphere of the cathedral's Latin Chapel. Over two weeks the Professor gave a general survey of theology and nominated further reading:

> it is undoubtedly the case that by far the majority of Oxford graduates take holy orders, there being only twenty-seven per cent of its masters of arts not clergymen. But Oxford does not teach clergymen. Its instructions in theology are of the scantiest and most meagre order, comprising ordinarily such information as would be given by any Christian parent to the members of his household, and in the case of those who purpose entering the Church, the attendance on one or two courses of professorial lectures. These are of very little profit. (Rogers 1861, p. 6)

Edward Bouverie Pusey complained in 1833: 'One fortnight now comprises the beginning and the end of all public instruction which any candidate for holy orders is required to attend previously to entering upon his profession' (in Butler 1983, p. 150). The Regius Professor of Divinity was thus the sole formal influence for the young ordinand.

Short was searching in his contemporary United Church of England and Ireland for the true roots of its Christian expression. He became aware that this search was shared with many others, and was gathering pace generally in the early nineteenth century — nowhere more so than in Oxford. Over the next two decades he became a spectator of, and sometimes a participant in, these debates and controversial events. Short revered holy scripture, yet the Church's history and traditions loomed just as vital to his religion. The apostolic teaching through the ages, the grace of God, and the presence of the Holy Spirit in the Church's community life and witness — all of the Church's rich symbolism and dynamism resounded with him. He resolved on ordination, and was made deacon by Bishop Legge of Oxford in Christ Church Cathedral on 21 May 1826. Charles Lloyd (Legge's successor as bishop of Oxford from March 1827) ordained Short to the priesthood in the same cathedral on 10 June 1827, the eve of Short's twenty-fifth birthday. Short was maintaining a family clerical tradition: his great-grandfather had been precentor of Exeter Cathedral, his grandfather a prebendary of the same cathedral, his uncle an archdeacon; and his cousin, TV Short, was also ordained.

What Short had discovered as an undergraduate was indeed that his university, often thought of simply as 'the nursery of the Church of England' (Green 1974, p. 134), did not in fact educate in theology at any depth at all, and religious instruction was minimal. His cousin expressed clearly the state of such instruction in the faith in those early decades of the nineteenth century:

> In one respect there was a sad deficiency in the College, I mean as to religious instruction. When I entered Christchurch [*sic*], there was absolutely none. The old system, in which the catechist, who was generally senior censor, gave a public lecture in chapel, had been done away, and never existed in my time. The new plan, by which the senior censor lectured three times a week in the public lecture-room, was soon afterwards set up, but it comprehended those undergraduates only who had entered on their third year, and the teaching concerned rather the preparation for the degree than religious instruction …
>
> As far as I remember, Lloyd began the custom of having his pupils in his own room, with their Greek Testaments. People may laugh at college religion taught over a Greek testament. I am sure that a religious man has, as tutor, no better way of leading his pupils to a knowledge of heavenly things, and that even when he himself is not strongly influenced by religious feelings, such a method of proceeding will probably render himself and his pupils better Christians. As far then, as teaching was concerned, I never had, as an undergraduate, any religious instruction. But the preparation for our public examination brought us into contact with Christianity, and among ourselves many of us read a good deal of the elements of divinity. (TV Short 1875, p. xlvix)

Nevertheless, most graduates, as Masters of Arts, took holy orders in Short's time, and many of the clergy sent from Oxford did fulfill an important function in English society, being a class of people acting as 'intermediaries' between groups in a rigidly stratified society (Rogers 1861, p. 9). This echoed a general belief that early in the nineteenth century an Oxford education, for clergy as for any other profession, was deliberately broad enough to be a means of conveying the moral and social expectations of a gentleman. Gradually, this view diminished and an education focused more on intellectual endeavours emerged by mid-century (Dowland 1997, p. 214).

Charles Lloyd's influence and example

> Had he not died at the early age of forty-five, Lloyd (1784-1829) would have played a great part in the stirring times that were in store for the Church. He was, says Mr. Gladstone, 'a man of powerful talents, and of character, both winning and decided.' He was a Christ Church don, and had Sir R. Peel among his pupils and constant friends. Lloyd warmly supported the Roman Catholic Relief Act in 1829. He was the first to publish the Prayer Book with red lettered rubrics. (Deamer 1897, p. 135)[19]

It was to Short's lasting benefit that his divinity lectures and ordination preparation were given by Charles Lloyd, elected Regius Professor of Divinity in 1822; a man who divided opinion greatly but was reforming in his teachings. Physically overweight,

---

19 The Roman Catholic Relief Act of 1829 removed longstanding discriminations against Roman Catholics in the United Kingdom, including Ireland. The Act, importantly, permitted members of the Roman Catholic Church to sit in the Parliament at Westminster.

socially often rude and abrupt, Lloyd was driven by ambition, and once he had become Regius Professor, he was determined to found a distinctive English school of theology at Oxford; in this he made himself the most influential Oxford professor of the 1820s. For ordinands he introduced the first postgraduate courses, with his characteristic High Church flavour. Most importantly, he introduced systematic reading and study of both the scriptures and the writings of the early Church fathers. Ward summed up the theological significance of this study of the early Church fathers when he quoted Newman's phrase, 'It was Lloyd to whom was "reserved to report to a degenerate age the theology of the fathers"' (in Ward 1965, pp. 52-3).

Lloyd often drew the ire of others by his outward manner; indeed, one commenter, Joshua Watson, referred to him as 'honest Lloyd, blunt and bluff' (in Churton 1863, p. 152). But his students soon responded to a much more friendly and even playful scholar:

> He had been for some years one of the senior tutors at Christ Church ... when the College numbered among its tutors [Thomas Vowler] Short and Longley, both since raised to grace the episcopal bench, and Levett, Bull, and Cranmer all names worthy of remembrance for private worth, ability and learning. But those who survive will readily admit that Lloyd was more than their equal for talents and acquirements of all kinds, for his varied knowledge, and the ease and skill with which he communicated his knowledge; and second to none in the conscientious vigilance with which he watched over the moral and religious training of his pupils. It was a penetrating sagacity guided by affection, which was irresistible. (p. 153)

The post of Regius Professor of Divinity was one of some antiquity. Founded by Henry VIII in 1535, the chair was joined five years later by Regius Professors of Hebrew, Greek, Civil Law and Medicine, the endowment of the chairs eventually becoming the responsibility of the dean and chapter of Christ Church. By Lloyd's time, the university statutes required public divinity lectures each Monday and Friday during term, at 9 am, dealing with aspects of scripture; the Professor was responsible for these lectures during at least one term in the year. All graduates in residence were expected to attend, but in reality only those seeking ordination were the ones present in the 1820s. As Keble put it, 'a Divinity class at the University naturally implies one of which the far greater part consists of those who are being prepared for Holy Orders' (Coleridge 1880, p. 401).

Lloyd was only briefly bishop of Oxford (he died on 7 August 1829), yet his theological lectures between 1823 and his death were noted for their determined anti-sectarian and anti-Erastian principles. His High Church approach focused on the English Church's historical continuity and emphasised the re-assertion of Church principles, arising in the Apostolic Church and developed by the early fathers; the Church's episcopal and sacramental life, the primacy of the scriptures and the creeds, and the spiritual independence of the Church. He shared with university colleagues a 'broad-based Anglican renewal against the opposing claims of Unitarianism and rational Dissent on the one hand and Roman Catholicism on the other' (Brock & Curthoys 1997, p. 201). Lloyd published little, but his book *The Formularies of Faith put forth by Authority during the Reign of Henry VIII*, published in 1826 clearly set before his students sixteenth-century beliefs upholding the importance of pre-Reformation ideas and principles inherited by the United Church of England and Ireland. All his students were referred to these readings in preparation for ordination. In its preface Lloyd asserted that

> these documents, though they carry no authority along with them as formularies of faith, are of great importance to all, who are anxious to acquaint themselves with the rise and progress of the Protestant opinion in this country, and who would examine critically into the history and intention of these formularies which were afterwards established, and are still of primary authority in the Church of England. It is in these works too that they may trace the last departure of that darkness, which had so long obscured the genuine form of Christianity, that they may hail the reappearance of the pure light of the gospel, and mark the first dawnings of a brighter day. (p. v)

Lloyd's aim, when lecturing on the Roman Breviary, was a constant: to remind his students of, and emphasise to them, the 'catholic' and 'primitive' and 'ancient' liturgical continuity of the established Church. William Palmer, when he published *Origines Liturgicae or Antiquities of the English Ritual and a Dissertation on Primitive Liturgies* in 1845, drew considerably upon Lloyd's earlier work. Lloyd knew that the history and tradition of the established Church had been neglected and warranted remedying; this went beyond just making scripture the focus of study for ordinands. In fact, the High Church tradition represented by Lloyd asserted that scripture was certainly the rule for faith but the corroboration or interpretation of the apostolic fathers was legitimate and sometimes required (Brock & Curthoys 1997, p. 237). A contrary view, from a Low Church perspective, was expressed years later by Reverend James Garbett, then Professor of Poetry. Writing at the height of the Tractarian disputes of those times, in October 1843, Garbett claimed 'that Romanism would naturally arise from studying Scripture through the Fathers, instead of studying the Fathers by the light of Scripture' (in Cox 1870, p. 331).

The influence of Lloyd's traditionalist views on Short became apparent time and again in Short's future role as bishop of Adelaide. He had seen in Lloyd a profound influence as he reminisced in 1882:

> My first theological examination was certainly somewhat perfunctory; but I must express my deep obligation subsequently to Dr Charles Lloyd, Regius Professor of Divinity, who delivered a series of lectures on the Epistle to the Romans, and then one

on the Roman Breviary as the source of the Book of Common Prayer. The catholic principle of Vincentius of Lerins, '*quod semper, quod ubique, quod ab omnibus*' was thus brought to my knowledge and conviction. (In Whitington 1887, p. 9)

The teaching of the early Church father, St Vincent of Lerins (died c. 445), while literally meaning 'what always, what everywhere, what by everyone', was the standard test for any authentic and universal Christian doctrine. In other words, the authentic in faith was that which had been held by believers 'always, everywhere, and by everyone'. This echoed the boast of Bishop Lancelot Andrewes in about 1600 regarding genuine orthodoxy: 'two Testaments, three creeds, four general councils, five centuries' (in Edwards 1978, p. 70). Short himself, several years later when he was select preacher before the university, expressed clearly how important to his theology and ecclesiology this view became. In a 'Notice' at the commencement of the published sermons (entitled *Sermons intended principally to illustrate the Remedial Character of the Christian Scheme, with reference to Man's Fallen Condition — Preached at Oxford before the University*), he wrote:

> In matters of practical difficulty we own, that 'in the multitude of counsellors there is safety.' May not such also be the case in abstruse subjects of speculation? According to the sound rule of Vincentius, quod *semper*, quod *ubique*, qoud *ab omnibus*; i.e. what *all* Christians *at all times* and *in all places* have held to be the sense, that most probably is the true interpretation of Scripture. (1838, p. vii, emphases in the original)

It was Lloyd's public lectures that drew so much attention and so clearly set the theological and ecclesiological framework for the young Short and others. The sense of the Church of England's Catholic and patristic heritage was dominant in Lloyd's divinity lectures and in this he had a profound influence on the future Tractarian Movement leaders (Brock & Curthoys 1997, p. 201).[20] In fact, what Newman recalled of Pusey, a contemporary at Lloyd's lectures, could equally be applied to Short; 'his [Pusey's] deep views of the Pastoral Office, his high ideas of the spiritual rest of the Sabbath, his devotional spirit, his love of the Scriptures, his firmness and zeal, all testify to the operation of the Holy Ghost' (Tristram 1956, p. 75).

Frederick Oakeley, Short's contemporary, recalled in 1865-66 that

> some of [Lloyd's] divinity-lectures were given before he became the Bishop of Oxford and some afterwards, but his elevation to the dignity did not produce the slightest difference in his demeanour, or even in his dress, the only symbol of it being his wig, which used to hang upon a peg in the door. He always wore a long loose coat, little removed from a dressing-gown, and carried in his hand a coloured pocket-handkerchief, as a necessary accompaniment of his habits as a professed snuff-taker ... [H]e never sat down, but always instructed peripatetically, making the circuit of his

---

20 These views Lloyd shared with TV Short; for more, see the preceding chapter.

large class once and again, and accosting several members … with a question which in its turn formed the handle of a reply of his own, full of information conveyed in a most attractive form … [H]e generally accosted [the students] by a kick on the shins, or by pulling their ears or noses to a degree which made them tingle … [T]he word 'special' was a favourite with him, and he always pronounced it with peculiar emphasis; and he generally drew attention to what he was saying by a copious use of the interrogative 'D'ye see?' (In Quiller-Couch 1892, p. 327)

Lloyd's eccentricities aside, his scholarship shone with a new method of lecturing, invigorating the public Divinity lectures, which had lost their lustre over preceding generations. In an Oxford where scholars were more acquainted with Homer and the Greek classics than with St Paul, Lloyd led his students into controversial scriptural areas, himself influenced by the insights of continental theologians and their debates. For example, he questioned, in the wake of German theological debates, the traditional view that Moses was the author of the Pentateuch, along with other provocative topics (Baker 1981, p. 98).

A forensic examination of scripture, verse by verse, became the lecture: 'he set the example of an elaborate study of the text and its interpretation, by occupying one whole lecture with the discussion of the four first verses of the Epistle to the Romans' (Ince 1878, p. 25). Introducing various interpretations of the text throughout the history of Christian theology, Lloyd would lead in to considering the current views within the English Church. Edward Bouverie Pusey concluded in 1877, when addressing the Oxford University Commission, that this approach enabled a whole generation (Short included) to embrace 'a very different idea of reading the New Testament from any that we had had before' (in Liddon 1894, pp. 62-3). Renown followed Lloyd for these lectures on St Paul, as Short was to testify. All this reflected that Lloyd was well aware of some elements of current German scholarship, and in particular, those concerning biblical criticism. To this end he ensured that one of his most promising students, Pusey, studied in Germany. Lloyd's popularity contrasted with the experience of other professors, whose public lectures were often openly neglected and derided: in 1832, the Regius Professor of History, Edward Nares, complained to the vice-chancellor of the university of 'being unable to procure any class … having difficulty even securing a room in which to lecture, and finding the whole experience defeating' (in Green 1974, p. 134).

Ffoulkes, writing in 1892, recounted how Lloyd's 'unmarried daughter … in kindness … [gave to Ffoulkes] a brief abstract of his unpublished Lectures, from April 1823 to February 1829' (p. 401). This abstract revealed a wide scope of subject matter in the Lectures, in a logical sequence, which could only have enhanced the theological and historical knowledge of his students: Lectures 1-3 — Genesis to Nehemiah, the New Testament referring to Roman history and the writings of Josephus; Lecture 4 — the study of ecclesiastical history, with special reference to Eusebius; Lectures 5-9 — the 'cautions' of atheism and deism, evidences of authenticity of scriptures and Church history, the crucial controversies and heresies; and Lectures 10-12 — the Reformation to 'mark how the Church of England did NOT adopt the Opinions of any distinct set or party of the Reformers, but chalked out a path for herself, by selecting from each what appeared most agreeable to Scripture' (Lloyd in Ffoulkes 1892, p. 403). In his final Lecture, Lloyd 'refers students to … the beauty of the offices of the *Book of Common Prayer*. The clergy should always use them in the way that will best serve for edification, and must not shrink from declaring the whole counsel of God' (Ffoulkes 1892, pp. 404; see also Lloyd 1838, p. xvii). Such teaching made a lasting impression on the young ordinands. Short recalled in his reminiscences of 1882:

> [T]hese lectures were the revival of those Theological Studies among the Clergy, which the University College Endowments were designed to foster; and to which in fact we owe the present advanced knowledge of Textual Criticism, as well as Patristic and Anglican Theology. I thus learned to value sound and accurate Biblical Knowledge, and the Primitive Theology which had enabled our Anglican Reformers to emphasise Scriptural purity of doctrine in the Anglican branch of the Catholic Church … together with Scripture as the <u>Supreme</u> Rule of Faith, became for me the Standard of Catholicity, and practically guided my views thro life and saved my Episcopal Administration from narrow and ignorant party exclusiveness. (SLSA, PRG 160/7, emphasis in the original)

For Short this was the history and tradition of orthodox English Christianity expressed within the established Church.

Lloyd's exemplary efforts were enhanced by private classes formed at his invitation, essentially a post-graduate education. An innovation, these classes were to be of great influence and importance to the revival of the Church of England:

> Dr Lloyd also formed small classes of persons, who could remain in residence in the University for some time after taking their degree. He read with them on a variety of subjects, giving them special books to get up, catechizing them upon these, and then adding his own thoughts and observations. Thus one term he discussed the criticism of the Septuagint, using Carpzov's Introduction; in others, Prideaux 'on the History between the Old and New Testaments'; Graves 'on the Pentateuch'; Paley's *Hoare Pauline*; Morsheim's 'Ecclesiastical History'. But his chief lectures were on the Epistles of St Paul. (Ince 1878, p. 25)

This reading list, 'giving them special books to get up', arising from the public lectures and private classes, does reveal an extensive study not then recommended in any university divinity course in England. Eventually Lloyd incorporated this list into a special publication of 1838, *A Catalogue of Books in Divinity, Ecclesiastical History &c. Including a Fine Collection of the Fathers of the Church* (pp. xxvi-xxxvi).

Figure 3.3 The Great Quadrangle. Note the small opening on the left, which was then the only entrance to the cathedral. The next door to the right leads to Charles Lloyd's rooms. The Hall is to the right.
Source: 'The Great Quadrangle, Christ Church', engraving by John Le Keux. Reproduced with permission from Memorials of Oxford, James Ingram, vol. 1, 1837.

In both the public lectures and, particularly, the private classes, Lloyd taught his students the rigours of the development of the English liturgies. Palmer recounts how, when preparing for holy orders, the study of ritual led him to discover that Lloyd himself had utilised his vast knowledge of the history and practice of the Church by entering his collections on the margins of a folio Prayer Book: 'Lloyd was also the first to publish the *Book of Common Prayer* with red-lettered rubrics at the University Press in 1829' (1845, p. vi). Lloyd traced, via historical analysis and word study of original sources, the English liturgies as they grew from the Roman missals and the Breviary. One of his students wrote much later:

> Bishop Lloyd's lectures had taught ... to the surprise of many, that the familiar and venerated Prayer Book [*Book of Common Prayer*] was but the reflexion of mediaeval and primitive devotion, still embodied in its Latin forms in the Roman Service books; and so indirectly had planted in their minds the idea of the historical connection, and in a very profound way the spiritual sympathy, of the modern with the pre-Reformation Church. (Church 1892, p. 47)

Another student, a close colleague of Newman, reminisced:

> Dr. Lloyd was a clergyman of great attainments, and unusual ability; one of those few men, under a corrupt system, who feel themselves strong enough to take a ground of their own, and to grapple fearlessly with existing prejudices. He had spent a portion of his earlier life in the company of French ecclesiastics, and from their conversation and example, had received an idea of Catholic doctrines, and Catholic life, very different from that which prevails among the great body of Protestants. (Oakeley 1855, pp. 4-5)

Lloyd, as the Divinity Professor, focused especially on the history, structure and intentions of the Anglican prayer book, a subject which led him, and with him, his pupils, to the examination of the Missal and the Breviary, as the sources from which the principal contents of the Prayer-book had been taken. There were a few other limited published works of Lloyd; however, some stood out. For example, in 1827, 'he put into the hands of his pupils a carefully prepared edition of the Greek Testament in 12mo, which is to this day the "*Textus Receptus*" at Oxford' (Ffoulkes 1892, p. 400).

Some of those invited to join Lloyd's private classes became famous names within the next decade: Edward Bouverie Pusey, John Henry Newman, Hurrell Froude, Robert Wilberforce, George Moberly, William Churton, Edward Denison. Newman, in time, became the most notable of Lloyd's pupils, and recounted in his memoirs of 1862 aspects of their encounters (here writing of himself in the third person):

> Lloyd was a scholar ... one of the high-and-dry school, though with far larger views than were then common ... Lloyd professed to hold to theology, and laid great stress on a doctrinal standard, authoritative and traditional teaching, and ecclesiastical history ... Lloyd made much of books and reading ... [A]n annual set of public lectures had been usual, attendance on them being made a *sine qua non* for ordination, but Dr Lloyd's new lectures were private and familiar. He began them in 1823, the year after Mr Newman's election [as a fellow] at Oriel and the year of Mr Pusey's ... [T]he subjects of the lectures betokened the characteristic tastes and sentiments of the lecturer. He had more liking for exegetical criticism, historical research, and controversy, than for dogma or philosophy. He employed his mind on the grounds of the Christian faith rather than on the faith itself; and, in his estimate of the grounds, he made light of the internal evidence for revealed religion, in comparison of its external proofs. (In Tristram 1956, p. 70)

Newman, when swirling in controversy by 1841 concerning his Tract 90, referred to Lloyd as someone who had taught him that beneath the errors of the Roman Church and its practices 'lay an essence of faith not unlike Anglicanism' (Baker 1981, p. 211).

Oakeley, writing in 1865-66, was effusive about Lloyd:

> Lloyd was the very prince of college-lecturers — a master in the art in which I have known so many failures ... Lloyd's peculiar excellence with his private Divinity class was, no doubt, the result in part of his former experience as a college-tutor, indeed, some of his pupils in that class had also been his pupils when he was tutor. As far as my recollections serve me, the tact and presence of mind which he showed with his class were characteristic of the Christ Church lecturers in general. (In Quiller-Couch 1892, pp. 325-6)

In 1878, Pusey went on to 'award [Lloyd] the palm of being the Oxford Movement's father' — high praise indeed, but not surprising, given Lloyd's audiences (in Butler 1983, p. 8). Undoubtedly, Lloyd's study and lecture room served as a nursery for the religious movement that brought turmoil to Oxford a few short years after his death. For Short, the legacy of Lloyd was his assertive character and infectious energy, his strategic sense of Church and state relations, his forensic approach to scripture, and his scholastic views on the historical origins of English Christianity, particularly its ecclesiology. Short's orthodox and traditional views of the faith and the Church owed much to Charles Lloyd's influence.

The ordained life: A curacy 1827-28

Following ordination, Short continued to reside in Christ Church. His father Charles reminisced: '1828 Augustus still residing in Ch Ch' (SLSA, PRG 160/32). The opportunity now arose for him to practise many of the teachings he had garnered from Lloyd's classes, and from his cousin, Thomas Vowler Short. Charles recollected: '[I]n July took the Curacy of Culham W. Oxford' (SLSA, PRG 160/32). Augustus himself, in 1882, wrote of this time:

> At the long vacation in 1827 the curacy of Culham near Abingdon, was offered to me, and I accepted the duty, which was to assist the vicar, he being in weak health. The population was small, and while I was thus initiated into the practical duties of a parish priest, the weekly visits and Sunday services afforded a pleasant variety from the routine of college life. In the hospitable vicarage, and in the family mansion of the squire I found very much to instruct and refine, counteracting at least the tendency of college tutorial duty to develop pedantry and dictatorial dogmatism. Thus passed two years very happily. (In Whitington 1887, pp. 9-10)

Culham, a tiny village just south of Abingdon, itself ten miles [sixteen kilometres] from Oxford, sat picturesquely in a bend of the Thames and thus was surrounded on three sides by water. Low-lying and flat, the parish was something of a rural backwater, run on the open field system for centuries until 1801 when the Enclosure Acts started to alter life for the local people considerably.[21] The manor house dated from the ninth century, originally part of Abingdon Abbey before it was dissolved in 1538. The village had three inns when Short went to live there: the Nag's Head, the Sow and Pigs, and the Wagon and Horses, but the pride of the village was twofold: the Culham Old Bridge, built in 1416 by the Abingdon Guild of the Holy Cross, with its five perpendicular arches, and the twelfth-century church of St Paul's. As Short viewed his parish church for the first time, he saw a building of some antiquity: a mediaeval church with tower, a north window with heraldic glass of local families, and much original Church plate (as the various precious metal items used in worship are known), including 'an Elizabethan silver chalice, dated 1575'. Adjacent to the church was a vicarage built in the mid-eighteenth century, where Short resided frequently over his time as a curate (Naylor 1962, n.p.). Here, materially, was the antiquity that Lloyd had so often referred to in his lectures, Thomas Vowler had highlighted in his private discussions, and Short had responded to in his cathedral church, regarding the traditions and continuity of English Christianity.

Short, however, soon became aware of a matter that touched him keenly: the educational deprivation of many children in his parish. It was only in 1808 that two small schools began teaching reading and writing to children, with a Sunday School underway by 1815 (Naylor 1962, n.p.). Short, who was so aware of the fortuitous nature of his own educational opportunities, saw that in Culham the Church did little for the education of the young; the attitude still prevailed that schooling was the privilege of private individuals. With the formation of the National Society in 1811 (further discussed in Chapter Five), the established Church had only recently begun to realise its corporate responsibility, and opportunity, to provide elementary education for all.

In other ways, Short was suddenly aware of the calling to which he now professed:

> In Culham the Church seems to have done little for education before 1815, but in other ways it had played a vital part in the lives of the villagers since Saxon times. It baptised their children, married them and buried them; the vicar was their guide, philosopher and friend. He counselled those in need of advice, he visited the sick, he presided over meetings of the vestry, the body that formed the local government of the parish. The members of the vestry were the better-off parishioners, who in turn served as churchwardens, overseers of the poor, and highway surveyors. The parish church was usually their meeting place. (Naylor 1962, n.p.)

---

21 The Enclosure Acts were a series of legislative changes over several centuries, particularly in the nineteenth century. They enclosed common lands and open fields, and thus extended legal property rights for some, while depriving many others of access to fields.

With the vicar in ill health, Short fulfilled many of the vicar's duties. He was engaged in an arduous learning curve, which abruptly ended when Dean Smith of Christ Church invited him to return to the house as a tutor and lecturer. In his reminiscences, he wrote:

> Just before the Long Vacation of 1827 commenced an offer of the Curacy of Culham was made by the Vicar, the Revd Robert Wintle, a Christ Church man, his health was precarious … I generally preached once each Sunday. The population being small, a visit to the village once a week usually sufficed for the infirm and sick … [T]he Squire John Phillips [then a minor] was at Cambridge, Culham House was occupied by Mrs Phillips [his mother] and her daughter Millicent Phillips — with whom I subsequently became acquainted. John Phillips' uncles were in the Coldstream Guards, my brother Colonel Short's Regt. As years passed on my relations with this family became of a more intimate character — I found much benefit in following set Parochial duty and may well reckon this period as amongst the happiest of my life but in 1828 being appointed by the Dean of Christ Church, <u>one</u> of the College tutors I felt it necessary from the pressure of College duties and Lectures to resign the Curacy of Culham. (SLSA, PRG 160/7, emphasis in the original)

Short's father, Charles, noted precisely in his diary that Augustus 'gave up the Curacy in Nov from having too many pupils attending Lectures at Christ Church' (SLSA, PRG 160/32).

The ordained life: Teaching student 1828-35

As Short began his first year as a tutor, Christ Church was still pre-eminent in academic achievement in the university. Dean Jackson's lead in reforming the examination system had led to this standing being maintained for the generation preceding Short's appointment (Bill 1973, p. 12). On being appointed a tutor in 1828, Short celebrated in typical academic manner by buying works of Classics that he would inevitably use. One was *Aristotelis de Rhetorica*, bound in two volumes and published in 1820, which he inscribed as 'Augustus Short Ch. Ch. Jan 30 1828'.[22] Short was confident in his academic abilities and, influenced by Charles Lloyd and Thomas Vowler Short especially, saw himself as an inheritor of a certain intellectual bias and firmness, centuries old in the English Church. There was a received faith, and its English expression reached well back to the early Church; it had integrity, tradition and a character of its own, and he would now have the opportunity to contribute to its further development. Christ Church had the good fortune of usually having five or six tutors when other colleges struggled to find more than one. This meant that large classes were rare at Christ Church, and attention to the reading and construing of Greek and Latin was much assisted (p. 13).

---

22   These volumes, with their inscription, are now held in the St Barnabas Collection, Special Collections, Flinders University Library.

The appointment of tutors was a much-valued prerogative of the dean, while the officers of the house — the censors, for example — were appointed by the dean and the chapter. As the tutors were the essential fulcrum of educational life, this meant that the dean strengthened his control of all educational arrangements (Bill 1988, p. 228). Intellectually, and often socially, the tutors were a cross-section of the house, being recruited in most instances from among the students, and former Westminster students at that: 'most still looked to a career in the Church rather than the university. Few then or later produced works of scholarship' (p. 233).

Charles Longley, a contemporary, who later became the archbishop of Canterbury (1862-70), and to whom Short refers in his memoirs of 1882 as one of 'the young men of mark' (in Whitington 1887, p. 11), wrote on becoming a tutor of the house in 1819:

> I am in receipt of a salary of 450 pounds a year, besides having apartments and a table throughout the year ... I should by my exertions in my profession, and in the occupation of public tutor, be making myself known to those whose good-will and esteem it is of importance to persons in every situation to deserve; and if I conducted myself in such a manner as to merit their approbation I should be securing a degree of connexion and interest as must ultimately prove beneficial to me. (LPL, Letters and papers of Charles Thomas Longley, MSS 1841, fo.110)

Here was an outcome much sought: not financial rewards, but the possibility of preferment through the connections that tutors might form with pupils' families.

The role of tutor at Christ Church, although enhanced from Dean Jackson's time, still rested upon the conscientiousness of the tutors: 'a student's task was to read. The tutor's role was to direct his reading' (Curthoys 2012, p. 247). In his diary of 1826, John Henry Newman, by then a tutor at Oriel College, contemplated the seriousness of his new role in an entry dated 21 March:

> I have a great undertaking before me in the Tutorship here ... There is always the danger of the love of literary pursuits assuming too great a prominent place in the thoughts of a College Tutor, or his viewing the situation merely as a secular office, a means of future provision when he leaves College. (In Ker and Gornall, 1961, p. 280)

It was not all reading and discussion, however. In Short's day, the tutor fulfilled the pastoral role of caring for his pupils and showing an interest in their life as undergraduates. Mozley's comment regarding Newman could be applied across Oxford to many tutors: '[T]here were plenty of college tutors in those days whose relation to the undergraduates about them was simply official and nominal. Newman stood in place of a father, or an elder and affectionate brother' (1882, p. 181). Short was conscientious, enjoying teaching yet often recording his pastoral concern in his diaries:

> Monday 3 February (1834) ... 10-11 Herodotus — pupils seems interested & anxious to learn ... 12 Ethics Lecture — it is a pleasure to teach sensitive minds ...

> Friday 7 February ... obliged to scold an idle pupil I explained to him I felt it my duty to be severe with him for his own sake. (SLSA, PRG 160/2)

Short tutored in the classics, and when Henry Vaughan commenced in 1829 the reading list was extensive: he listed the works of Herodotus, Thucydides, Livy, Polybius, Homer, Virgil, Cicero, Xenophon, some Plato, the plays of Euripides, Aeschylus, Sophocles, and Terence, along with Euclid and Aristotle. Diligently, he studied logic and theology as well, using Butler's *Analogy of Religion* (Bill 1973, p. 15). Augustus taught, among others, Thucydides. William Ewart Gladstone, in later life four times Prime Minister, recalled, 'began Thucydides ... had first Lecture with Short' (Foot 1968, vol. 1, p. 81). Short reminisced later, 'Gladstone for two years attended my Lectures on Thucydides' (SLSA, PRG 160/7).[23]

Not all Short's students were as successful as Gladstone. In a generous gift to Short of six volumes of *The Works of George Bull D D, Lord Bishop of St David's*, by Edward Burton, 'late Student of Christ Church', Short found enclosed the following letter addressed to him:

> Ch Ch June 1832
>
> Dear Sir
>
> Allow me to add to your Library the Accompanying set of Books as a mark of the Obligation which I feel myself under to you for all your kindness and attention to me during my long course of Tuition. I wish that I could return for it in the schools, but the fault was my own, and whatever had been the issue your assistance and kindness would always have been remembered with gratitude by
>
> Dear Sir
>
> Yr very sincerely obliged
>
> Chas: E Lefroy (St Barnabas Collection, Flinders University Library [FUL])

It seems that even those who failed appreciated the young tutor's pastoral approach!

Short was immediately involved in the life of the house. In 1829, the dean instituted an entrance examination for commoners. In the Censor's Book (a record of house proceedings) it was reported:

> The Dean desired the censors and Mr A Short, his 'tutor designatus' to examine Mr ----- before he was entered as a commoner. The examination consisted in a short trial in classics, in which he was well prepared; in arithmetic and mathematics, in which he knew less than he ought to have known; and in divinity, which he had attended to.

---

23 Short's annotated copy of *Thucydides de Bello Peloponnesiaco*, with an inscription reading 'A Short, St of Ch Ch — "Student of Christ Church" — Jan 21 1822', is held in the St Barnabas Collection, Special Collections, Flinders University Library. This was Short's undergraduate copy, from which he taught in subsequent years.

The object of the first was to discover whether he was likely to do us credit, and himself benefit by the instructions of the place; of the second and third, that some effect may gradually be produced in the public schools, where these subjects are apt to be grossly neglected. (Thompson 1900, pp. 192-3)

It was no surprise that the relationship of dean and tutor was vital. Dean Smith resigned from Christ Church in 1831 and was replaced by the Regius Professor of Greek, Thomas Gaisford (who remained dean until 1855). Gaisford (1779-1855) had held his chair since 1812, retaining that post while he was dean, and his scholarship was renowned. With a first class in ancient Greek, Short shared much with his employer but despaired somewhat at Gaisford's resistance to educational reform and progress. Patronage, not merit, mattered to Gaisford. For Short this was disappointing. Thomas Vowler, who had only just departed Christ Church in 1829, had been a major proponent for reform, suggesting improvements to the examination system. On this, Augustus came under his cousin's spell.

Gaisford polarised his colleagues and students, feelings oscillating from admiration to bewilderment; he was described as 'a strong man who knew his own mind' (Thompson 1900, p. 194) but also as

an amiable, kind-hearted man, much misunderstood, especially when, some years later, he became Dean of Christ Church, and was thus placed in a false position. He was not a man of the world, and had no notion of dealing with young men as a class, nor of supporting the dignity of the head of a college like Christ Church, and, as Dean, he always seemed out of his element. (Quiller-Couch 1892, p. 316)

Gaisford was a firm dean, often regarded as single-minded and authoritarian. The measure of Christ Church had always been the effective leadership of the dean, and Gaisford did much to uphold the dignity and traditions of Christ Church, often at the expense of the university. He excelled in administration, showing financial acumen, and his priority to academic matters meant his 'rule was all-pervasive' (Bill & Mason 1970, pp. 6-7).

It was said that in an effort to thwart the attraction of the university honours examinations, and raise the independence of the house and its education, Gaisford highlighted the importance of the internal end-of-term Collections as the measurement of academic progress (Brock & Curthoys 1997 p. 342). He aimed at keeping Christ Church true to 'its ancient customs and traditions, and was careful to oppose, or at least ignore, all reforms which introduced novelties inconsistent, as he deemed them, with the spirit of the foundation' (Thompson 1900, p. 195). Although the dean cared little for distinctions gained outside the walls of the house, his discouragement took time to have effect. During Short's appointment as tutor (1831-35 especially), Christ Church continued to excel in the university examinations: twenty-eight first classes were gained by members of the house. The decline came in later years. Short records in 1882 that:

> At the end of March 1833, I was appointed public examiner in the classical schools, and, with my colleagues, had the pleasure of placing in the first class one afterwards known to fame as Archbishop Tait.[24] (In Whitington 1887, p. 11)[25]

Dean Gaisford obviously saw in the young priest leadership qualities, and in 1833 invited Short to be both librarian and junior censor. As a public examiner in Classical Honours, Short, with fellow examiners Moberley, Michell and Sewell, awarded 'firsts' to AC Tait (mentioned above); John Jackson (later bishop of Lincoln, then of London — a self-made man, the son of a small tradesman in a provincial town); Charles John (later Earl Canning); Henry George Liddell (later headmaster of Westminster School, then dean of Christ Church); Robert Scott (later dean of Rochester); and Robert Lowe (later Lord Sherbrooke and Lord Chancellor). Not all the pupils examined excelled academically — Short bestowed a 'fourth' on Lord Ramsay, who afterwards, nevertheless, as Marquis Dalhousie, was appointed Governor-General of India.

The role of junior censor, *Censor Naturalist Philosophiae*, was responsible for undergraduate discipline (the senior censor, *Censor Moralis Philosophiae*, oversaw all academic matters on behalf of the dean). Short thus lectured to the undergraduates and moderated in disputes. While neither censor had a place on the governing body, each was central to the smooth and appropriate conduct of the house. There were highlights, one being speeches each censor gave near the end of Michaelmas term. On a Wednesday evening at dinner, before the dean and chapter and Christ Church staff, the senior censor delivered a Latin oration summing up and commenting on his year in office. The junior censor (Short was one) gave a similar oration the following Saturday to the same audience. The censors enjoyed another highlight:

> The Chapter dinners, to which the tutorial staff were invited, continued to be given yearly … [T]hey were interesting ceremonies. The Dean and Canons, the hosts, sat together at the top of the table; their guests, the Censors and Tutors, sat together at the bottom. All were in academical dress; the beautiful pewter service, as lustrous as silver, was always used, and the custom of 'taking wine' with the guests was carefully observed. (Thompson 1900, p. 139)

---

24 Tait was archbishop of Canterbury from 1868-82.

25 In retirement during 1882, the relationship with Archbishop Tait was renewed: '"March 13th — Lambeth. Walked in the garden with the archbishop. Lunched afterwards"'. Two or three times the bishop's diary speaks of Lambeth Palace and the pleasant religious and social gatherings he attended there. For the late archbishop he had a sincere regard, though he by no means agreed with him in what he could not help calling his 'Erastian tendencies' (in Whitington 1887, pp. 261-2).

The place of the university in the activities of state and society was never lost on Short. There were occasions when the young clergyman was reminded of the vital, dynamic relationship of education with society. During 1834 Short witnessed both the election and the installation of the Duke of Wellington as chancellor of the university. The Convocation of the university met on 29 January 1834, elected the Duke, and then called him to office with an election ceremony on 7 February. The following June, Short, as he celebrated his thirty-second birthday, participated in the formal installation of the chancellor. In June 1834 Mr Croker, a close friend of the Duke of Wellington, described the great event:

> [T]he view of the [Sheldonian] theatre was certainly the most beautiful thing I ever saw in my life. The sight of the women dressed in all the colours of the rainbow … the burst of applause from all the benches as the Duke entered the theatre, the shouts of the men, and even the voices of the women were heard, and waving of the handkerchiefs — and all lasted for ten minutes in a degree of beauty and enthusiasm which I had never before seen before. (In Ffoulkes 1892, p. 491)

He went on to add:

> The dinner at Christ Church Hall was very fine, the members of the College, old and young, dined with us. I suppose we were about 200, rather more, perhaps. The Hall itself is very fine, and the enthusiasm of the young men was as great as in the theatre. We dined at five, and went away by daylight. (pp. 493-4)

A splendid lithograph of the day ('Commemoration of the Installation of His Grace the Duke of Wellington as Chancellor of the University of Oxford in the Theatre on the 10th, 11th, and 13th June 1834', by Thomas Dighton) shows the doctors and noblemen seated in the semicircle of the theatre; the masters of arts, Short being one of these, in the main floor area, women seated separately, and bachelors and undergraduates in the upper gallery. These events underlined how the university was a pivotal participant in affairs of state. The grand occasions were seen by some as a polite rebellious exhibition by the conservative elite in a political climate where pressure had removed the public discriminations against Dissenters and Roman Catholics. Conservatives saw Oxford as a bastion of the established Church and thought it should remain so, yet there were by then debates about removing the religious test (affirming doctrines of the established Church) for matriculation to the university.

This reinforced for Short how much education mattered in his society, how contested a ground it was, and how privileged was the position of his Church in this. His time as a staff member of the house, however, was reaching its conclusion. One year later, 10 June 1835, he was, in his own words (1882),

> presented by the dean and chapter of Christ Church to the vicarage [of Ravensthorpe] … Dean Gaisford would have had me retain my tutorship at Christ Church if I had

been willing to reside at Oxford, but such a position was distasteful both to myself and wife. We preferred the country and parish work to Oxford and university life, and so migrated to Northhampton. (In Whitington 1887, p. 12)

Short was engaged by this time to Miss Millicent Phillips, from Hints Hall, Staffordshire. As described earlier in this chapter, they had met during his Culham curacy, and the two were married on 10 December 1835. Short had been in Oxford for sixteen years; despite excelling as a scholar and exhibiting great promise as a teaching fellow, he believed that

my work, however, in college and university, diversified though it was by parochial duty in the neighbourhood of Oxford and Culham, did not remove my distaste for tutorial life. (1882 in Whitington 1887, pp. 11-12)

Why did he forgo this position of some privilege and certain intellectual challenge at such a stirring time in the life of English Christianity, for the apparent obscurity of rural Northamptonshire? The dean was keen for him to remain, which was a sincere acknowledgement of his academic and pastoral skills, although being married would have meant living away from the house.

While Short declared his growing 'distaste' for the academic life, there is little doubt that the somewhat dubious reputation of Christ Church, and aspects of fellow student behaviour, worried and disturbed him. A decade later, when delivering the Bampton Lectures to the university, he made an allusion to this possibility:

[N]ot only do the refined enjoyments of our present social life render it difficult to train the child of God to 'endure hardness.' The spirit of the world penetrates into our seminaries of religious learning, mingling visions of ease and wealth with the associations of boyhood, and perverting to sloth and luxury the noblest institutions of Science and Education. The tares are freely sown among the wheat while men sleep; they grow together in the same vineyard and even healthy plants imbibe noxious ailment from a tainted atmosphere. Yet 'the word of God standeth sure. Ye though the Spirit must mortify the deeds of the body, if ye would live'; and it is your duty therefore, 'young men,' to consider, how far systematic self-discipline may be necessary to give you the victory over those fleshly lusts which war against the soul. (1846, pp. 97-8)

While he was a student, he had discovered his calling to ministry, with all its seriousness of commitment, yet the house was not exactly a scholastic or devout institution for the bulk of the undergraduates. Many of 'the young men of mark, and noble and landed gentry, as well as the more promising pupils of the great public schools' (Whitington 1887, p. 11) were not interested in education or the Church. Short was also irked clearly by the social exclusiveness prevailing among many students and other undergraduates, and the inevitable prejudices and snobbery accompanying it.

Another probable reason Short declined Dean Gaisford's offer was that it would have entailed being an absentee vicar, simply visiting Ravensthorpe from time to time.

The practice of absenteeism was the cause of much social and political criticism of the established Church, and was regarded widely as a scandal. Short's principles would have nothing of it. He was acutely aware of Lord Henley's attack in 1832 on 'non-residence of beneficed clergy' (see Chapter Four). Perhaps he was also becoming more conscious of the integrity of his calling. The episcopal exhortation at his priestly ordination proclaimed, quoting from 'The Ordering of Priests' in the *Book of Common Prayer* (1662):

> … and now again we exhort you, in the Name of our Lord Jesus Christ, that you have remembrance, into how high a Dignity, and to how weighty an Office and Charge ye are called: that is to say, to be Messengers, Watchmen, and Stewards of the Lord; to teach and to premonish, to feed and provide for the Lord's family; to seek for Christ's sheep that are dispersed abroad, and for his children who are in the midst of this naughty world, that they may be saved through Christ for ever. (p. 593)

There was not only the distaste Short felt for certain aspects of the academic life, but also the fact that Oxford was a university town dominated by academics. He was keenly aware of the disparity between the privileged life in the colleges and that of the local population. A dramatic illustration of this came in 1832 with a cholera outbreak that caused forty deaths in the town. It was close to home for Short, as the source of the epidemic was thought to be adjacent to Christ Church:

> A great cry was raised against the filthy stream, which empties itself into the Isis at Folly Bridge, and whose banks were lined with 'pigsties and other abominations.' The Christ Church authorities, however, succeeded in making the stream partially cleanse itself, by a system of *flushes* of water, and at a very great expense shut it out, at least *from the eye*, by carrying a wall along its course on the west of Christ Church meadow. (Cox 1870, p. 265, emphases in the original)

The abrupt contrasts of Oxford, where the local people knew 'as much about deprivation and fever' as anywhere in England, and where the sentimental view of the 'casket of architectural jewels in mellow stone rising out of unspoilt countryside' (Prest 1993, p. 20) jarred with reality, were making an impression on the earnest Augustus Short. His call to a parochial ministry, and married life, offered him the opportunity to implement many of his ideas and change direction. At the same time, he could do whatever was possible to counter some of the social discrimination that disturbed his Christian views, not least in education.

4

Reform and revival in Church and society 1800-50

Who and what, in the early nineteenth century, was the 'English Church' or 'English Christianity', 'Anglicanism', or the 'British Empire', and what constituted the 'United Kingdom' or 'Great Britain'? Who were the 'British'? What we do know is that between the defeat of Napoleon in the Battle of Waterloo (1815) and the rise of a united Germany under Bismarck (1871), British imperial power throughout the world reached its height. Its economic and industrial strength, the physical reach of the Empire, and the standing of its political culture climbed to a zenith for the United Kingdom. Rarely, however, did people speak of themselves as 'Britons'; more likely the designations were English, Scottish, Welsh or Irish. Within a quarter of a century from the end of the Victorian age, it could still be written:

> It must be remembered that no Englishman, & perhaps no Scot even, calls himself a Briton without a sneaking sense of the ludicrous. How should an Englishman utter the words *Great Britain* with the glow of emotion that for him goes with *England*? He talks the *English* language; he has been taught *English* history as one tale from Alfred to George V; he has known in his youth how many Frenchmen are a match for one *Englishman*; he has heard of the word of an *Englishman* & of *English* fair play, scorns certain things as *unEnglish*, & aspires to be an *English* gentleman; he knows that *England* expects every man to do his duty, & and that to the foreigner his nation is the *Anglais & Englander & Inglesi*; in the word *England*, not in *Britain*, all these things are implicit ... [W]ho speaks of a British gentleman, British home life, British tailoring, or British writers or condemns with 'unBritish'? (Fowler 1926, p. 139, emphases in the original)

Within the United Kingdom (which from 1801 had included England, Scotland, Wales, and Ireland), the various national groups were divided linguistically, historically, often religiously, and clearly geographically. In these nations people sometimes struggled to see themselves as part of one greater, unified whole; the Irish especially felt that their relationship to the United Kingdom was more colonial than anything else. The dominance of the English, especially people from southern England, in aristocratic and social, economic and political terms meant more often than not a condescending view of the provincial nationalisms of the other members of the United Kingdom, even within England itself. What this meant, away from London, was that with the industrial revolution underway, the provincial centres were taking on their own distinctive characteristics, thus challenging the rural image of England. After 1815, for example, the question of agricultural protection, exemplified in the Corn Laws (repealed in 1846), divided England and gave a political focus to the differentiation between urban and rural life which the industrial revolution was making more marked every year.

Between 1800 and 1850 the population of the United Kingdom grew rapidly. The 1801 census showed that England's population was 8.3 million, with nearly 0.6 million people living in Wales and 1.6 million in Scotland, giving a total of 10.5 million people, with a further 5 million in Ireland. The population of England, reaching almost 16 million by 1840, had doubled by 1850 from the 1801 figures, with slightly less growth in Wales, Scotland and Ireland. Population growth was just as significant overseas and throughout the Empire, and it was estimated that by 1850 only half the English-speaking population lived in Great Britain or Ireland, down from three-quarters sixty years earlier (Wolffe 2006, p. 22).

Poverty increased in crowded urban settings, especially in the north of England, and there was a failure of infrastructure to keep pace with the changes: housing, education, legal services, public health, and political representation were some of the issues of concern often provoking agitation. No wonder emigration to the 'new world' of North America, or to the British colonies, reached significant heights.

> [T]he number of emigrants was enormous by modern standards, reaching 368,764 in 1852; of these perhaps one-third were Irish, or of Continental, mainly German, origin. Of the 1852 total, 244,261 went to the USA, 32,876 to Canada, and 87,424 to Australia and New Zealand (Clarke 1924, p. 167)

At the same time a distinct 'Englishness' prevailed over the social and cultural landscape of the United Kingdom, something Short experienced in Oxford. Birth, education or occupational place in the hierarchy usually brought social favour and privilege, and encouraged the sense of self-importance and self-assuredness that accompanied the spectacular growth of British power and might over this first half of the nineteenth century. The barriers to social mobility for many were real, and forcibly defended at first, with many devices operating to protect the English in their dominance and social privilege: manners, accent, dress, housing and entertainment; and also, certainly, access to education and the professions, political representation, and some spheres of religion. The period under discussion saw immense changes and adaptations to this social landscape.

Reform in England

An enduring reality for English life was clearly the combination of monarchy, aristocracy and hierarchy (especially evident in the House of Lords), and an established Church. The 1789 revolution in France and its subsequent history meant that in the following generation reform was discussed openly throughout the United Kingdom, yet the strong conservative reaction to affairs on the Continent meant that an English radicalism focused more on the adaptation of society's institutions rather than on their abolition. As the nineteenth century progressed, the economic and industrial revolutions in the United Kingdom clearly pointed to a time of exploration for markets, expanding trade and manufacturing, colonialism and opportunities with emigration, and increasing national wealth.

Politically and socially, calls for reform were widespread. However, from where would the impetus for reform within the Church come? Dissenters (Congregationalists, Baptists, Presbyterians and Quakers, now joined by the Methodists) had for quite some years pointed to the many shortcomings in equal treatment for them before the law. In religion, it was not just the privileged role of the established Church that some people railed against, for in some aspects of faith and order many saw a complacent established Church failing to address both people's needs and contemporary practices of discrimination. The prevailing traditional belief, in the post-Napoleonic era, in state and Church as one was effectively ended by the twin moves to repeal the *Test* and *Corporation* Acts, which on one hand had limited the civil rights of Dissenters, and on the other hand had politically and socially disenfranchised Roman Catholics.

In the first thirty years of the nineteenth century the Dissenters, including the tiny percentage of Roman Catholic 'Romish Dissenters', had been chiefly occupied with the campaign to remove their civil and political disabilities. The *Corporation Act* of 1661 had required all municipal office holders to be worshippers in the established Church, and the *Test Act* of 1673 had required all Crown office holders to swear an oath to the same effect — that they accepted the doctrines and practices of the established Church. Both measures effectively excluded dissenting Christians from Parliament; thus reform was advocated on political as much as religious grounds by the 1820s.

By 1828, the *Test* and *Corporation* Acts had been repealed, and the following year political and civil rights were granted to Roman Catholics. Both these significant reforms meant that Dissenters and Roman Catholics were now eligible for election to Parliament. The Houses of Parliament, for several hundred years the final arbiter in the affairs of the established Church, would in future have members who owed no allegiance to that Church. Did this herald a new era in which the established Church's endowments, episcopacy, buildings, liturgy, formularies and even its creeds would be threatened? Did it mean that effectively the theoretical basis of the establishment, where Church and state were identical, would now be challenged, even abandoned?

'No Peel'

Short, when he was an undergraduate, was well aware of the example set before all his contemporaries of Robert Peel (1788-1850), former student of the house, and now Member of Parliament for the university. Peel had relished Dean Jackson's reform of the university examination system and in 1808 won the first double First degree in the university's history. Then, at twenty-nine years of age, he had been elected to be the university's parliamentary representative. The example was not lost on Short; Peel had not come from any position of advantage in society — his social and political connections were few, as his family was not linked to the aristocracy. Merit alone had taken him to his position of power, and of promise. Short identified with this: were not merit, born of hard work and diligence, along with a strong sense of character, characteristics he had come to avow? Thomas Vowler Short, a significant influence on Augustus, was unsurprisingly also an enthusiastic Peel supporter. Likewise, Short's Professor of Divinity and ordaining bishop, Charles Lloyd, who was similarly influential in Short's life, had been Peel's tutor and remained his closest confidant. Both men saw in Peel the moderate and conservative reformer England needed.

At the University of Oxford, in the 1820s, with so much talk of reform in the air, no political issue had resounded more strongly than the prospect of emancipation for the Roman Catholics. Each year the University of Oxford Convocation (all Masters of Arts and staff of the colleges) had moved its motion rejecting Roman Catholic emancipation, confident that its parliamentary representative would follow suit. In 1828, however, Prime Minister Lord John Russell had proposed a motion to repeal the *Test* and *Corporation* Acts discussed above; the time had come to remove discriminations based on religious affiliation where participation in civil matters was at stake. Peel, dependent for his seat on the anti-Roman Catholic majority at Oxford, could nevertheless see that discrimination had run its course, and in January 1829 he had changed his mind. No longer opposed to the repeal, he informed both Charles Lloyd, as his confidant, and the vice-chancellor.

Figure 4.1 The anti-Roman Catholic cause showed their opposition to Sir Robert Peel by hammering nails in the door to spell out the words 'No Peel'. The door is at the foot of the stairs to the Great Hall, Christ Church. The author is pictured here in 2016.
Source: Photograph courtesy of the author.

On 5 February 1829, the University Convocation was to meet and approve the annual motion of a united petition to Parliament against Roman Catholic emancipation. The vote was 164 to 48 against repeal, but then:

> [a]fter a vote in Convocation against the 'Roman Catholic Claims', a Letter was read from Sir Robert Peel, offering to resign his seat for Oxford, on the ground that he, as a Minister, had recommended to His Majesty *an Adjustment* of those Claims. He had changed his opinions, but the majority of his Oxford constituents had not changed theirs; his resignation was, of course, accepted ... Peel was again nominated, a great number of the voters (myself amongst the number) being unwilling ... to part with our Alma mater's most distinguished son. On the 26th of February the University Election began, and, at the end of the polling (which was kept up for two days), [Sir Robert] Inglis had 755 votes; Peel 609. (Cox 1870, p. 126, emphasis in the original)

So within the month, his resignation accepted, Peel — having been renominated despite his views — had lost the election. The anti-Roman Catholic cause was vehement in opposition to its once-favoured son, some of whom made their protest by hammering in a door, at the foot of the hall stairs in Christ Church, the words 'No Peel'.[26] Peel's most vigorous supporter in Christ Church was Thomas Vowler Short, then senior censor of the house. As a conservative reformer, Thomas Vowler saw that Peel was in tune with political change and reform and respected his change of mind. He had urged support for Peel's re-election, even initiating a committee in London to organise for Peel's re-election (Ward 1965, pp. 71-2).

The opposition to Peel among students and dons had its lighter moments, especially in a poster lampooning the 'Peelites'. Appearing around Christ Church was the advertisement for a 'Grand Concert under the patronage of Rev. Thomas Growler, For the Benefit of Mr PEELigrini, on Wednesday, February 25, 1829'. 'Growler' was a reference to Thomas Vowler, and 'Mr PEELigrini' echoed the most famous European violinist of the day, Niccolo Paganini. Ridiculed also were Bishop Charles Lloyd, who was listed as singing a song, 'There's No Place like Home', and a ballad, 'No Churchman am I for to Rail and to Write', and Dean Smith, who was to sing the words of an old English song, 'The Miller of Dee': 'I care for nobody — no, not I, and nobody cares for me' (in Brock & Curthoys 1997, p. 57).

Peel's loss dismayed Thomas Vowler Short, and he soon after departed Christ Church for a parish ministry at King's Worthy, Hampshire. From 1834-41, he was rector of St George's, Bloomsbury, where he was often spoken of as a possible future bishop, as JH Newman's letters reveal. Writing to Thomas Mozley on 6 May 1839, Newman shared the gossip: '[T]hey say Short of Bloomsbury is to be the new Bishop [of Peterborough]'. Again on 10 September 1840, the *Times*, when announcing the appointment of a new bishop of Chichester, commented that others who 'would have very gracefully borne the addition of "Right Reverend" were Hampden, Arnold, Hinds and TV Short' (Tracey 1995, p. 73). Thomas Vowler was eventually consecrated for the see of Sodor and Man in 1841, a see nowhere near in the same standing as Peterborough or Chichester.

Peel's most public supporter in the House of Lords was Bishop Charles Lloyd.[27] In late March he rose to speak in favour of emancipation: anarchy in Ireland threatened the United Kingdom, parliamentary indecision needed to end, and public opinion wished for there to be change. In an appeal to warm Short's heart, Lloyd focused on the young in society: they wanted emancipation for Roman Catholics, and the House of Lords, with many members in their senior years, should not stand in the way of reform.

---

26 The words remain hammered into the door to this day.
27 Charles Lloyd was never anti-Roman Catholic, as his upbringing had been close to a community of French Catholics. See Chapter Three for more detail about Lloyd's life.

To the anti-Roman Catholic claim that the *Roman Catholic Relief Act 1829* involved surrendering to idolatrous Catholic ways, he referred to a publication of his own in 1826, which had sought to show that the principles, if not many of the practices, of Protestants and Catholics were all but the same.

At the same time, Charles Lloyd had argued to Peel on 21 March 1828 that the established Church had already actually lost some of its spiritual power and independence by its close, and exclusive, attachment to the state:

> [The legislature] has placed the Church of England under so severe a cognizance, has passed such severe laws in relation to her exertion of such spiritual power, has so impeded & controlled the action even of the Ecclesiastical Courts that the spiritual power of the Church of England is not only virtually but positively taken away by direct acts of the Legislature … The Legislature in fact say [*sic*] to the C. of E., 'So long as we guarantee your property we will take to ourselves the right of controlling your discipline & of preventing you from exercising any spiritual Power over your members'.
> It is a villainous argument, & as oppressive as it is mean. (In Baker 1981, pp. 176-7)

The stance of those in favour of public reform was for equality before the law for all (that is, male) citizens, regardless of religion. However, the stance taken by those in favour of private reform, within the established Church, differed. They were concerned about how the Church's right to govern its own affairs and to meet in ecclesiastical Convocation could be regained. This Convocation, the meeting of the episcopate with the clergy, had been suspended in 1711, thus depriving the Church of its independence. Indeed, it would not be revived until 1852.

Short watched this drama unfold just as the invitation to return to Christ Church as tutor was extended to him.

The 1830s

The 1830s were a momentous period of change: railroads and the penny post arrived; there were parliamentary and municipal reforms; the *Poor Law Amendment Act 1834 (PLAA)*, known commonly as the New Poor Law, was enacted; London University was inaugurated; Queen Victoria came to the throne; and writers such as Tennyson, Keble, Browning and John Henry Newman came to public prominence.

> Nowhere was the breach with the past more sundering than in Oxford. The University over which the Duke of Wellington was installed as Chancellor in 1834 … the seeds of the changes which awaited it — of Church movements, Museums and Art Galleries, Local Examinations, Science Degrees, extension Lectures, Women's Colleges … were to begin their transforming growth before the period which he adorned had found its close. (Tuckwell 1908, pp. 2-3)

More political and social upheaval was to come as the new ministry of Lord Grey and the Whigs moved to reform Parliament, bringing forward in 1832 a Reform Bill effectively acknowledging that the United Kingdom was now an emerging industrial nation and not just a society dominated by the landed aristocracy. The Reform Bill involved the most significant changes to the electoral basis of the Parliament for centuries with a widening of the franchise, inclusive of Dissenters and Roman Catholics, and a recognition of the fact that a range of electoral abuses needed cancelling. Legislation changes of 1828, 1829 and 1832 confirmed for some a view of what the established Church was now facing: the Church was not the state, nor was it identical with Parliament. The Church could no longer hope to dictate what the governing powers should do, and in the future all laws affecting the Church would be made in a Parliament composed of men of differing Christian denominations and religions, or none. A noted historian of Victorian England has written:

> [After 1829-32] the question was not usually framed, ought there be an established church? England continued to believe in a church as by law established, which in many eyes was part of Englishness as well as wise Christianity. The question was framed, how is an established church compatible with equality before the law? Or, does equality before the law include religious equality? (Chadwick 1970, p. 3)

In just a few years the first steps of a bold experiment — that of enhancing representative government in order to achieve compatible religious and political equality — had occurred. The question remained whether English Christianity, whatever its denominational forms, would be able to adjust to the rapid growth of population and of the urban centres, the revolutions in agriculture and industry, and the emergence of a significant and widespread empire across the seas. Reality was that Parliament in an industrial England was diverted from ecclesiastical affairs by more pressing and urgent issues. Society was increasingly pluralist, yet the established Church maintained that it had a mission as the Church of all the people and to all parts of society (Bowen 1968, p. 375).

English Christianity: Revivals and reforms

The first half of the nineteenth century in England was still a time when one was born into the Christian faith rather than formally converted to its doctrines and practices. Yet, in the nations comprising the United Kingdom marked differences of Christian religious affiliation and practice prevailed: in Scotland, the dominant Church was the established (Presbyterian) Church of Scotland; in Wales, the legacy of Methodism and Nonconformity raised the chapel over the established Church. In Ireland — the Church of which had been incorporated with the Church of England in 1800 to form the United Church of England and Ireland — the Roman Catholic majority felt most aggrieved about the denial of their religious and social independence, and about the privileges accorded to the minority established Church.

This established United Church of England and Ireland comprised the clergy and laity of the two provinces of Canterbury and York, with dioceses broadly corresponding, with some exceptions, to the county boundaries of England, supplemented by the Channel Islands and the Isle of Man, and now including the four provinces of the Irish Church. The four Welsh dioceses were part of the province of Canterbury.[28] The two archbishops of the established Church (in England) and all twenty-four diocesan bishops sat in the House of Lords, and after 1801 they were joined by one archbishop and three diocesan bishops from Ireland (selected by rotation from four archbishops and twenty-two diocesan bishops). The political identification of the established Church was clearly confirmed by these arrangements and seemed to cement the Church within the English aristocratic and hierarchical society.

Legally, and historically, the United Church of England and Ireland was continuous with the Church of past centuries in England; it was, to many, part of what being English meant. There was a firm belief among some in the Church that this continuity was founded on a regular succession of bishops from not just the primitive Church but also even from apostolic times, and the Reformation upheavals had not broken this link.[29] Many saw the Church as part of the 'One Catholic and Apostolic Church', named in the Nicene Creed. The argument was that while it had never initiated a break in communion with churches recognising papal jurisdiction, or the orthodox churches of the East, it maintained firmly its position as an independent branch of the Catholic Church and was not subject to any authority external to the realm of England other than a 'general Council' of the whole Christian Church, if one were to be agreed upon. Many in the established Church, especially within England, saw the episcopate as the cornerstone of its communion and thus refused to recognise the legitimacy of other religious bodies in England, or elsewhere, which were not dependent on the episcopate for their identity and organisation. The Church of Scotland may have been a 'sister' Church because it had not broken away from the established Church as had the Baptists and Methodists, but it had rejected the episcopacy nevertheless.

After 1801, the established Church was regarded, by the English at least, as coterminous with the newly constituted United Kingdom, although this was clearly not the case north of the border in Scotland. For some centuries the commonwealth of the United Kingdom, and the established Church, had been legally treated as identical;

---

28 The Church of Wales was not separately constituted until the *Welsh Church Acts* of 1914 and 1919.

29 Others in the established Church, the Evangelicals in particular, did not regard this issue as a central Church principle.

members of one were also members of the other. As the civil and ecclesiastical bodies had been the same, there was no sense of Church and state being in contention with, or separated from, each other. Moreover, the argument from within the Church was that, like the monarchy, the Church had not been 'by law established'; the English Church had preceded the English state in history and in continuity. Its constitutional position and its establishment were from the remotest times of English history, long before any laws or statutes of Parliament. How this was to change during the nineteenth century and before Short's very eyes!

The United Church of England and Ireland possessed a common liturgy, a shared episcopacy, with roots reaching down to the very early Church. Common prayer was emphasised over doctrinal uniformity; centralised bureaucratic structures were avoided; Catholic and reformed understandings of Christianity were held in an uneasy relationship. In the nations of Scotland and Ireland, English Christianity first adjusted to a non-established, non-privileged and minority reality. The established Church in England had now to make changes in understanding its present and future role.

The more common understandings of an established Church were well known: it was seen as an institutional expression of a system of religious beliefs, open to all and meant to be inclusive of all the population, and in a traditional relationship with the other major institutions of the society in which it operated. Moreover, probably at no time since the proroguing of the established Church's Convocation, in both the provinces of Canterbury and York in 1741, had the established United Church of England and Ireland been more clearly identified with the political and social fabric of the nation than by the 1820s. Yet as the decade progressed, this was becoming the touchstone for criticisms, and there came calls for reform of the established Church, particularly from those who did not identify with the United Church of England and Ireland. By 1832 calls for reform were increasing.

There were several obvious issues as a focus for reformers. The established Church's rites of marriage and burial still ruled for most citizens regardless of Christian denomination. All episcopal leaders were political appointments, and were often selected from within the wealthy nobility who also provided the political leaders, thus minimising any possible rivalry between Church and state. Life as a clergyman tended to be viewed more often as a career choice alongside the law, trade, public service or the military for many men of wealthy or prominent families. The ordained life was not generally spoken of as a vocational calling from God. Individual bishops, or cathedral chapters, only appointed one in ten parish clergy, while the colleges of the universities (Cambridge and Oxford) and the prominent public schools retained the right of appointment in about four out of every ten parishes. It was the local lord of the manor, or squire, who held the exclusive right to nominate the incumbent in half the parishes in England and Wales.

At the same time, the organisational life of the established Church appeared often chaotic or contradictory, with considerable inequities within, creating room for debate and criticism. Alongside a certain amount of organisational disarray, two other related contentious matters competed for attention: first, the compulsory tithes to fund the clergy and the Church organization; second, the confusion of roles when the members of the clergy served in both civil and social roles — local magistrates were an example of this. Change was inevitable. Parliament's concern also was becoming clear: how was it to honour its obligations to the people at large and yet uphold its duties to an established Church?

Methodism and the Evangelicals

It was one thing to survey the changes coming externally in the late 1820s and early 1830s, but the established Church had already been shaken by two great revival movements from within: that of Methodism (part of a general Evangelical revival across protestant denominations) from the mid-eighteenth century, and the other a specific Evangelical revival within the established Church slightly later. A century before Keble and Newman and Pusey, the Wesley brothers had their own 'Oxford movement'. John and Charles Wesley (1703-91 and 1707-88 respectively), both former students of Christ Church and both ordained in Christ Church Cathedral, formed, with others, the society given the sobriquet of 'Methodists', because of their focus on practical and evangelistic theology.

> John Wesley maintained (when writing to the Bishop of Lincoln in 1790) that
>
> Methodists in general ... are members of the Church of England. They hold all doctrines, attend her service, and partake of her sacraments. They do not willingly do harm to anyone, but do what good they can to all. To encourage each other herein they frequently spend an hour together in prayer and mutual exhortation. Permit then to ask, *Cui bono*, 'For what reasonable end' would your Lordship drive these people out of the Church? (In Gill 1956, p. 232)

By questioning the ecclesiology of the established Church, particularly its episcopacy and its forms of ordination, and by reaching out to a population largely estranged from the Church, Wesley ensured that Methodism would be an embarrassment and a reproach to the established Church. After the death of John, who was still an ordained member of the established Church, as was Charles, the movement had splintered into several groups: the Methodist New Connexion in 1797, the Primitive Methodists in 1810, and the Bible Christians in 1815. By the late 1820s, the prominent groups of Methodists were the Wesleyan, Primitive, United, Bible Christians and the New Connexion. For many, the most important question was whether the phenomenon of Methodism was the result of the Erastianism which denied the established Church an independence in its own affairs, or not.

The Evangelical revival within the established Church could have been a belated response to the Methodist movement. However, the Evangelicals were distinctive in the established Church, as they cared less about the institutional Church and more about the saving of souls; scripture had precedence over tradition and ecclesiastical authority (Symondson 1970, p. 88). For Evangelicals, personal conversion and primacy of a faith in the atoning death of Christ were linked to a focus on personal piety and stricter moral conduct. For many, this found expression in humanitarian causes, a great advocate of this being William Wilberforce (1759-1833). Wilberforce and his Evangelical colleagues (collectively known as the Clapham Sect) spurred concern and action about many unacceptable traditions and habits: among them child labour, duelling, cruel sports and (especially) slavery. At the same time, other Evangelicals like Charles Simeon (1759-1836), vicar of Holy Trinity, Cambridge (1782-1836), focused on promoting foreign missions and distributing the scriptures; on ensuring that new church buildings appeared where the urban population was growing; and on attacking the Church's sins of non-residential clergy and sinecures. In fact, the *Church Building Act 1818*, set up to fund the construction and maintenance of new churches, especially in the rapidly growing urban areas, owed much to pressure from Evangelicals.

Some in the established Church by the late 1820s were concerned that, although the Evangelicals had been effective in bringing to light the ethical concerns facing English Christians, they seemed to have raised the Bible to a position of such exclusive importance that other aspects of the English tradition were overshadowed. Some critics even felt that the ministry of clergy, and especially bishops, and even the creeds themselves, were being put to one side by this revival. It was argued by some that the sacraments within the Church's faith and order, along with the ordinances of the Church, were being ignored by the Evangelical revivalists because of their emphasis on preaching and prayer, rather than on sacraments, as the channels of divine grace (p. 88). The criticism heralded the cry that nonconformity belonged outside the established Church, not within it.

The major criticisms of the Evangelicals came from the strand within the established Church referred to as the High Churchmen. Here, the doctrinal emphasis took precedence and, rather than the atoning death of Christ, it was the Incarnation that took central place; along with this, the institutional Church, in its sacramental life, was central to each person's salvation. The High Churchmen shared the Evangelical zeal for humane and philanthropic causes: their most prominent initiative to meet the challenges of urban growth and to rouse their Church was the formation in 1811 of the National Society for Promoting the Education of the Poor in the Principles of the Established Church in England and Wales. This pioneering move in the general education of children was a deliberate counterpoint to the British and Foreign School Society (founded 1808), which had been developed and promoted by the nonconformists.

Pamphleteering for Church reform

What, therefore, was to be the future for the established Church? From where would reform of the Church come and who would make the decisions? As the ferment built regarding the Reform Bill, many in the Church were arguing for ecclesiastical reforms. The key pamphlet stirring this debate was released in early 1832 by Lord Henley (1789-1841 — a fervent Evangelical lawyer and a Tory Member of Parliament 1826-30, having succeeded his father in the House of Lords in 1830). This occurred before the introduction of the Reform Bill in June. He and his close friend, Sir Robert Peel, had been contemporaries as students at Christ Church before 1811, and, significantly, Henley had married Peel's sister, Harriett Eleanora, in 1824. Lord Henley called his pamphlet *A Plan of Church Reform*:

> [S]everal Corruptions exist in [the Church] which secularise and debase its spirit, contract the sphere of its usefulness, and lessen its hold on the affections and venerations of the People. (Henley 1832, p. 4)

Plural parish appointments, the scandal of non-residence of many clergy, the sinecures which often accompanied non-residence, the gross disparities in clerical income: these were some of the 'corruptions' Henley addressed: 'the most prominent Evil in the Church, is the Non-Residence of the Beneficed Clergy and the System of Pluralities' (p. 9).

Clearly, some of the established Church's practices for many had become a scandal; however, Henley went further and focused on a redistribution of the endowments of the Church from the cathedrals and the episcopal sees to the parishes; the creation of new episcopal sees; and the removal of bishops from the House of Lords. These were not new proposals, but it was the blunt and direct manner in which Henley asserted that the Church needed to govern its own affairs which drew public attention. He suggested the creation of a commission to manage all Church property:

> The plan which is here submitted proposes to vest all Episcopal and Chapter Estates in the hands of a Corporation for the exclusive management and controul [*sic*] of this species of Ecclesiastical property. (p. 34)

Furthermore, he wrote:

> The residence in his diocese is the first duty of every Bishop ... [and] Prelates in Parliament [were a barrier] to love and goodwill to man ... [T]he admixture of the Ministers of Religion in politics, is bad every way ... [I]f, therefore, the Parliamentary Peerage of the Prelates be prejudicial to the cause of Religion, the next inquiry will

be, whether a sufficient substitute for it can be provided by an Ecclesiastical Synod or Church Assembly. (pp. 51-2)

Before the Tractarian appeal to the apostolic roots of English Christianity, and its claims to holiness, Henley made a resounding call to his readers:

> Let the influence of all who possess influence, and the zeal and the holiness and the talents of all who are endowed with those graces and gifts, be united to render her constitution, in temporalities, in government, and in practice, what she has long been in profession, in doctrine and in faith, an APOSTOLICAL CHURCH [sic]. (p. 63)

Given our knowledge of the character of Short by the time he came to South Australia in 1847, it is clear that the strategic and organisational emphases, and the practical and ethical tone, of Henley's proposals must have made an immediate impression on him. Here, in all likelihood, were some of the earliest ecclesiastical influences on the young clergyman. These were to come to the fore when he became an ecclesiastical reformer and innovator in Adelaide.

Henley's publication was an immediate sensation and rapidly ran to eight editions, culminating in September 1832 in the formation of the Church Reformation Society of which he was the initial chairman. Here were courageous, and often radical, suggestions for the established Church to put its house in order, as Lord Grey had demanded. The response was speedy. Thomas Arnold (1795-1842) led in January 1833 with a pamphlet entitled *Principles of Church Reform*, the Preface of which summed up his argument:

> Church Establishment is essential to the well-being of the nation; that the existence of Dissent impairs the usefulness of an Establishment always, and now, from peculiar circumstances, threatens its destruction.[30] (1833a, pp. iii-iv)

Arnold believed that the focus must be on the relationship between the established Church and Dissenters, rather than just on the correction of the abuses within the United Church of England and Ireland. To this end, then, it was necessary to consider something radically different:

> Is it not, then, worth while [sic] to try a different system? And since disunion is something so contrary to the spirit of Christianity and difference of opinion a thing so inevitable to human nature, might it not be possible to escape the former without the folly of attempting to get rid of the latter, to constitute a Church thoroughly national, thoroughly united, thoroughly Christian, which should allow great varieties of opinion, of ceremonies, and forms of worship, according to the various knowledge, and habits, and tempers of its members, while it truly held one common faith, and trusted in one common Saviour, and worshipped one common God? (1833a, p. 28)

---

30   This is a reference to Dissenters and Catholics in Parliament.

Arnold argued for a truly national Church inclusive of all Dissenters, whilst acknowledging that others might dismiss his appeal as 'visionary and impracticable' (p. 87). This is precisely what happened, as his latitudinarianism appealed to few and within a short time Arnold had to issue a new explanatory pamphlet, *Postscript to the Principles of Church Reform*:

> The substance of what I endeavoured to shew [*sic*] was this, — that a Church Establishment is one of the greatest national blessings; that its benefits have been lessened and are now in danger of being forfeited altogether, by it being based on too narrow a foundation, and being not so much the Church of England, as of a certain part only of the people of England and that in order at once to secure it from destruction and to increase its efficiency as an instrument of national good, it should be made more comprehensive in its doctrines, its constitution, and its ritual. (1833b, p. 3)

Short clearly was not enamoured with the broad Church arguments of Arnold; if anything, this is borne out by his later experience when, as bishop of Adelaide, he had to deal with the latitudinarian appeals of some his own Church people in 1858 to allow a prominent English Nonconformist preacher, Rev. Thomas Binney, to preach in Church of England pulpits — appeals that Short refused amidst great controversy. Indeed, Arnold's general approach found few supporters among Short's contemporaries.

However, in the *Postscript*, Short would have positively responded to an argument in which Arnold appealed to the history of the early Church (a constant inspiration to Short in later years) in reference to episcopacy, and thus the leadership of the Church. Lord Henley had brought the issue of episcopacy to the forefront of the debate, and Arnold's observations were timely:

> … now the primitive bishops were appointed the members of their own order, with the approbation of the people of the diocese: — bishops in England are appointed solely by the crown. The primitive bishops could legislate for the Church, laity as well as clergy: — the bishops in England can legislate for no one without the consent of the crown, — and if they are allowed to meet in synod they can legislate only for the clergy, — over the laity their canons have no authority whatever. The primitive bishops fixed the doctrine of their Church, and ordered their ceremonies: — no single bishop, nor all the bishops in England united, can order a single prayer to be added to or taken from the Church services, nor can they so much as alter a single expression in its language. No bishop can ordain any man unless he will take certain oaths imposed by Act of Parliament, and subscribe to the Articles of religion as required by Act of Parliament. No bishop can refuse to institute any man regularly ordained to any cure of souls in his diocese, to which he has been appointed by the patrons; nor can he, except as patron, and not a bishop, confer the cure of souls on any one. Finally, in the primitive times the bishops were the judges in the civil matters amongst their people, and thus possessed a temporal influence and authority as well as spiritual: — whereas

in England they are accounted solely the governors of the clergy, and the bulk of the people are hardly aware of their possessing any authority at all. (Arnold 1833b, p. 16)

This stark analysis in the *Postscript* drew out for Short and others the central issue facing the Church: where lay the Church's authority, and how independent was the Church to order its own affairs? Arnold's comments on this point struck home. Many now joined in the debate during 1833: Edward Burton, *Thoughts upon the Demand for Church Reform*; Uvedale Price, *Reform without Reconstruction*; Hastings Robinson, *Church Reform on Church Principles*; A Country Gentleman, *Hints for Church Reform*; A Non-Beneficed Clergyman, *A Letter to His Grace the Archbishop of Canterbury on Church Reform*; LLB, *The Curate's Plea*; and William Palmer, *Remarks on the Rev. Dr. Arnold's Principles of Church Reform*. However, the most significant and detailed response to Henley and Arnold came late in 1833 from EB Pusey: *Remarks on the Prospective and Past Benefits of Cathedral Institutions, in the Promotion of Sound Religious Knowledge and of Clerical Education*. Nevertheless, political events quickly overshadowed this ferment in the established Church, diverting and redefining the debates and arguments, and igniting fresh passions.

The Church Temporalities Act 1833

The established Church, reform or no reform, as a corporation established by law, was now prone to investigation by a reforming Parliament. The attention of the politicians shifted in 1832 and 1833 to one of the most public areas of abuse, the state of the established Church in Ireland. The anomalies in Ireland were glaring. There were four archbishops and twenty-two diocesan bishops of the established Church, in a society that was predominantly Roman Catholic; members of the established United Church of England and Ireland numbered only 850 000, or 12 per cent of the Irish population. The combined episcopal income meant that the average income for each bishop far exceeded that of most English bishops (Knight 2008, p. 14). The Irish Church was partially funded by tithes levied on all Irish citizens, and this was a particular source of grievance. The ministry of Lord Grey proposed suppressing two of the archbishoprics, amalgamating ten of the diocesan bishoprics with other dioceses, and diverting some of the surplus revenues for use in the parishes. Grey's Bill, however, delayed dealing with the question of tithes, instead focusing on this rationalising of ecclesiastical structures.

There was a conundrum for the established Church. For many generations, the Church had looked to the state for protection and had benefited in an arrangement which had brought its clergy influence, social position and sufficient emoluments to support what was seen as their dignity or privilege, and had ensured the maintenance of hundreds of churches and cathedrals. The advantages had been worldly and considerable.

The state, in essence, had been the Church's protector. What now — was the Church to become totally Erastian, or was it to lose the support of the state altogether? Was secular authority to become either 'the Church's master or the Church's foe' (Lewis May 1933, p. 60)? Was the suppression of the Irish bishoprics the first ominous sign of things to come? How could such a vital question of the Church's order, the episcopate, be determined, so it seemed, by Parliament and not by the Church itself?

These were stirring times, yet even more was in store within the life of the Church as the conservative devout reacted to the reforming zeal of Parliament. The central question posed and embraced by many clergy was now not only concerned with the issues of authority in, and independence of, the Church, but with what was to be their conception of the Church. The new Whig government of Lord Grey clearly held to a more utilitarian view of Church government. The opposing view within the established Church found a voice: this held the Church to be a supernatural institution, immune in its spiritual life from political interference. Bishops might sit in the House of Lords, but they were successors to the apostles; clergy had divine vocations and were not 'primarily English gentlemen with a mission to behave like characters in a Jane Austen novel' (Knight 2008, pp. 14-15).

What in these changing times was to comprise the established Church? That one question implied many more issues: hierarchy, sacraments, creeds, doctrines, the *Book of Common Prayer*, the Bible, ecclesiastical discipline, historical tradition — all these were now worried over, especially by the ordained men of the Church of England. Morley (1908) summed it up in terms of differing views:

> The stupendous quarrel of the sixteenth and seventeenth centuries again broke out. To the erastian lawyer the church was an institution erected on principles of political expediency by act of parliament. To the school of Whateley and [Thomas] Arnold it was a corporation of divine origin, devised to strengthen men in their struggle for goodness and holiness by the association and mutual help of fellow-believers. To the evangelical it was hardly more than a collection of congregations commended in the Bible for the diffusion of the knowledge and right interpretation of the Scriptures, the commemoration of gospel events, and the linking of gospel truths to a well-ordered life. To the high Anglican as to the Roman Catholic, the church was something very different to this; not a fabric reared by man … but a mystically appointed channel of salvation, an indispensable element in the relation between the soul of man and its creator. To be a member of it was not to join an external association, but to become an inward partaker in ineffable and mysterious graces to which no other access lay open … [O]f this immense mystery … the established church of England was the local presence and the organ. (p. 117)

Was the established Church one institution with rival schools of thought and practice, or simply a collection of rival ecclesiologies cohering around the convenience and material benefits of what might be called the folk religion of the English?

'The religious movement of 1833'

On 1 July 1933, the *Waiapu Church Gazette* printed the following prayer, known as the 'Oxford Movement Centenary Prayer':

> Almighty and Everlasting God, we desire to offer to Thee most high praise and hearty thanks for Thy mercy and loving kindness to us during the last one hundred years. We praise and bless Thy Holy Name for the increase of devotion and reverence, for the more frequent administration of the Holy Sacraments, and for the teaching of the Faith once for all delivered to the Saints. And we pray Thee, as Thou hast cleansed and defended Thy Church in the past, so Thou wilt preserve it evermore by Thy help and goodness; through Jesus Christ our Lord. Amen.

With its references to 'the increase of devotion and reverence', the 'Holy Sacraments', and above all, to 'the teaching of the Faith once for all delivered to the Saints', this prayer encapsulates the breadth and depth of the religious movement which began in Oxford and swept the established Church from 1833. The Rev. John Keble (1792-1866) was regarded as the pioneering saint of this movement:

> Blessed be Thy Name, O God and Father most high, for Thy servant John Keble, whom Thou madest strong by humility and faith to proclaim awakening unto Thy Church ... (p. 2)

We do not know where Short spent July 1833: earlier, in March, he had been appointed a public examiner in the classical schools, in addition to his positions as a tutor and lecturer in the Classics. July saw the university in recess. It is unlikely that Short was in St Mary-the-Virgin, the university church, just under one kilometre from Christ Church, on Sunday 14 July. John Keble (1792-1866, former fellow of Oriel College and professor of poetry from 1831) had been invited to preach to His Majesty's Judges of Assize. For his text he chose 1 Samuel 12:23: '[A]s for me, God forbid that I should sin against the Lord in ceasing to pray for you: but I will teach you the good and the right way'. What followed was momentous, a sermon that quickly assumed the name 'National Apostasy'. It focused on the independence of the Church in its spiritual life, as expressed in the integrity of an episcopal order which derived its authority over the centuries from the apostles themselves, and which was now severely compromised by the actions of Parliament. In an 'advertisement' printed eight days later, on 22 July, to introduce the sermon to the wider public, Keble (1914), wrote:

> The Legislature of England and Ireland ... has virtually usurped the commission of those whom our Saviour entrusted with *at least one voice* in making ecclesiastical laws,

on matters wholly or partly spiritual ... [I]t is a moment, surely, full of deep solicitude to all those members of the Church who still believe her authority divine, and the oaths and obligations, by which they are bound to her, undissolved and indissoluble by calculations of human expediency ... [W]hat answer can we make henceforth to the partisans of the Bishop of Rome when they taunt us with being a mere Parliamentarian Church? And how consistently with our present relations to the State, can even the doctrinal purity and integrity of the MOST SACRED ORDER be preserved? (p. 541, emphases in the original)

The legislation bringing the changes to the Church in Ireland — that is, the *Church Temporalities Act* — was, at the time of the sermon, before the House of Lords; a week later, it passed into law. Many in the Church, especially in that bastion of orthodoxy Oxford, saw the suppression of the Irish bishoprics and their absorption into other dioceses, in defiance of Church protests, as an indication that the reforming Parliament would continue to target the rights and the endowments, and even the constitution and creeds, of the established Church. Would English bishoprics be next? The apostasy lay in the apparent renunciation by Parliament, for the first time, of the identification of the state with the established Church. In Keble's view the English had maintained for centuries that an essential part of their theory of government, as a Christian nation, was that the nation was part of Christ's church. Thus, he argued, all legislation and policy were bound by the fundamental rules of the Church of England (p. 546). Keble further saw this apostasy as a rejection of apostolic succession and thus hostility to the Church.

It is doubtful that Short embraced, in the heated atmosphere created by the sermon, the full implications of Keble's contentions that not only was the established Church a legal and constitutional cornerstone of government and civil order, but it was also, by the work of divine providence, the apostolic Church in England and Ireland, and its endowments and its Church order were therefore immune from the expediencies of parliamentary action. The sermon excited widespread interest and debate, overtaking the debate brought to life by Lord Henley. Certainly, two of Keble's questions lingered in the minds of the young clergyman and his contemporaries:

What are the symptoms by which one may judge most fairly whether or no a nation, as such, is becoming alienated from God and Christ?

And what are the particular duties of sincere Christians whose lot is cast by Divine Providence in a time of such dire calamity? (p. 546)

Keble's sermon was later regarded, primarily by John Henry Newman (1801-90), as the 'start of the religious movement of 1833', what became known as the Oxford or Tractarian Movement. Keble may have been forty-one at the time, but his soon-to-be colleagues were younger men — Edward Bouverie Pusey was thirty-three, John Henry Newman thirty-two, Hurrell Froude thirty, Isaac Williams thirty-one. Augustus Short was just thirty-one. It was soon clear, even in the cloistered world of Oxford, that the established Church was in ferment, not just over the encroachment of the state on its affairs, but also over renewed debates regarding the essential nature of the 'Holy, Catholic and Apostolic Church' of which the United Church of England and Ireland was, in the eyes of many — especially those of most of the ordained — the local expression in the British Isles. The 'religious movement of 1833' soon took shape and a series of *Tracts for the Times* commenced, inspired largely by John Henry Newman and Edward Bouverie Pusey.[31] Here was a movement that was to revolutionise the practical life of the established Church. Its leaders came from some unexpected places — the poet and pastor in his rural parish, Keble; the restless university professor with an encyclopedic knowledge of Hebrew, and canon of Christ Church, Pusey; the refined and erudite vicar of St Mary's, the university church, Newman. Their mastheads, the *Tracts*, were not to be original writings so much as a revisiting, a reproducing and a rebirth, of the writings of the early Church fathers and the Caroline divines of English Christianity.

To defend and promote Church principles soon became the purpose of the *Tracts*: the sacredness of the ordained ministry, the apostolic nature of the episcopacy, the episcopacy as the enduring source of the Church's authority, the sacramental and divine nature of the Church, and, pre-eminently, the independence of the Church from any worldly power, especially secular government. In fact, what characterised the movement was the pursuit of holiness, held to be the vital characteristic of being a Christian, recalling clergy to an often ascetic commitment to serve Christ above all else and to see their vocation as God's grace and gift. Newman's sermons, along with the *Tracts* that commenced as brief leaflets within two months of Keble's sermon, eventually became more detailed discourses, culminating in Tract 90 in January 1841. Their subject matter often concentrated on the question: What is the Church? In this, the *Tracts* generally asserted the dogmatic and supernatural element in the Church of England, affirming it as part of the wider Catholic Church and transcending any state. Central at all times was apostolic succession, the divine link with Jesus and the apostles (Lewis May 1933, p. 68).

Those early years of the Oxford Movement stirred the ecclesiastical and political world of Oxford, and to a certain extent, the world beyond. The exuberance was, for some, infectious. JB Mozley, Newman's brother-in-law, fellow of Magdalen College and enthusiastic participant in the Oxford Movement, wrote:

> The year 1834, in respect of events, was as the calm which precedes the storm, but it was one of vast preparation and incessant labour ... The tracts took time to write, and perhaps more time to read. Sermons were preached everywhere, even in the Chapel Royal, but mostly in country places, and published with long introductions

---

31 The *Tracts* were published between 1833 and 1841 and were made up of ninety separate publications, with many authors. They varied greatly in length and subject matter.

and copious appendices. High and Low Church stood by amazed, and very doubtful what it would come to; but meanwhile equally pleased to see life in the Church, which the House of Commons seemed to think incapable of thought, will, or action. The correspondence grew. Oxford resumed its historic place as the centre of religious activity. This was the golden age of the movement, and men talked rather gaily. (1890, pp. 340-1)

Newman and Pusey were the dynamos of the movement in Oxford, with Keble distant in rural Hursley, Hampshire.[32] In addition to the *Tracts*, the three men, reaching back to the influence of Charles Lloyd and others during the 1820s, pursued the ambition of compiling *The Library of The Fathers* ('*A Library of Fathers of the Holy Catholic Church: Anterior to the Division of the East and West*') and signed the prospectus for the project in 1836. This was to be a series of translations into English of selected writings of the fathers of the early Church. Here was the kernel of the movement, the endeavour to recall the foundations of the Catholic faith inherited by the established Church, especially its doctrine of the Church. The first volume of the *Library* in 1838 was by Edward Bouverie Pusey, being St Augustine's *Confessions*: '[I]t is the first book of patristic theology put by the French Seminarists into the hands of their pupils' (Mozley 1890, p. 416). It was intended, with its successors, as a provocative and innovative contribution to theological study for English Christianity also.

Short never wrote in any detail of his feelings regarding the Tractarian movement. He knew several participants personally, especially Pusey, and obviously had sympathy with many of the starting points of the *Tracts* but then parted company. Perhaps he concurred, as often before, with his cousin. Many years later, Thomas Vowler Short (1875) recalled:

> The *Tracts of the Times* began to be published after I had ceased to reside at Oxford. They are written by many different people in different tempers, and the mass of them I have never read. They attracted most attention while I was rector of Bloomsbury, but I did not think they were likely to have much influence on my own flock, and did not bring them forward by preaching upon them. In the Isle of Man the people had heard little and knew less about the controversy, and in Wales it was never agitated. As far

---

32   There was a deeply moving postscript to the Oxford Movement. Keble, Pusey and Newman soon took different paths after 1833: Keble in his country vicarage; Pusey to the heights and depths of scholastic Oxford; and, Newman to the Roman Catholic Church in 1845. Thirty-two years after 1833, in the year before Keble died, Pusey decided to meet his old mentor again and went to Hursley to dine with Keble and his wife. While talking together for the first time in decades Keble was called to the door to speak to a parishioner. While speaking with his parishioner, the white-haired Keble looked up and saw approaching a man not much younger than himself. It was John Henry Newman coming to visit Keble for the first time in decades. At first the two men did not recognise each other. The coincidence of this occasion was remarkable, and the three ageing stalwarts of the Catholic English Church sat down to a meal together, alone, for the first and last time in their lives!

as I have been able to judge, they have done much harm and much good, but not so much of either as has been attributed to them. (p. lv)

From 1835 Short, while vicar of Ravensthorpe (see Chapter Five), retained a keen interest in the religious excitements of his university. He was asked, by Newman — who, like Pusey, had been an academic colleague from the 1820s, although not a confidant — to contribute to the *Library of the Fathers*. Short chose to translate the work of St Hilary (c. 315-c. 368, bishop of Poitiers) on the Trinity (*De Trinitate*), and it is no surprise that Short chose St Hilary as his subject. Sometimes referred to as the 'St Athanasius of the West', Hilary was the leading Latin theologian of his time, and his standing rested on his defence of orthodoxy against the Arians (who denied the divinity of Jesus Christ); *De Trinitate* was the great work in this regard. Parish work centred on the proclamation of the gospel; what and how to proclaim was Short's daily companion. He knew he was orthodox in his beliefs, and thus found comfort and encouragement in St Hilary's words in Book 1:37-38 of *De Trinitate*:

> Bestow on us then the right use of terms, give light to our understanding and agreeable style to our words, grant us loyalty to the truth. Grant that what we believe we may also speak, about you the one true God the Father, and the one Lord Jesus Christ, as we learn from the apostles and prophets, and that we may succeed now in proclaiming against the denial of the heretics that you are God, yet not alone, and in preaching Jesus Christ as true and no false God. (In Kenneth 1983, p. 630)

Short also found encouragement in Book 2:33-35:

> There is one Creator of all, for there is one God the Father, from whom all things are. There is one Only-begotten, Jesus Christ our Lord, through whom all things are. There is one Spirit, the Gift, in all things. (In Kenneth 1983, p. 382)

In the prospectuses of the *Library*, for several years, Short's translation of *De Trinitate* was referred to as 'preparing for publication'; Newman had a draft from Short in 1840 for consideration. He wrote on 28 August 1840:

> Dear Short,
>
> Your MS shows at first sight what trouble you have given yourself with it, for which all the subscribers to the Library must be grateful. In so difficult an author it is not wonderful if some further alterations should still be wanting; and I think that is the case. I would have without scruple altered the MS, had <u>it come from a person of junior standing; but of course I cannot even wish to take such a liberty with yours</u>, though I am sorry that in consequence I shall be putting you to some further trouble. (Tracey 1995, pp. 381-2, emphasis in the original)

Short replied immediately, 1 September:

> I was quite prepared to find errors … With regard to being literal I should wish it to be so except where the English would be *irreverent*, tautological, or obscure. In the

> passages you have sent me I certainly have been too careless and in the part decidedly mistaken. (In Tracey 1995, p. 381, emphasis in the original)

Nevertheless, despite this involvement, no-one regarded Short as a Tractarian, least of all Newman. Writing to Pusey in August 1842, Newman commented that a translation of Tertullian's *Apologetic and Practical Treatises* was the contribution of a non-Tractarian, the Christ Church student and tutor Charles Dodgson (later famous as 'Lewis Carroll'); and that Augustus Short was clearly another (Tracey 1995, p. 61). If Newman did not acknowledge Short as a fellow Tractarian, then this assists in refuting suggestions later in life for Short, when in Adelaide, that he was inclined towards Tractarianism:

> No one who intimately knew the first bishop of Adelaide would ever have spoken of him as a profound sacramentarian, or as a ritualist. Bishop Short remained to the end a moderate representative of that early school of Oxford high churchmanship, which was of a literary and doctrinal rather than of a mystic or ceremonial character. (Whitington 1887, p. 242)

Short had been invited to contribute to the *Library of the Fathers* based on his abilities in scholarship alone, but in the end his translation failed to be published. Speculation about why this was so varies. There was the discouragement that Short may have felt at Newman's demands as an editor (Brown & Nockles 2012, p. 108.). There was also the fact that this work, as important as it was to the Movement, was, for Short, soon swamped by the controversies surrounding Tract 90, and by the appointment of Keble's successor as professor of poetry, all of which occurred in 1841 (see Chapter Five).

Oxford's religious movement did pass through many stages, before and after the secession of Newman to the Roman Catholic Church in 1845. Its legacy is much debated but, as one partisan account records, over the remainder of the nineteenth century there were

> revived studies of Patristic Theology, greater depth, and freedom from narrow party-shackles ... [T]he care of students to be acquainted with the truth of Ecclesiastical History; and at the same time the advancement of works of Christian popular instruction, increased services, and concern for the beauty and order of the house of prayer. (Churton 1863, pp. 280-1)

Politically, the movement did not halt parliamentary action. Reform for the established Church, once started, did not cease as far as the Parliament was concerned. Ecclesiastical Commissioners were inaugurated in 1835 to manage the financial affairs of the established Church, and various acts of Parliament, passed between 1836 and 1840, removed the worst ecclesiastical abuses: the distribution of endowments was revised; plurality was restricted by law (*Pluralities Act 1838*); members of cathedral chapters could only hold one benefice; cathedral clergy were reduced in number; and the inequalities of episcopal revenues were revised.

Within the university the movement was a powerful influence on many undergraduates, as spiritual guidance remained a central responsibility of the tutor. For people such as Pusey, the aims of the movement within the university were to restore the university as an ecclesiastical institution (Evans 2010, p. 252). The Oxford Movement inspired an ecclesiastical dynamism that reached back to the early Church; the young men caught in its appeal became involved in ecclesiastical history, art, architecture and music. What attracted Short's attention was that this movement, centred on several former colleagues, had revived the doctrine of the Church. His sympathies were clearly High Church in the old fashioned sense, thanks to Charles Lloyd and Thomas Vowler Short. During Short's lifetime, the established Church had largely been High Church, with most clergy identifying with it. This broad and sometimes vague theological emphasis, with which Short had grown up, endured until the rise of the Oxford Movement and its radicalisation of High Churchmanship (Strong 2007, p. 39; Nockles 1994, pp. 27-31). While sharing the Tractarian search for holiness, Short was, nevertheless, wary of too subjective a religion. For him, the *Book of Common Prayer* would suffice as guardian and guide. He had decided to dedicate his life to the established Church; and to a significant extent the Oxford Movement affirmed and supported that calling.

5

Rural vicar and Oxford matters 1835-47

The Ravensthorpe village church, built in AD 1315, was a fine specimen of early English architecture. The tower remained intact, and though the aisles had been rebuilt the whole fabric needed repair and restoration … [The vicarage was in] a poor and dilapidated state. It was absolutely necessary to rebuild the office and to add new rooms. A grant of one hundred pounds from the dean and chapter of Christ Church, Oxford, and a loan from the Queen Anne's Bounty office enabled me to expend six hundred pounds on the premises. (Short 1882 in Whitington 1887, p. 13)

Vicar of Ravensthorpe

The Ravensthorpe fourteenth-century church, dedicated to St Denys, had been under the control of the Knights Hospitallers at Dingley before the Reformation. In Short's time the parish of Ravensthorpe (in the Brixworth district of Northamptonshire), was within the diocese of Peterborough. Short recounted in 1882:

> The village of Ravensthorpe is situated on a moderate range of hills, separated from Haddon on the west and Guilborough [sic] on the east by deep valleys of fertile soil. The hamlets of Teeton and Coton stood in the latter, containing about one-third of the seven hundred residents who made up the population. Of the laboring class the majority were Baptists. (In Whitington 1887, p. 15)

In his reminiscences, he described Ravensthorpe as follows:

> [it] was a neglected out of the way village well nigh obliterated from the Ecclesiastical references. I see in the story of my new Incumbency how providential a preparation

it was for my call to the See of Adelaide over which I was to preside … whilst leading the usual quiet life of an English Country Clergyman from 1835 to 1847. (SLSA, PRG 160/7)

Ravensthorpe shared with a multitude of rural parishes the aspiration and expectation of the established Church to be a presence in every part of England, and to persist in a belief in the Church's responsibility to all residents, especially the rural poor: 'the conservative ideal was that the parish should be a coherent community' (Wolffe 1994, p. 50). For Short there was another dimension. His Oxford experiences had given him a zeal for real energetic activity, and he focused not just on rebuilding the church and the vicarage but also in creating new opportunities for the parish in other ways, especially by building a schoolroom. His approach was a mix of sincere caring for the people as called for through his vocation with an instinct for the self-preservation of the established Church in a religious environment that was at times turbulent both nationally and locally.

Energy, imagination and creativity came to the fore. Over the ensuing eleven years Short ministered in his village, where the majority of residents were Dissenters, outside the established Church, and where religious rivalry was prominent. Short found he was engaged in a social revolution that was gathering pace in England. Clearly, society was changing, embracing more democratic forms with all its contingent debates and arguments about change, as he described in 1882:

> The labourers at that time were ill-paid, ill-fed, ill-housed, and of course discontented. There was no sick club, and the 'Union allowance' was little favourable to the sick man's convalescence. During the miserable period in England between 1836 and 1847 twice I found it necessary to purchase bags of good rice and retail them at half-price to the poorer labourers, whose wives thankfully received this boon to eke out their scanty meals. No wonder Chartism flourished under such conditions of life. (In Whitington 1887, p. 16)

What personally concerned him was that there existed 'no parochial school, and so much sectarian feeling prevailed'; he soon was determined 'to build a schoolroom and try whether fellowship in education would not lessen religious rancour in after-life'. Here there was an echo of his cousin's views that school education had a role in arbitrating the conflicting and complicated claims of both the working and governing parts of society. TV Short maintained that widespread school education, conducted by the Church of England and inculcating religious values, would ensure more harmonious relationships between the English social classes (1835, pp. 5-6). Augustus Short, as he often did, took his inspiration from the pioneering and decisive initiatives of his cousin when the latter was the vicar of King's Worthy, Hampshire, from 1826:

> At King's Worthy [TV] Short proved to be a reforming cleric. By preaching, catechising, visiting the schools and establishing a Sunday School he and his family taught, attending an evening school taught by the parish clerk, and holding a weekly Bible class for young men and establishing occasional lectures, he became aware of the possibilities of rural ministry … [TV] Short also acted as secretary of the Hampshire Society for National Education, which meant he superintended the work of Church education in those parts. (Brown 2014, n.p.)

The schooling debate in English Christianity, at this time, was not so much between religious education and secular education as it was between rival notions of religious education. Some held that a general and simple religious education without any Church instruction was preferred. To achieve this, the British and Foreign Schools Society had been organising schools since 1814, an approach that was popular with Dissenters and nonconformists. Others maintained that religious instruction without education in membership of the established Church was all but pointless. The established Church had begun the National Society for Promoting the Education of the Poor in the Principles of the Established Church, in 1811 (later known as The National Society for Promoting Religious Education, or simply The National Society); by 1831 it was reaching through its schools a quarter of a million children. The liturgy and catechism of the United Church of England and Ireland were taught, the vicar or rector was in prime control of his school, and he employed the schoolmistress. One side argued that the Bible was all that was necessary and common to all denominations, and that it could be taught without denominational interpretation and divisiveness. The other side argued that religious instruction was not a subject like mathematics; it entailed a tradition of community life and purpose. Education in worship and the life of the Church made sense of the gospels.

Warily, Short trod a fine path between these two competing ambitions, practising a consensual and neutral approach, as he described in 1882:

> I went round to some of the Baptist parents and asked them if they objected to their children learning the Creed, the Lord's Prayer, and the Ten Commandments. To which I purposed to limit the religious instruction of *their* children. To this they readily assented and thus, in the case of dissenting children … the experiment succeeded, in spite of the 'religious difficulty' as it is called, of teaching children the catechism. (In Whitington 1887, p. 16, emphasis in the original)

Many years later, in evidence before a Select Committee of the House of Assembly appointed to the South Australian Parliament, Short was to recall:

> I undertook, in 1836, the charge of a parish, which numbered 700 inhabitants, containing a large body of Baptists, and a large body of Independents. There was no school, and the children of that village were grossly ignorant, and animated by a very

sectarian feeling. My first attempt to build a school, which I succeeded in doing, and I put in a Church of England mistress, and invited all to come; and gave a pledge that their religious principles should not be interfered with. I know that even the catechism of the Church of England was taught there, but I made it a rule never to ask any child not of the Church of England any question, except with regard to the Lord's Prayer or the Ten Commandments, or the Creed. The school flourished and numbered sixty or seventy children, and was a great blessing and benefit to that population. I carried it on for ten years. (SAPP, pp. 18-21; see also 'The Report of the Synod of the Diocese of Adelaide' 1869)

Thus, in the relatively isolated society of Ravensthorpe, Short, learning how to lead, practised policies of consensus which he would later seek to follow on a greater scale in South Australia. Here was his conviction that religion in society had a prime function in expressing collective values and promoting a moral unity, a key framework for which was school education. Short saw all residents of the parish as his parishioners, whether they were Church of England or not: 'the bulk of the parishioners were staunch Baptists or Congregationalists. I was, however, by my intercourse with this mixture of religious professions well trained for my future diocese in South Australia' (SAPP, pp. 18-21). This approach, deliberate by Short, was part of the landscape in England, where the acknowledgement of nonconformity, and a high degree of social respect for it by the established Church, prevented the anti-clericalism so common on the Continent. Dissent and nonconformity provided a valuable alternative to the established Church for many and prevented a sharper distinction between belonging to the United Church of England and Ireland or rejecting the Christian faith altogether.

Such experiences confirmed for Short that elementary schooling for all was a growing necessity. Yet there emerged a persistent fear in the established Church of a growing impetus towards a secular education — schools maintained directly by the state. In the wake of the 1832 *Reform Act* (which was the background to Short's rural efforts in education) came the innovative 1833 vote by Parliament to provide unconditional grants of £20 000 to the voluntary societies. However, there were arguments growing for increased state intervention in, even state administration of, elementary education, primarily because the voluntary societies could not cover all the demands.

One of Short's contemporaries at Christ Church, Archdeacon George Denison, a friendly colleague who was becoming a major figure in the established Church, expressed the conservative view in an exchange with William Ewart Gladstone, who was now, as his political star rose, most prominent in his religious affiliation. Denison wrote to Gladstone asserting, in the face of the gathering momentum for state intervention, the traditional Church principles:

> [T]he clergy are directly and solely responsible for all that is taught in the parish schools, for the matter and the manner of it. For the clergy are in virtue of their office 'the dispensers of the Word of God and of His Holy Sacraments' and it is upon the Word of God and upon His Holy Sacraments that all Christian Education in any sense of the word must be based. (In Bowen 1968, p. 233)

Here was an issue of some vulnerability for the established Church: many churchmen feared the threat of secularity that an education provided by the state might encourage. Short was relieved during the 1840s as the established Church moved towards a conviction that the moral purpose of education would be best served by its support of the state in providing universal elementary education. He shared with his cousin TV Short (bishop of St Asaph in Wales from 1846) a belief that the Church should influence a state system of education to prevent it becoming totally secular. In all its facets, education of the young mattered greatly to Short. To supplement the income of his parish and to continue the essential building maintenance, he agreed from time to time to take into his home private pupils, sons of the wealthy:

> So many parochial wants and improvements to be effected led me to accept the offer of private pupils, the income from which source enabled me to accomplish these objects. In addition to the schoolroom I was then enabled to make some restorations in the church, add a rood of ground to the churchyard, purchase the cottage and yard where the Chartist meeting had been held and add them to the glebe, exchange other land for the field in front of the vicarage house, carry on successfully the sick club, and provide on the annual village feast-day some amusements for the labourers as well as prizes for the best shearers in the village. (Short 1882 in Whitington 1887, p. 17)

Lord Grosvenor (later Duke of Westminster) was one parent grateful to the young vicar and his wife, writing on 12 September 1843:

> My dear Sir
>
> As my son is about to quit your roof you must let me trouble you with a line to thank you for the kindness & attention he has received from yourself & Mrs Short during his agreeable residence at Ravensthorpe — a residence which has been a real service to him, and one which he will look back on, I trust, in future years with affection. (SLSA, PRG 160/2)

Short was not alone in the style of his approach to elementary education, and in creating, by its means, social harmony in his parish. The Rev. Thomas Mozley, writing in 1882, recalled a visit he made in 1834 to Northamptonshire, at the beginning of the religious controversies associated with the Oxford Movement:

> [The Reverend] Sikes was a fine-looking, elderly man, with a dignified bearing and a very kind expression, ready to talk about everything, but with a certain languor and sadness which might or might not be more his wont … Sikes made the kindest

inquiries about the Oxford people ... but all his talk was against pushing Church principles too hard, and making breaches never to be healed. There were zealots in Northamptonshire, he said, who would bring Church teaching to a point that would necessarily exclude dissenters. As things were there was inconsistency on both sides, on the side of the Church managers as well as the dissenters. But he had always urged privately that these inconsistencies should be endured. If the dissenters will bear it, surely we may. Their children are often the best in our schools. The Northamptonshire schools, he said, stood high, and he believed it was owing to a quiet, conciliatory policy. Avoid disturbance if you can. (p. 333)

The time in Ravensthorpe was significant in another way: it was the beginning of family life for Augustus and Millicent. Children were born: Sophia Millicent in September 1837, Charles in July 1839, Isabella Emily in December 1840, Henry Augustus in March 1843, Albinia Frances in February 1844, Alfred Newton in January 1845, and Caroline Phillipa Augusta in February 1847. The couple knew tragedy amidst the joy of family life, however. Charles and Alfred died in infancy and were buried in the Ravensthorpe churchyard.

In 1878, Short, nearing the end of his time as bishop of Adelaide, made a return visit to Ravensthorpe, as described in 1882:

> I had the satisfaction of finding the sick club with one hundred and thirty members, and four hundred pounds in the Savings Bank, the schoolhouse enlarged, the church and chancel thoroughly restored, the vicarage and ground in nice order, such as might well satisfy the modest wants of a country clergyman. I went down to preach on the re-opening of the church after the restoration. About twenty-five clergy met in the schoolroom to welcome me, some of them former neighbours. The old parishioners came afterwards into the vicarage garden, and were not a little pleased by my remembering most of them well. (In Whitington 1887, p. 17)

Select preacher 1838

It was not long into his rural ministry before Short was invited to renew his Oxford links with an invitation to be the select preacher before the university for 1838. The title of the seven sermons he was to give in response to this invitation was *Sermons Intended Principally to Illustrate the Remedial Character of the Christian Scheme, with Reference to Man's Fallen Condition* (1838). The first sermon was a repeat of an earlier one, indicating that Short had already been prominent in the university before his departure for Ravensthorpe. On Trinity Sunday in 1835, he had delivered the Ordination Sermon in Christ Church Cathedral — a rare honour. The titles of the other sermons were: 'The Gospel Good Tidings of Great Joy to all People' (Romans 5:19, 20); 'The Holy Ghost shed on Christians Abundantly' (Luke 11:13); 'No Respect of Persons with God'

(Romans 2:14, 15); 'All Things Work Good to them that Love God' (Matthew 13:27-30); 'The Increase of Faith through Obedience' (Luke 17:5-8); and, 'Who are Christ's' (Romans 8:9).

The first sermon revealed much of Short's understanding about ordained ministry. Entitling it 'The Blessedness of the Peace of God' and inspired by John 16:33, Short described in it some key foundations to his ministry, upon which he would rely, not only at Ravensthorpe but in later years in his episcopacy in South Australia:

> There is then a *spiritual happiness* to be looked for in spite of outward circumstances, even in this world; the reward of faithful obedience: to which in turn it gives increased strength, and a wider sphere of action. (p. 3, emphasis in the original)

Further, he wrote that the Apostles' 'experience of spiritual joys enabled them to endure afflictions, to do the work of evangelists, and to make full proof of their ministry (pp. 4-5)'. He wrote that he believed in the importance of 'God's word and sacraments' and stated that 'one evil effect of pushing the liberty of private judgment to an extreme length is the practical denial of the obligation to maintain the unity of the visible Church … [It can lead to] the *apostolic commission* [being] lightly regarded' (p. 13, emphasis in the original).

In sum, he wrote in the first sermon:

> I would draw no exaggerated picture of the ministerial life, nor present it as the unalloyed exercise of pleasurable benevolence. It unquestionably has its trials and discomforts; but this I say, that, 'one day spent in thy courts, O Lord,' spent, that is, in devotion to thy service, 'is better than a thousand' passed amidst the highest pleasures of refinement and society. (p. 27)

Significantly, these sermons were dedicated 'To The Rev. Thomas Vowler Short, DD, Rector of Bloomsbury as a mark of my affectionate respect'. Here was a rare public acknowledgement of the influence Short's cousin had had on the development of his theology and ecclesiology: 'the train of thought pursued in the second, third, and fourth [sermons], was suggested by a question asked many years ago at [TV Short's] private Divinity Lecture in Christ Church' (1838, n.p.).

The 'Notice' following the dedication (pp. v-vii) also revealed the influences of Charles Lloyd's teachings, with wide-ranging references to the 'leading theologians of the Reformation, Lutheran as well as Anglican'; to 'even the Swiss divines', Calvin included; and to 'the Fathers also', including Augustine. Not least, the Notice showed how 'our Tenth Article' (of Religion) was relevant to Short's sermons. Short was keen to show the comprehensiveness of his theology and how rooted in antiquity it was:

> in matters of practical difficulty we own, that 'in the multitude of counsellors there is safety', referring again to 'the sound rule of Vincentius, quod *semper*, quod *ubique*,

quod *ab omnibus*; i.e. what *all* Christians *at all times* and *in all places* have held to be the sense, that most probably is the true interpretation of Scripture. (1838, pp. v-vii, emphases in the original)

The professor of poetry 1841

Immersed as he was in the life of a country parson, the scholar in Short hankered for the chatter, for the lively intellectual exchanges only a university could give. Oxford still mattered to him and, over the eleven years at Ravensthorpe, he was drawn into three momentous events at Oxford: the disputed appointment of a new professor of poetry in 1841; the publication of the final and most controversial *Tracts of the Times*, Tract 90 in 1841 and the ensuing controversy until 1845; and, the personal honour of an invitation to deliver the Bampton Lectures before the university in 1846.

The Reverend John Keble had been professor of poetry in the University of Oxford since 1831, although he was not resident, and was to retire from his post in 1841 after serving the second of two five-year terms. Keble had had a distinguished career in Oxford: awarded a double first at the age of eighteen (Robert Peel had been twenty, and Gladstone twenty-two, when they shared this distinction), he was elected to the Oriel fellowship four days before his nineteenth birthday (Hylson-Smith 1993, p. 133). It had been little surprise when he was elected professor of poetry in 1831.[33] Yet Keble's most stirring contribution to his Church, and to English Christianity, had been his sermon on Sunday 14 July 1833, preached in the university church before the Judges of Assize (see Chapter Four).

For the post of professor of poetry there was an obvious successor to Keble in the Reverend Isaac Williams (1802-65), who was a fellow and tutor at Trinity College. A poet and a scholar of considerable standing in the university, 'one of the gentlest and most saintly of scholars' (Ollard 1925, p. 62), he was Keble's choice. He was, however, much identified with the Catholic revival in the 'religious movement', by then known as the Tractarian movement, and had authored a controversial Tract 80. In the atmosphere of the day, opposition quickly formed to his election. While no actual contest eventuated, much debate and campaigning ensued before it was clear that Williams was unelectable. Former students of Christ Church were lobbied, as they would be asked to vote, being members of Convocation, and Short received a circular from Pusey on the issue. The circular, dated 17 November 1841, outlined the virtues of Isaac Williams and claimed that Mr Garbett, the other contender, 'would not even now have been brought forward except to prevent the election of Mr Williams' (in Whitington 1887, p. 20).

---

33 His volume of poems, *The Christian Year*, published in 1827, ran to over 150 editions within fifty years.

Privately, Pusey attached a note for Short;

> My dear Short — I hope you will be able to help us at ye [*sic*] present crisis. There is no question but that Williams is every way ye superior. He has great poetic talent, tastes, deep thought, and devotion. The only question is, whether he is disqualified by his connection with us. It is to be made a condemnation of us and our teaching in ye mass ... [I]t would seem like a formal rejection of ye Tracts, and of all we have been for these many years, not I trust without fruit, inculcating.
>
> Your sincere friend,
>
> EB Pusey. (In Whitington 1887, p. 22)

What intrigues is whether Pusey's letter, in its references to 'us', meant he identified Short with Tractarianism as a supporter, or whether he was simply one Christ Church academic appealing to another to stand by one of their own.

A few days later, on 23 November 1841, Short replied. His letter, acknowledging Williams's superior claim to the position, is nevertheless circumspect and revealing regarding the revival movement:

> Is it not an object with yourself and friends to influence the public mind in the views (special as well as general) of the Tracts through the Chair of Poetry? And do you not seek to stamp with University authority the system and views you advocate? ... At the same time your party never were at any pains to disconnect the University from the system of the Tracts ... <u>For myself I can say that I believe in *some* of the main positions of that system — a visible Church, Episcopacy, a Succession, and Sacraments as means, not merely signs, of grace to them who rightly receive them.</u> (In Whitington 1887, p. 22, emphases in the original)

Short then listed his misgivings: disapproval of the tone in various Tracts when referring to the Reformation; the issues of the sacrifice of the Mass in Tract 90; Newman's views on prayers to the Saints and the Virgin Mary; other proposed changes by the movement regarding divine worship; and (most interestingly, given how later events unfolded for Short) rejection of the movement's views regarding the colonial bishoprics. Short concluded in friendly terms: 'I have written fully and candidly my impressions, because besides private esteem and respect I can publicly thank you for much of your labours' (in Whitington 1887, p. 23).

Now thirty-nine years old, Short showed in this reply some of the ecclesiological and doctrinal views he had formed which were clearly in sympathy with some of those promoted by the Oxford religious movement. This did not make him a Tractarian, however. Pusey understood this and wrote again on 26 November 1841, enclosing a copy of a letter sent to one of those opposing Williams. In his letter addressed to 'my dear Short', Pusey referred to the matter of 'reserve', which Williams had discussed in Tract 80:

> If you had not read both tracts on 'reserve' I should feel satisfied that you would not object to [Williams's points of view in his Tract] as a whole ... Williams is supported as ye [*sic*] best man, taking in of course the *general tone* of his religious views, and not disqualified because of his connection with us. (In Whitington 1887, p. 25, emphasis in the original)

Short replied promptly; he had done what Pusey requested, 'I have read Tract No. 80 with attention' and continued to question Williams's argument about the Atonement, particularly the use of the term 'reserve'. He went on:

> [I]t will not do to let the younger clergy fancy that they are at liberty to *withhold* that which sets forth the exceeding sinfulness of sin and the love of God in Christ, viz,. the Atonement, because it will be a saviour unto life or death. The word 'reserve', is, in my humble opinion, most unfortunately chosen, as calculated to convey a notion of *keeping back* the grand features of the Gospel scheme, rather than of teaching them with *awe and seriousness*. (In Whitington 1887, p. 26, emphases in the original)

Short then suggested a way forward (to avoid a direct election) by requesting from members of Convocation an indication, a 'comparison', of 'pledged' votes: 'surely it is as well to seek the things which make for peace, if it can be done without compromise' (in Whitington 1887, p. 26).

Events progressed, nonetheless:

> On the 20th January, however, while every one was discussing the comparative merits of the two candidates (one being decidedly a poet, certainly a scholar, but unfortunately a Tractarian; the other a clever man, a classical scholar and critic, but rather a Low Churchman), all the hubbub and all the discomforts of a contested election on a large scale were quietly put a stop to by a challenge to a comparison of *promised votes* from one side [Mr Garbett's] and an acceptance of the challenge on the other. (Cox 1870, p. 324, emphasis in the original)

Short's suggestion of a compromise process was obviously widely shared: what eventuated was an indication of 921 votes for Garbett and 623 for Williams, resulting in Williams withdrawing his candidacy.

Short had participated directly in a touchstone of one of the leading religious conflicts in English Christianity of the time — between those who followed the path of Keble, Newman, Pusey and their colleagues, and those who distrusted the 'Romish' implications of the Catholic revival. While Short's contributions were in private correspondence, the public 'storm of angry words and a heavy shower of controversial letters' (Cox 1870, p. 323) underlined how such an event was defining for many.

Tract 90 (1841)

Within a month of this resolution, another episode occurred, indicating both the high standing in which Short was held and his continuing interest in Church politics and affairs at Oxford. However, his recollections, which he shared with Whitington forty years after the event, indicate something of his concerns regarding how history might regard him. While sometimes accused of being a Tractarian, and thus peremptorily dismissed because of it by some Evangelicals in his own church and by Protestants of other denominations, Short seemed determined to show that his religious attitudes were never that simple or obvious. While he publicly accused some of the Tract writers of obscuring religious truth, nevertheless, he was not reticent either to reveal to his first biographer material regarding his defence of one of the major controversies of the Tractarian movement, John Henry Newman's Tract 90.

One constant theme of the *Tracts of the Times*, since 1833, had been the inherent Catholicism of the *Book of Common Prayer*. This universal integrity of the cornerstone of English Christianity, some thought, had been hindered by the consistent failure of many clergy to observe, and obey, the Prayer Book's rubrics. The failure was episcopal as well, in that discipline on such a pivotal matter had been missing. Tract 90, appearing on 27 February 1841, was a turning point. In this work Newman sought to argue that the Thirty-Nine Articles of Religion, appended to the *Book of Common Prayer* and printed in every copy, were open to a Catholic interpretation. These were the very Articles to which all graduates of Oxford and Cambridge, and those being ordained in the Church of England, were required to subscribe in order to matriculate, to graduate or to be ordained, as the case might be. Thus they were also central to the authority of the heads of colleges and halls in the administration of the university. For many in Oxford, Tract 90 appeared to undermine the enduring ecclesiastical conception of the university as a part of the established Church.

The Articles, approved in 1563, had always been intended to show the reformed nature of Anglican doctrine, but the question for some was: were they also able to show its reformed Catholic nature too? A somewhat rigid and Protestant interpretation of the Articles had become the norm within the established Church by the nineteenth century, and Newman asked if the time for this emphasis to be balanced was not overdue. Newman contended that the purpose of his Tract was

> merely to show that, while our Prayer Book is acknowledged on all hands to be of Catholic origin, our Articles also, the offspring of an uncatholic age, are, through God's good providence, to say the least, not uncatholic, and may be subscribed by those who aim at being Catholic in heart and doctrine. (1841, p. 4)

The argument was that the Articles were expressed, at times, with a vagueness and indecision that deliberately encouraged as comprehensive and an inclusive reading as possible. The Articles did not condemn many Catholic practices at all. The words of the framers of the Articles were what mattered, not their sentiments and emotions as protesting reformers. The Articles in fact reflected the views of the early Church before the accretions of the Roman Catholic Church in the middle ages. The controversy was immediate:

> The Tract had sufficient novelty about it to account for most of the excitement which it caused. Its dryness and negative curtness were provoking. It was not a positive argument, it was not an appeal to authorities; it was a paring down of language, alleged in certain portions of the Articles to be somewhat loose, to its barest meaning. (Church 1892, p. 288)

For the family man and scholar at work in rural Northamptonshire, it was not possible to resist a contribution to this ecclesiastical controversy. The resounding questions arising from Tract 90 for Short were: what did the Thirty-Nine Articles of Religion mean, and to what did men bind themselves when subscribing to them? In all the talk of reform and revitalisation of the established Church, these were legitimate questions for discussion. The edge to this controversy was that there persisted until the mid-1840s a determination by the opponents of Tractarianism to attack Tract 90 and have the established Church formally condemn it.

By 1845 Short felt called to write an *apologia* for the Tract and sought the advice of two clerical friends. What motivated him were his leanings (deriving from his education at Christ Church) towards a view of the established Church as having been founded on the undivided Church of the first five centuries, and thus fully Catholic in its doctrines and practices. Here were clear reflections of the influences of earlier years: Charles Lloyd and Thomas Vowler Short. Newman, in his view, had simply demonstrated more often than not, in Tract 90, that this was the case. Short's research, study and thought convinced him of the Catholic principles of English Christianity: that the established Church did conform with the four gospels, Creeds and councils of the undivided Church of the first five centuries.

In an undated letter to his friend the Rev. Charles Swainson (1796-1871), Short argued for the true method of interpreting and regarding the Thirty-Nine Articles.[34] He referred to several aspects of the Tract including the Rule of Faith, the Holy Scripture

---

34 Swainson had been junior proctor of the university in 1829 when Augustus Short returned as a tutor at Christ Church. Swainson, a fellow of St John's College from 1815-37, had a distinguished career at the university, being dean of divinity in 1831 and senior bursar in 1836. In 1837 he was appointed as vicar of Crick, where he remained for thirty-five years until his death.

and the Authority of the Church, the 'Justification by Faith ... of Works Before and After Justification', the 'Romish Doctrine of Purgatory', Masses and the bishop of Rome (in Whitington 1887, pp. 31-40). He continued:

> [T]he English Church was essentially complete without Rome and naturally independent of it ... I have now gone through the various parts of the Tract, and on the whole do not see how its explanations are either foreign to the 'literal and grammatical sense' or to the Convocation of 1662, from whose authority we receive them; or are consistent with 'Roman Catholic errors' ... I for one will not consent to narrow their [the Articles] meaning to an un-Catholic, Lutheran sense, miserable in its results as at this time exhibited in the theology of Germany ... or help to cast a stigma on that singularly able writer, [Newman] whose retirement from public notice since the first edition of the Tract [in deference to the wish of his bishop] shows that he is far above the vulgar ambition of leading a party, but that to advance the cause of God's truth is the single purpose of his self-denying life. (p. 31-40)

His correspondent replied generously, with fine understanding, yet urged great caution on his colleague given the existing atmosphere of tension.

Another confidant and long-time friend, the Rev. Henry Bull of Lathbury (1798-1884), in a succinct summary of the prime issues of Tract 90, wrote:

> [T]he tone of your remarks is, I think, too universally *apologetic*. I believe with Newman that the framers of the Articles had much more of the *Catholic* spirit than the Low Churchman of our day will allow. But I think he has given this Catholicism a Romish tincture in the Tract. I do not believe that the interpretation of this Tract is *generally* consistent with Roman Catholic error. But I think it too much to *defend it from the charge altogether*, as you do more or less, and I question the expediency of publishing what you have written without some qualifications. (In Whitington 1887, p. 29, emphases in the original)[35]

These cautionary remarks from his friends were enough to persuade Short not to publish his views. Not publishing his own defence of Tract 90 was prudent:

> [P]robably had he not done so the Colonial Church would not have reaped the advantage of his wisdom and learning in helping to mould her early history, for — in the then state of Anglican opinion in England — a champion of Tractarianism would scarcely have been likely within two years of so stepping into the arena of theological controversy to have been asked to go forth as the first bishop of the Church in an English colony avowedly founded upon the broadest basis of religious toleration. (Whitington 1887, p. 30)

It was also unlikely that a more immediate honour would have come Short's way — the invitation to deliver the prestigious Bampton Lectures to the University of Oxford in

---

35 For more about the Rev. Henry Bull, see Appendix B.

1846. However, before the prestige of that invitation, Short was consumed by another controversy at his university.

WG Ward and the Convocation of 1845

William George Ward (1812-82) was a fellow of Balliol College from 1834-45. An enthusiastic Tractarian, Ward was regarded as a second-generation Tractarian, and in the lead-up to 1844, when he published *The Ideal of the Christian Church Considered in Comparison with Existing Practice*, he was casting doubt regarding the Church of England as part of the wider Catholic Church, and affirming the attractiveness of Roman doctrines (McGrath 2006, p. xxii). When *The Ideal* appeared in 1844, therefore, many in the established Church were prepared to read it as unashamedly praising and promoting Roman Catholicism: 'in this book the ideal seemed always to be realized in Rome and never in England' (Ward 1965, p. 120). While Ward argued that the established Church failed as a true Church, he also touched a raw nerve by declaring provocatively that when he had subscribed to the Thirty-Nine Articles of Religion he in no way renounced any Roman doctrines and practices. Here was the opportunity that opponents of Tractarianism had waited for. They demanded that Convocation should and must act to discipline and censure Ward.

WG Ward's son Wilfred published a biography of his father in 1889 and detailed his father's examination for his BA in 1834. Of the four examiners, one was 'Mr Augustus Short', and as the examination in Classics was *viva voce* large numbers of undergraduates and graduates attended. Curiosity centred on Ward's performance:

> One of Cicero's letters to his brother Quintus is chosen, and the examiner [Short?] tells Ward to turn to a particular part. Ward reads it admirably, his voice being excellent, his intonations and inflections faultless, and his sense of meaning and spirit of the passage leaving nothing to be desired … [T]he construing comes next, which, if not quite so exceptionally good as the reading, still bears out the expectations of a display of first-class ability. (pp. 26-7)

Apart from a rare insight into Short's life as an examiner, Wilfred's account is revealing in two ways. It shows the relative obscurity of colonial bishops — Moberly was noted as 'afterwards the bishop of Salisbury', but Wilfred seemed oblivious that 'Mr A Short' was later the first bishop of Adelaide. It also describes the *viva voce* style of examining which in time was complemented — and in some cases replaced — by written examinations.

Short recounted these events in his retirement in 1882:

> The proposed condemnation of Mr Ward's 'Ideal of a Church', by the university convocation, drew me about this time to Oxford once more, and I journeyed thither in company with Dr Tait, then head-master of Rugby, and the Rev. C Swainson, of Crick. The hushed and serious demeanour of some seventeen hundred clergy and masters of

arts in the theatre, while listening to Ward's defence of his book, much impressed me, and having recorded my vote for the first resolution condemning the book, I took no further steps in the following penal resolutions. (In Whitington 1887, p. 18)

No doubt as Short travelled with Tait and Swainson in their coach the trio discussed in detail this extraordinary event ahead of them. Tait had been examined by Short for his degree in 1833 (see Chapter Three), and had won election as a fellow of Balliol, Ward's own college, before succeeding in 1842 the distinguished head of Rugby School, Thomas Arnold. He had written a letter to the vice-chancellor on the controversial matter and shared his views with his companions that, while he intended to vote for the condemnation of the book and the academic degradation of Ward, he was concerned that the third proposition (commonly called the 'New Test'[36]) went too far and was outside the province of the university to declare:

> When [Ward] wrote his book it was in the full hope that his challenge would be answered, and the question finally settled by competent authority, whether or not a Clergyman of the Established Church, and [as a graduate] an authorized teacher in one of its Universities, is entitled to retain all the authority and influence which this double position gives him, while he glories that he rejects no one doctrine of the Church of Rome. (Tait 1845, p. 9)

Another of Short's close colleagues and a fellow examiner of Ward in 1834, George Moberly — by then headmaster of Winchester College — was also moved to write, drawing the distinction between being offended by the book but yet allowing a person to express his opinions freely. His letter (1845) was to the master of Balliol where Moberly too had been a fellow. He began:

> This interest I share with many. But it is rather as a Balliol man, as one not wholly unconnected with Mr. Ward's early Oxford life, and deeply interested in the proposed degradation of a brother-fellow, whom I myself examined and helped to elect to his fellowship, that I am induced to break my silence on this occasion. (p. 3)

Moberly continued:

> It is a heavy and serious thing to pronounce, by a judicial decree, against a man's personal honesty. I am ready to condemn these passages, or the book at large, upon clear, intelligible grounds. I know enough of it to know it to be a dangerous book; but the University must pardon me, *I know Mr. Ward too*; and I know him to be a man of the most thorough and upright integrity. I will not and cannot be a party to a sentence, which goes out of its way to declare that he is not an honest man. (p. 7, emphasis in the original)

---

36   The term 'New Test' (or 'New Religious Test'), while a way of condemning Tract 90, was a measure that would have empowered the Vice-Chancellor to launch an inquisition into the orthodoxy of any university member at any time.

Short obviously shared his disapproval of the publication with his colleagues from years past, but would himself have no part in any further condemnation of Ward. Convocation met on 13 February 1845 during a burst of a cold and snowy weather. The conditions were uncomfortable for those travelling from rural England: 'the weather was most inclement; snow falling fast all day. Graduates came from all parts of the kingdom at the risk of their lives' (Ffoulkes 1892, p. 460). Ward's son (1889) wrote:

> February 13, 1845, the date fixed for the great meeting, arrived. The Sheldonian theatre, the scene of the day's proceedings, was filled with Masters of Arts from all parts of England. It was no merely personal event, it was a crisis in the history of the constitution of the English Church, which was in some measure to decide the legal rights and theological position of thousands of her sons. 'A great proportion of those who arrived,' writes an eye-witness in the Times of 14th February, 'were men distinguished in public life, who came up purposely to be present at the Convocation.' Prominent amongst them were Mr. Gladstone, Lord Shaftesbury, the Earl of Romney, Archdeacon Manning, Mr. J. R. Hope (afterwards Mr. Hope-Scott), Lord Sandon, Lord Faversham, Dr. Tait, Dean Merrewether of Hereford, Sir Thomas Acland, Dr. Moberly (afterwards Bishop of Salisbury), Sir W. Heathcote, the Bishop of Llandaff, the Bishop of Chichester, Lord Kenyon, the Earl of Eldon, Sir John Mordaunt. The Oxford authorities also were present in large numbers. Dr. Pusey supported Mr. Ward by his presence, in spite of his disapproval of the tone of *the Idea*. (p. 334, emphasis in the original)

Once the Registrar had read selected passages from Ward's book, Ward himself 'was allowed to read, from the rostrum, a lengthened defence in English. He did not appear at all distressed or excited by his position, but, in his usual, cool manner, *took it easy*' (Cox 1870, p. 344, emphasis in the original).

Ward's book was overwhelmingly condemned by a majority of 777 to 386. Ward's demotion (then called a 'degradation') to undergraduate was carried much more narrowly, 569 to 511. Short himself noted his vote for the rejection of the book, but declined to participate in the decision to demote Ward. The Convocation erupted on the third resolution — that Tract 90 be censured. Drama ensued when a tradition of the university was acted out. For many centuries, the proctors had retained the right to intervene and veto proceedings of Convocation, without giving reasons. At this point the two proctors did so, the senior proctor standing and proclaiming '*Non placet*'[37]:

> Then came the proposal for the condemnation of Tract 90. The Vice-Chancellor read the resolution. But now the two Proctors rose, Mr. Guillemard and Mr. Church, and

---

37   The phrase '*Non placet*' translates as 'It does not please' — meaning, in an ecclesiastical or university setting, a negative vote.

uttered the words which, except on one memorable occasion, the Hampden case, no one living had ever heard pronounced in Convocation. When the resolution was put, a shout of 'non' was raised, and resounded through the whole building, and 'placets' from the other side, over which Guillemard's 'nobis Procuratoribus non-placet' was heard like a trumpet and cheered enormously. The Dean of Chichester threw himself out of his doctor's seat and shook both Proctors violently by the hand, and, without any formal dissolution, indeed, without a word more being spoken, as if such an interposition as the Proctors' veto stopped all business, the Vice-Chancellor tucked up his gown, and hurried down the steps that led from his throne into the area, and hurried out of the theatre; and in five minutes the whole scene of action was cleared. Mr. Ward was cheered by the undergraduates as he left the theatre, and the Vice-Chancellor was saluted by hisses and snowballs from the same quarter. (Ward 1889, p. 343)

This was, apparently, followed by 'a storm of indignation' (Cox 1870, p. 345), but 'Mr Ward was cheered by the Undergraduates [on his way to Balliol] "as a *plucky fellow*"' (p. 345, emphasis in the original).

Proceedings ended and Convocation dispersed, but Tractarianism in Oxford never recovered from this debacle. A footnote was Ward's own decision to marry, and be received into the Roman Catholic Church in September of the same year, followed soon after by Newman's decision to secede to Rome on 8 October. Short, however, returning to Ravensthorpe, found now a new challenge placed before him: the Bampton Lectureship for 1846. He had been invited once before, in 1838, to preach before the university; an election to be Bampton Lecturer, however, was of another level of importance and prestige.

The Bampton lectures 1846

As outlined in the Preface to Short's *The Witness of the Spirit with our Spirit* (1846), the Reverend John Bampton (1690-1751) had been a canon of Salisbury Cathedral and bequeathed his estate to the University of Oxford with the following instructions:

> I direct and appoint, that, upon the first Tuesday in Easter Term, a Lecturer be yearly chosen by the Heads of Colleges only, and by no others, in the room adjoining to the Printing-House, between the hours of ten in the morning and two in the afternoon, to preach eight Divinity Lecture Sermons, the year following, at St. Mary's in Oxford, between the commencement of the last month in Lent Term, and the end of the third week in Advent Term. (pp. iii-iv)

The lectures in the school of theology were to focus on defending and explaining the Christian faith as found in the scriptures, expressed in the Creeds and by the fathers of the early Church. The lectures had 'been filled at various times by many of the prominent

Bishops and theologians of the English Church' (SLSA, PRG 160/25, 1 March 1882).[38] Short reminisced after his retirement, in 1882:

> In April 1845, I was elected to the Bampton lectureship, and visited Oxford in 1846 to preach the course. The Tractarian Controversy was still at fever height. Newman had published his tract, No. 90, in February 1841, nearly five years before he seceded to Rome — on October 8, 1845, at Littlemore. I purposely chose a subject important alike to all parties, viz., 'The witness of the Holy Spirit with our spirit, as stated by St. Paul in his epistle to the Romans, xiii, 5-27.' The lectureship was proposed to me by my old friend Dean Gaisford, and following the principle I had previously acted on in life, viz., to follow the path opened to me rather than 'choose my way', I accepted it, though I found myself, from my previous tutorial employments, inadequately furnished for so important an office in the school of theology. (In Whitington 1887, p. 18)

Prudent and careful as Short was in these lectures (1846), he still set out clearly the doctrinal positions he had come to hold. The influences of Charles Lloyd and Thomas Vowler Short, as much as the retreating turbulence of the 'religious movement of Oxford', can be detected. For many years prior to the 1840s, the annual Bampton lecturers had faithfully upheld the conservative High Church views held in Oxford, especially the importance of tradition in the doctrines of the established Church. Tractarianism had highlighted this when an energetic and determined Newman asserted that some traditions, such as the apostolic succession, could not just be corroborated by scripture but could also evolve dynamically under the guidance of the Holy Spirit.

Referring to the Church of Rome and apostolic succession, Short stated in a footnote in Lecture II (1846, p. 29, fn. h,) that 'the Crown and Church of England ... in throwing off the supremacy of the Bishop of Rome' had been 'secured to us by Canon viii of the Council of Ephesus', and the 'Papal church excommunicated us, not we that church'. In other words, Rome, not England, had 'made the schism'. Central to the English Church was its apostolic succession:

> He who rejects the Universal, Concurrent, Uninterrupted *testimony* of Apostolic tradition (*so far as it will go*) as the means of ascertaining the 'mind of the Spirit' revealed in the Scriptures, throws the Church back on the dictation of an assumed infallibility; or casts it loose on the multitudinous sea of *individual opinion*; which (humanly speaking) renders unity of sentiment impossible. By the aid of Apostolic Tradition illustrating Scripture, unity of doctrine and discipline might, under the grace of God, be attained; so far at least as were needful for communion between independent National Churches. (p. 30, fn. k, emphases in the original)

---

38 A personal copy of these lectures is held in Special Collections in the Barr Smith Library at the University of Adelaide. It is inscribed by Short to his son-in-law as follows: 'George Glen, with the author's kindest regards Feb.#1 1864'.

Short confronted the contentious issue of baptismal regeneration and the protestant challenge of 'inspired conversion'. He claimed in Lecture III that the ninth Article of Religion, and the spirit and letter of the baptismal office, ensured that 'a fanatical claim to conscious, inward, immediate inspiration' was foreign to the beliefs and practices of the English Church (p. 49, fn. i). In fact, he went on, the English held to 'a visible and *organised* Church, an authorised ministry; holy mysteries as pledges of His Love; and the day of His resurrection to be kept holy … [T]hese are the appointed means and channels of His grace' (p. 55, emphasis in the original):

> [T]he service of God has been enshrined, even since the coming of the Holy Ghost, in a visible temple … ministering outward signs as means of grace to *faithful* partakers; witnessing *to* the canonical Scriptures … presenting to the eyes of men everywhere a *sign* that God has sent His Son to be the Saviour of the world. (p. 56, emphases in the original)

In Lecture V, Short wrote:

> The duties, for example, of fasting, almsgiving and prayer, as the Christian's protection against the flesh, the world, and the devil, are enforced in the Sermon on the Mount; the very same authority on which rests the Liturgical use of the Lord's Prayer. Again, they are commended to our observance by the perpetual and concurrent practice of the church in all ages and countries at least for *private* and *personal* discipline. (p. 92, emphasis in the original)

In his eighth and concluding lecture, Short emphasised the 'sober principles of our reformed Church' (p. 171), adding that 'she holds the Catholic Church to have been both the witness and the keeper of the canonical Scriptures' (pp. 171-2); and 'that nothing be taught to be held or believed, upon the account of religion, but what is agreeable to the doctrine of the Old and New Testament, which the Catholic Fathers and ancient Bishops have gathered from *thence*' (p. 172, emphasis in the original). His rousing summary spoke of 'God's *appointed* way', namely

> the instrumentality of the holy Catholic Church; the Scriptures interpreted by the Creeds of the oecumenical councils; the Sacraments ordained by Christ himself; an Apostolic ministry and ordinances; diligent use of the primitive Liturgies, and the constant practice of private prayer and meditation. (pp. 175-6)

Diplomatic in his approach, Short reflected on how he was greatly influenced and shaped by the ecclesiastical debates of the previous twenty years and on the significant people — Thomas Vowler Short, Charles Lloyd, Edward Bouverie Pusey and John Henry Newman, among others — to whom he had listened and with whom he had corresponded. After almost two decades as a clergyman, including several years as an academic, Short now had a firm view of his faith. He was conscious that the divine was a revelation, by God's grace, and that it came in the wake of his own obedience to the established Church, its ministry and its sacraments.

Thus Short's lectures addressed a relatively closed ecclesiastical world. Nevertheless, these lectures not only confirmed Short's spiritual devotion, and the academic standing in which he was held, but were also a personal triumph for a rural clergyman, and did much to bring him to the attention of the leaders of the established Church. Early in 1847, he received an invitation from the archbishop of Canterbury, William Howley, to become a colonial bishop.

6

A bishop of the colonial Church
1847

In early 1847 William Howley, archbishop of Canterbury, wrote to Augustus Short:

> Rev. and dear Sir — It being a matter of the utmost importance to obtain the services of men who are qualified by ability, attainments, judgment, and temper for important stations in the Church as bishops in the newly-constituted dioceses in Australia, I trust that you will be disposed to accept an office in which, from all I have heard, I consider you will be eminently useful. In temporal respects these bishoprics have little to offer; the salaries of the bishops are little more than eight hundred a year. But this, I understand, is sufficient to bear all the expenses in a country where incomes in general are small, and money goes further than in England. The diocese over which you would preside is situated in the north-east of Australia. It is not yet determined whether the see shall take its name from Newcastle or some other town. I have reason to think that in point of situation it is the most desirable of any of the sees. The climate is uniformly represented as very fine.
>
> I remain, dear sir,
>
> Your faithful servant,
>
> Rev. Augustus Short   W. CANTUAR
>
> P.S. — a new see is also to be established at Adelaide, in South Australia, and it is indifferent to me which of the two you would choose. Before you determine, however, you might consult Mr. Hawkins, the secretary of the Society for the Propagation of the Gospel, who can give you full information of all particulars. (In Whitington 1887, p. 44)

The other turning point of 1840-41

As the 1840s arrived, the clergy and congregations of the established Church, abroad in other lands within the Empire, were under the jurisdiction of the bishop of London. The good fortune was that Charles Blomfield was the bishop in question. Blomfield (1786-1857) had been translated to the see of London in 1828 from the see of Chester, where he had won notice as an ecclesiastical reformer. The keys to his reforming reputation had been his open acknowledgement of the new reality, the encroachment of the state upon the independence of the established Church since 1828, and his promotion of greater efficiency and courage in the Church's parochial and social mission. He transferred this reforming zeal to London (having formed the Church Building and Endowment Fund in London in 1836). There was an added responsibility, however:

> 'I have,' Bishop Blomfield himself observed, in speaking of this anomalous jurisdiction, 'references continually made to me upon matters of great importance to the cause of religion and the Church, from English clergymen and congregations in foreign parts, which I am obliged to settle as well as I can, without any means of inquiring personally into the facts which form the subjects of their appeals to me'. (Biber 1857, p. 272)

What was 'anomalous' to Blomfield was the absence of local diocesan bishops for such gatherings of English people belonging to the United Church of England and Ireland 'residing amongst and superintending his own clergy, and giving unity, consistency and efficiency, to their pastoral labours' (p. 273).

Blomfield was not alone in his concerns. Some years before, in March 1836, WE Gladstone (at the time Member of the House of Commons for Newark), anticipating perhaps the initiatives of the established Church at some time in the near future, wrote to the Society for Promoting Christian Knowledge [SPCK], the oldest missionary organisation in the established Church. He asked the society to take the lead in caring for the spiritual welfare of emigrants through their publications. Gladstone had served for a brief period, January-April 1835, as Under-Secretary of State for War and the Colonies in Robert Peel's first ministry. He followed this in 1838, publishing his book, *The State in its Relations with the Church*, the main argument within it being the responsibility of the state in the United Kingdom to promote and defend the established Church. Arguing at that time against public opposition to an established Church, Gladstone saw governments as having 'active duties towards religion', especially 'Christian governments towards the Christian church' (1839, pp. 318, 323). By 1841, Gladstone had progressed his opinions and was suggesting the principle of missionary bishops separate from, and independent of, the state (Brown & Nockles 2012, p. 92).

The Methodist and Evangelical revivals, the repeal of the *Test* and *Corporation* Acts in 1828, the emancipation of the Roman Catholics in 1829, the pamphleteering for Church reform from 1832, the profound change in the composition of Parliament with the Great Reform Bill from 1832, the *Irish Temporalities Act* and the 'religious movement begun in Oxford' in 1833, and the legislative initiatives to reform the United Church of England and Ireland, had all caused a continuing crises in English Christianity. The accompanying outbreaks of public dislike and hostility to the established Church shook its confidence. Yet by the end of the 1830s something profound was stirring within: churchmen were realising, and accepting, new understandings facing their Church, not least the financial realities of the temporal authorities seeking stringent accounting for the privileged position it held. At the same time, the needs and the opportunities of the established Church beyond the boundaries of the United Kingdom brought to the fore much imagination and thoughtful daring. The imperial expansion required fresh thinking about organisation and mission from the Church, as hundreds of thousands of people emigrated from the United Kingdom to the various colonial outposts. Where was English Christianity, especially the United Church of England and Ireland, in this Empire?

Bishop Charles Blomfield's initiatives and influence

It was no surprise that a rapidly expanding Empire and its ecclesiastical needs became another arena of Church debate. In this regard, it was Bishop Blomfield who became the man of the moment for English Christianity. On 24 April 1840, Blomfield composed *A Letter to His Grace The Lord Archbishop of Canterbury, upon the Formation of a Fund for endowing Additional Bishoprics in the Colonies*, stating in it that 'an episcopal Church without a Bishop is a contradiction in terms … [E]ach colony must have not only its parochial, or district pastors, but its chief pastor, to watch over, and guide, and direct the whole' (in Hawkins 1855, p. 14), and forwarding it to Archbishop William Howley. He argued that it was time for the United Church of England and Ireland to provide in the colonies appropriate episcopal leadership, thus ensuring that the established Church's ordinances and doctrines were followed in all parts of the Empire. Blomfield's arguments were considered and well reasoned: 'The government of a Christian country [ought to make] provision for the spiritual wants of its colonies', he said (p. 16), yet the reality was that 'at present … there does not appear to be much hope of … any considerable aid from the national resources, for the purpose of planting and maintaining the Church of this country in its colonies'(p. 13).

The established Church must take the initiative and create a fund for voluntary contributions, he went on, to be 'administered by the Archbishops and Bishops of the English Church', such funds to be used to endow new bishoprics and buy suitable colonial property. If such a step was taken, then 'we may reasonably expect that the Great Societies will contribute liberally from the funds entrusted to their administration' (p. 17). Here Blomfield was principally referring to the Society for the Propagation of the

Gospel in Foreign Parts [SPG, later SPGFP], which had been founded by Royal Charter in 1701, and to the Society for Promoting Christian Knowledge [SPCK], founded in 1698. In a flourish, Blomfield concluded:

> My own deeply-rooted conviction is, that if the Church of England bestir herself in good earnest, and put forth all the resources and energies which she possesses, and for the use of which she must give account, she will in due time cause the reformed episcopal Church to be recognized, by all the nations of the earth, as the stronghold of pure religion, and the legitimate dispenser of its means of grace. (p. 18)

Some years before, Thomas Vowler Short, then rector of St George's Bloomsbury, (1834-41), had associated himself with the SPG and in 1832 he had written:

> The next society in which I engaged was the Society for the Propagation of the Gospel ... I feel sure that this Society is, of all human instruments, the one which seems best adapted to spread the pure and holy doctrines of our Church over the face of the globe ... In looking at a Church, there are two points which must always be kept in view — one is the vital Christianity, the other that the government and rites of the Church are according to apostolic regulations. Without the first, there is no salvation; without the second, there will never be permanency and orthodoxy ... Wherever Englishmen dwell, let there be a Church of England, headed by a bishop, and let us pray that a gradual approximation may take place throughout the world, till there is one fold and one Shepherd. (p. lxi)

Twelve months following Blomfield's letter, on 27 April 1841, Archbishop Howley presided at a public meeting where the Colonial Bishoprics' Fund was created: 'His Grace presided on the occasion, and was supported by the Archbishops of York and Armagh, the Bishops of London, Durham, Winchester, Bangor, Llandaff, Hereford, Chichester, Lichfield, and Salisbury' (Hawkins 1855, p. 20). The presence of these episcopal leaders underlined the fact that the succession of crises in the 1820s and 1830s had made apparent to the established Church that if Parliament was intent on supressing bishoprics in Ireland, ostensibly for financial reasons, it was unlikely that the same Parliament would fund creation of new episcopal sees throughout the Empire. The principal speakers were Howley and Blomfield, assisted by WE Gladstone and the Rev. E Hawkins (later secretary of SPG), who became the first secretary of the Fund. A Colonial Bishoprics' Fund would enable the Church's financial independence, and with the granting of Letters Patent from the monarch issues of government funding would be avoided. If the established Church was to be one among several (equal-in-status) Christian denominations in the colonies, then the Church must look to its own resources for its development and consolidation outside the United Kingdom.

In June 1841, 'the Tuesday in Whitsun week', four archbishops and twenty-five bishops of the Church of England and Ireland met at Lambeth Palace to consider issues facing the established Church as it spread with British colonisation. A Declaration was issued highlighting 'insufficient provision … for the spiritual welfare of members of the National Church residing in the British Colonies', 'the want for a systematic supervision of the Clergy and the absence of those ordinances, the administration of which is committed to the episcopal Order', and, thus, the need for a 'Fund for the Endowment of additional Bishoprics in the Colonies' (in Flindall 1972, p. 94). The Declaration had two lists of locations requiring an episcopal presence. Among six in the first list was Van Diemen's Land and in the second list of seven were South Australia, Port Phillip and Western Australia. The Declaration concluded with the statement: 'In no case shall we proceed without the concurrence of Her Majesty's Government' (p. 94).

While the Declaration was an appeal ostensibly to raise funds for colonial bishoprics, the discipline and good order of the spreading Church was the prime concern for the bishops. Only new colonial bishops, superintending colonial Church life, would secure that. It is interesting to note that one of the treasurers of this fund was Gladstone, Short's former student and by then the leading parliamentarian for ecclesiastical colonial issues. One of the signatories to the Declaration was Thomas Vowler Short, who had only recently been raised to the episcopate as bishop of Sodor and Man. The ecclesiastical world was indeed small and intimate.

Enabling legislation was necessary from Parliament in order to provide the machinery by which new bishops could be consecrated. This was rushed through during the ensuing months, so that by October 1841 the first bishop under such legislation was consecrated at Lambeth Palace — George Augustus Selwyn for New Zealand. By 1841, only ten colonial sees had been erected throughout the Empire; fourteen new ones were to be established between 1841 and 1850! The *Bishops in Foreign Countries Act 1841* (often referred to as the *Colonial Bishoprics' Act*) was thought to go a long way in solving the emerging problems of episcopal oversight for the colonial expansion in India, South Africa, Australia, New Zealand and Canada. The Colonial Bishoprics' Fund would underwrite this innovation. However, time showed that the Act actually caused many of the problems which were to beset the colonial churches during the ensuing decades, not least the device of using Letters Patent issued by the Crown to create the colonial bishoprics.

If there were to be new bishoprics in the large and cumbersome diocese of Australia then the progress to that end owed as much to the ecclesiastical situation in the Australian colonies as to initiatives in London.[39]

---

39   The diocese of Australia existed from 1836 until 1847. The dioceses of New Zealand and Tasmania were founded in 1841 and 1842 respectively. In 1847 the dioceses of Sydney, Newcastle, Melbourne and Adelaide were founded.

Bishop Broughton and the Reverend Edward Coleridge

William Grant Broughton had been appointed an archdeacon in the colony of New South Wales in 1829 under the authority of the bishop of Calcutta. At first he felt confident that his Church would be the established Church, as it existed in England. To this end, the Church and Schools Corporation, established in 1826 and endowed with revenue from Crown lands, would be the means of the Church's viability. However, the spirit of political reform, and circumspection regarding ecclesiastical matters, had preceded him to the colony, and these generous provisions for the United Church of England and Ireland in the colony were revoked. The governor of New South Wales from 1831-38, Sir Richard Bourke, was conscious of instructions that costs to the United Kingdom Parliament of education and religion in the colonies were to be kept to a minimum. Though he made a trip to England in 1834-36 to reverse these local decisions, Broughton's appeals were denied, and then he was diverted by being consecrated the first bishop of Australia.

For Broughton, as increasingly for other colonial bishops throughout the Empire, there were difficult questions ahead for the United Church of England and Ireland in the colonies, particularly if it was not to retain its role as a distinct English national institution. If colonial political developments, particularly colonial representative government leading to self-government, meant severing such ties, then what doctrine of the Church would prevail, and more importantly, whither episcopacy and Church government? The reality was that each Christian denomination in the colonies would, in theory, be of equal standing. Traditionally, the established Church in England viewed the Dissenters and nonconformists as not belonging to acceptable Churches — they had neither apostolic succession nor sacramental theology or practice. The Roman Catholics may have had apostolic succession and the sacraments, but corruptions and innovations over time meant that their Church, too, lacked validity.

As bishop of Australia, Broughton maintained a vigorous correspondence with supporters and leading figures in England. When he was visiting England in 1834-36, he visited Dr Keate, at Eton. The Reverend Edward Coleridge (1800-83) recalled in 1876 that this was 'my first connection with that remarkable man, the Bishop of Australia' (in Cooper 1990, p. 259). Joshua Watson, treasurer for the Society for Promoting Christian Knowledge, also facilitated contact between Broughton and Coleridge. Edward Coleridge came from a noted ecclesiastical and society family. He was the youngest brother of John Keble's close friend, John Taylor Coleridge, and nephew of the poet, Samuel Taylor Coleridge. Following schooling at Eton (Pusey was a classmate), he was tutored at Corpus Christi, Oxford, by Keble's brother, Tom. He married Mary Keate, the daughter of the Eton College headmaster, having returned to Eton at twenty-four.

He remained there for the rest of his working life primarily as a housemaster, later being promoted to lower master, then fellow. His enthusiasm for the established Church, especially its mission abroad, knew few bounds. He was a stupendous and boundless letter writer and fundraiser, especially through the SPG (Cooper 1990).[40]

Between July 1836 and his death in 1853, Broughton corresponded almost 100 times with Edward Coleridge (Hobbs 1984, pp. 8-28). This is not surprising, given Edward Coleridge's enthusiasm for the 'Church abroad'. When writing to John Keble on 18 December 1851, Coleridge insisted on a theme that the Church at home would be renewed by the Church abroad: 'for the SPG and its supporters, the spiritual health of the nation could not be separated from what was happening to its branches around the world; that the "Church at Home" would be reinvigorated by "the Church abroad"' (in Maclear 1888). Earlier, in 1836, Coleridge had written to a despondent Broughton:

> Do not think it necessary to thank me … Your names are 'Great in Israel' — pre-eminently so, and there are hundreds and thousands of thoughtful Churchmen who are expecting a reflux of new life to the Mother Church from Australia, New Zealand and Tasmania. (In Whitington 1936, pp. 71-2)

Archdeacon Manning, a vigorous supporter of episcopacy for the colonies, saw the Church abroad as a divine initiative intended to redress the failure of the empire in its moral responsibilities to both Indigenous populations and English settlers (Strong 2012, p. 91).

Coleridge had already argued that mission work was an essential ingredient in the religious life of the nation and the established Church, not an added extra. Broughton's correspondence with Coleridge covered much, reporting on Church and political affairs in Australia and seeking Coleridge's advice and assistance in ecclesiastical matters. Coleridge was of great assistance through the SPG in the supply of clergy and money for the Australian colonies. In a 'Circular Letter recently sent to The Head-Masters of the chief Free Grammar Schools of England and Wales', on 18 December 1842 (NLA, AJCP, Miscellaneous series M1517-1534), Coleridge brought to attention the situation facing the colonial bishops of Australia, Tasmania and New Zealand. This document focused on the need for clergy and how these schools might respond to the need. Broughton had attended King's School, Canterbury, and Selwyn, Eton College; there are references throughout to costs and to the fact that each of these bishops 'has gone forth'. Eventually, the creation of St Augustine's College in Canterbury for the training of clergy as missionaries was hoped to be the fulfilment of a joint dream for both Broughton and Coleridge. In 1845, writing to Joshua Watson, Broughton commented:

---

40   Coleridge attended Broughton's ordination and consecration as bishop of Australia in Lambeth Palace on 14 February 1836; and he was present at Broughton's funeral in Canterbury Cathedral on 26 February 1853.

> But alas, it is too true and too evident that Christianity cannot be propagated, nor its general influence impressed upon a nation, by the mere building of churches. We need in addition the services of *men*, with heads and hearts filled with the love of God, and with correct principles and sound learning, and willing to devote themselves and all that they have to working out the great purpose upon which we are sent forth. Coleridge sends me from time to time encouraging and hopeful, accounts of the progress of St Augustine's ... [T]he entire character of the colonial Church will be moulded according to what St. Augustine's shall be during the next twenty years. (In Churton 1863, p. 266, emphasis in the original)

Earlier, on 14 October 1839, Broughton had confided with Coleridge on the vexed question of the future independence of the colonial Church:

> My augury is that before long we shall be called to defend Christian truth not in alliance, incorporation, union or connection with the State, but in positive opposition to it ... My reliance, I assure you, begins to rest very little on external aid, but rather on that internal strength of the Church herself. (In Hobbs 1984, p. 10.)

Broughton was searching for the identity of his Church in this challenging colonial setting: weeks earlier, on 27 August 1839 in his *Speech in the Legislative Council on Education* in Sydney, he had spoken in the New South Wales Legislative Council. In his speech, he focused on his Church's inheritance centred on the Holy sacraments, the ministerial office and the Church's authority (Brown & Nockles 2012, p. 100).

The correspondence with Coleridge was Broughton's prime avenue in discovering the impact of the Tractarian movement. If the future of his Church in the colonies was to be a form of self-governing Church, episcopally led, then he found quite a deal of intellectual and theological support in the *Tracts*. The United Church of England and Ireland possessed its own independent authority, divinely given, and centred on the doctrine of apostolic succession. The *Tracts* affirmed for Broughton that his Church possessed a form of ecclesiastical government and theology able to be independent of monarchy and the legislature.

Edward Coleridge was not only indefatigable in raising funds, he was also determined to provide a theological library. This became a prime means of education for colonial clergy in the debates in the established Church. In 1839 Coleridge 'reported a large consignment of "The Anglo-Catholic Library" publications, and add[ed]: "they are given nominally by the publications committee but really by that man of men, Dr Pusey"' (in Whitington 1936, p. 131). Broughton was overwhelmed with the books Coleridge sent, and wrote in a letter to the latter on 25 February 1839:

> With regard to the library I am every day more and more convinced that familiarity with ancient literature, generally diffused among the clergy, will alone render them able

defenders of the evidences of revealed religion ... if we wish to find and keep the true path of the Church of England ... [directing] us to preserve our distance from Geneva without running, as some seem half inclined, back to Rome. (In Cooper 1990, p. 261)

Following the inauguration of the Colonial Bishoprics' Fund, and Selwyn's consecration as bishop of New Zealand (1841) and FR Nixon as bishop of Tasmania (1842), Broughton's difficulties of episcopal pastoral care and administration were eased considerably. The questions of episcopal authority and Church government endured, however, raising them to a more urgent level. On 23 December 1843, Broughton wrote to Joshua Watson:

> My description, in brief, of a colonial bishop is that he must be a man ready for everything and everybody that may require of him; whilst himself must require nothing but just what he happens to find. My two dear brethren and colleagues in the neighbouring sees [Tasmania and New Zealand] are altogether men of that stamp. (In Churton 1863, p. 265)

In 1836, the New South Wales legislature had passed the *Church Act*, which altered the position of the Church of England profoundly. Financial assistance was now available to all denominations, especially for the recruitment of clergy. In 1836 Broughton had fifteen clergy; by the mid-1840s he had fifty-three. The background to this was extraordinary population growth: Australia's population was estimated at 5000 in 1801 but by 1850 measured 438 000 (Wolffe 2006, p. 22). This underlined Broughton's concern that the further subdivision of what was now the diocese of Sydney (essentially all of Australia excluding Tasmania) was urgent. In 1844 he urged upon Archbishop Howley of Canterbury the establishment of a see in South Australia but received no encouragement. Lord Stanley (Secretary of State for Colonies) was 'immovable.' To all of this, Broughton wrote to Coleridge on 15 October 1844, 'we must have Bishops, whether we get money or not, either married or single' (in Bailey 1891). In an extraordinary gesture by a colonial bishop, Broughton himself was prepared to surrender half his own income for the benefit of funding additional bishoprics:

> The Bishop of Australia ... felt so strongly the need for a more efficient superintendence over the clergy, that he offered to give up one half of his own life income towards the endowment of Bishoprics for the Northern and the Southern division of his vast diocese. So noble and disinterested a proposal could not fail to be favourably received and responded to at home, and an arrangement was soon made between the Secretary for the Colonies on the one part, and the Colonial Bishoprics' Committee on the other, for the Northern Counties of N.S.Wales, and for another at Melbourne for the Port Phillip district ... [T]he voluntary surrender of 5000 pounds a year from a life income, is an instance of liberality — too rare in any profession. ('The Rise and Progress of the Colonial Episcopate' 1847, p. 10)

A turning point was 1845, when WE Gladstone, treasurer of the Colonial Bishoprics' Fund, became the Secretary of State for War and the Colonies (23 December 1845 to 27 June 1846) in Sir Robert Peel's second Conservative ministry. Within a short time, Gladstone had royal assent for new sees to be created at Port Phillip and Morpeth (Shaw 1978, pp. 184-5).

A diocese for South Australia?

The Episcopal Committee created in June 1841 had several Special Committees report to it on the locations most in need of episcopal appointments. In May 1842, such a committee reported the following in regard to a 'Bishopric of South Australia':

> South Australia was created a British province by an act of Parliament in the year 1834. It contains an area of 300,000 square miles. The Colony was founded in December 1836. Its progress has been singularly rapid — the population having, in the course of six years, increased from a very few labourers to the number of 16,000. The healthiness of the climate and the numerous inducements to emigration, give every reason to expect that the Colony will advance in prosperity. Some churches have been built in and near Adelaide, the capital of South Australia, and others are in progress; but the want of Episcopal control has been already sensibly felt, and questions have arisen which could only be satisfactorily determined by a Bishop. For, although the Colony is nominally with the diocese of Australia, the distance is so great, and the means of transit are so uncertain, that the Church is practically beyond the limits of Episcopal superintendence. (In Hawkins 1855, p. 25)

The churches were also unconsecrated; young people were not confirmed; the clergy had no episcopal guidance; and there were the constant dangers of disunity without effective leadership and oversight of the doctrines and practices of the Church of England.

Short did not attend the public meeting in London — Oxford matters were foremost for the rural vicar at that time. Nevertheless, he was well aware of these momentous moves on behalf of the Church abroad, not least through correspondence with his cousin. Like many clergymen, he was also well aware of the work of Bishop Blomfield, especially his call for the established Church to take initiatives for the colonial Church. His was an example not lost on Short. Well briefed regarding the colonial ecclesiastical needs, Archbishop Howley, from 1842, thus knew of the requirements of the new colony of South Australia.

> The Episcopal Committee further reported in a pastoral letter of 23 June 1843:
>
> Attention was directed, in our first Report, to the want of a Bishop in the rapidly-growing settlement of South Australia; and the offer of land which has been made by a zealous proprietor of that Colony, renders it especially desirable that no

unnecessary delay should occur in completing the organization of that infant Church. (In Hawkins 1855, p. 30)

The pastoral letter then referred to the bishop of Australia being 'lately relieved from the care of New Zealand and Van Diemen's land', adding that he nonetheless still cared for 'a diocese vastly too large for his effectual superintendence'. The letter went on to plead 'earnestly for the erection of a distinct Bishopric in the thriving settlement of Port Phillip' (p. 30). The understated issue, as always, was funding.

Discussion about likely candidates for such a colonial bishopric was widespread, and even Edward Coleridge found his name being mentioned. Broughton promptly rebuked Coleridge in a letter dated 12 October 1846:

> If you are to come to a colonial bishopric the only station worthy of you will be India or [Sydney] ... [D]o not go to South Australia. There is no opening worthy of you there ... [M]y dear Coleridge, when South Australia is offered to you, as you say it probably will be, let me entreat you to ponder well, to consult your own conscience, and the judgement of your friends, before you agree to accept it. (In Whitington 1936, pp. 165-6)

Nevertheless, a bishopric for South Australia could not be considered, apparently, until significant funding materialised. In the end, this came as a benefaction from the unlikely person of a young heiress, Angela Burdett Coutts, as discussed below.

Miss Angela Burdett Coutts and a benefaction

The *Third Report of the Episcopal Committee* reported on 18 May 1845:

> Of the Colonies still remaining without Episcopal superintendence, the Cape of Good Hope and South Australia have been mentioned in preceding Reports as presenting the strongest claims; and it would have been the duty of the Committee on the present occasion to renew the appeal on their behalf, had it not pleased God to put it into the heart of an individual member of the Church, by an exercise of almost unexampled liberality, to guarantee adequate Endowments for a Bishopric in each of these Colonies. (In Hawkins 1855, p. 33)

On 21 August 1848, the *Fourth Report of the Episcopal Committee* recorded:

> We cheerfully acknowledge the ready concurrence and aid which, in these great measures for the extension of the Church, we have received from Her Majesty's Government; and we desire once more to record our high sense of the permanent services to religion, which have been rendered by the disinterested liberality of the Bishop of Sydney and Miss Burdett Coutts. (In Hawkins 1855, p. 39)

In August 1837, at twenty-three years old, Angela Burdett Coutts (or Miss Coutts as she was then known), daughter of the radical politician Sir Francis Burdett (who was once

Figure 6.1 Angela Burdett Coutts.
Source: 'Lady Burdett-Coutts, ca. 1840'. Reproduced from Wikipedia.

a pupil of Westminster School and later the MP for the area) inherited a fortune accumulated by her grandfather, the banker Thomas Coutts, and bequeathed to her by his widow. When Miss Coutts inherited this money, it was said that she had only just over £900 in her bank account; her inheritance multiplied thus sixty times. Overnight, she was one of the richest women in Europe (Healey 1978, p. 49). A supporter of the SPG and of a determined Christian faith, Miss Coutts believed her inheritance was a gift of God and was intended for her 'to feed my sheep'. The parable of the Good Shepherd recurs in her letters (p. 77). During the 1840s, in the wake of Bishop Blomfield's reforming work in London, Miss Coutts had responded by assisting two funds that Blomfield had created. The first was for church buildings in London, the second to establish bishoprics in the colonies.

Her interest in the colonies may well have been spurred on, not just by the creation of the Colonial Bishoprics' Fund in 1841 and Blomfield's influence but also by the receipt, unannounced, of correspondence from Edward Coleridge: 'His whole soul was filled with the idea of doing all in his power for the spread of the Colonial Church' (Maclear 1888, n.p.). This was the kernel of Coleridge's correspondence with Miss Burdett Coutts (as she now became known). In 1845, Coleridge's brother-in-law, James Chapman, was appointed as bishop of Colombo, and with the existing interest in the colonial episcopacy now heightened by family connections, Coleridge approached Miss Burdett Coutts for support. In his first letter to her, written on 26 January 1846, he wrote about his brother-in-law as one 'who has left all he loved and valued in this world … for the sake of Christ, and is, I am quite sure, ready to die in the holy cause'. Acknowledging the many demands on Miss Burdett Coutts, Coleridge concluded guilelessly, '[Y]ou will, I doubt not, do what you can' (LPL, Burdett-Coutts Papers, MSS 1384/1-2). Miss Burdett Coutts was entranced, and requested more information, prompting a lengthy six-page letter a few weeks later, on 21 March. The importance of this communication is apparent:

> When I have told you as much as you desire to hear from me on this subject generally, then I will undertake from time to time to send you ... such letters as I am frequently receiving from the Bishop of Australia, Tasmania, N.Z., Newfoundland, Colombo, and other friends in the Colonies, so that you may be able to feel ... what is the condition of each Church in each settlement. I can assure you that by the aid of Books, Letters, Prints, & c, and above all, actual friendship with those abroad, I am able almost to live as much in the Antipodes as in England, and in thought and Prayer to hold Communion with members of some Colonial Church in every successive hour. (MSS 1384/5-6)

Being assertive, Coleridge was adamant early in this letter that his appeal was about the fundamental principles of the established Church — sacraments, episcopacy, apostolic succession, good order and discipline:

> [I wish to] disapprove and dissuade you from supporting the *Church* Missionary Society, as it is called, but which really does not deserve that name, seeing it has (numerous) supporters who hate Episcopacy, deny Apostolic Succession, and do not hold some of the most sacred and essential doctrines of Christianity. (Emphasis in the original)

Coleridge did not let up: his challenge was to further inform Miss Burdett Coutts. On 10 April 1847, which was Good Friday (the day after Augustus Short first met his future episcopal colleagues at Lambeth), Coleridge sent Miss Burdett Coutts a 'Short Account of the Church of England in Australia from the First Settlement of the Colony to the Present Time', containing a preface and two documents he had written, one in 1837 and the other in 1841. He noted:

> [T]here are moreover the following Religious and Charitable Societies in Sydney and the Country district, at present in full and active operation:— The Diocesan Committee of the Societies for the Propagation of the Gospel in Foreign parts, and for the Promoting Christian Knowledge, instituted on the 20th June 1836, and embracing the following designs:—
>
> 1. The foundation and encouragement of Public Schools for the education of the youth in the principles of the United Church of England and Ireland.
>
> 2. The distribution of Holy Scriptures, the Book of Common Prayer, the Homilies, and other religious Books and Tracts contained in the catalogues of the Society for the Promoting of Christian Knowledge.
>
> 3. The establishment of Churches and Christian Ministers of the United Church of England and Ireland in the Colony of NSW and its dependencies ... (MSS 1384/5-6)

His two 'Appeals' of 1837 and 1841 highlighted: 'The wants are chiefly three — Churches throughout the whole Colony ... funds to maintain Parochial Schools ... [and a] great want of additional Clergymen and Schoolmasters' (MSS 1384/5-6).

On 30 April 1846, Coleridge wrote to Burdett Coutts of 'great and holy works' (MSS 1384/5-6), regarding himself as Miss Burdett Coutts's 'guide and advisor' and referencing the practicalities of interest rates, budgets and investments. In a short time he had thus established an affinity with a benefactor who was ready to join him in the financing of 'more colleges and more Bishops' as the 'grand desiderata'. Miss Burdett Coutts was drawn in by his larger theme that the moral destiny of the Empire depended on the extension of the United Church of England and Ireland, through its episcopate. Coleridge entered the debate where benefaction was most needed. He recounted conversations with the archbishop of Canterbury, Mr Gladstone and the Rev. Hawkins about the news of two bishoprics to be founded in the Cape of Good Hope and Adelaide. While acknowledging that the Cape had a more urgent claim, he wrote of South Australia to Burdett Coutts on 30 April 1846:

> Adelaide is a very growing and thriving Colony, while Cape is not …It will take a year at the least to obtain answers from South Australia to any letters now written to an Agent or to the Governor there on the subject of an Investment in Land … [I]n this way much time would be gained, a Bishop might be selected — a temporary residence be purchased for him, and a subscription made by the Settlers for House and a Cathedral …
>
> Supposing this plan to succeed thoroughly in South Australia, it might proceed afterwards according to your means to do the like good work for the Cape of Good Hope; meanwhile you will have the happiness of feeling that in God's hands and by his guidance you have been made the instrument of completing the Episcopate for the present in Australia, that vast country, which must within a century become the centre of a great & independent Empire, attached or non-attached to Christ's true Church. (MSS 1384/5-6)

On 6 May, Coleridge, having received a confirmation of a most generous benefaction, wrote to Miss Burdett Coutts that he 'went with a heart full of joy and thankfulness to Lambeth and there laid your noble offering to the Colonial Church at the Archbishop's feet … your truly noble disposition of that treasure, which the Almighty has not placed in your hands in vain' (LPL, Burdett-Coutts Papers, MSS 1384/33). Later, in a letter to Burdett Coutts dated 24 November 1846, as if to reinforce the needs in Australia, Coleridge praised his long-suffering friend Bishop Broughton:

> [H]e is so holy and primitive —has seen so much affliction — and yet has never allowed himself to (wander?) from the straight path of duty. He is a higher kind of Joshua Watson — not better, not more loving or to be loved — but wiser, more learned, more scholar-like, less prejudiced. (MSS 1384/5-6)

In what became her largest single benefaction to date, Miss Burdett Coutts (late in 1846) announced to Hawkins that she intended to endow new bishoprics in Cape

Town and Adelaide with £50 000 each. Of this, £25 000 was to go towards Church endowment; £15 000 was intended for the bishopric and £10 000 was to go to the clergy (Healey 1978, p. 80). There was genuine praise and gratitude:

> A noble-minded English lady, who had but recently shown her regard for the best interests of religion, by devoting a munificent sum for the erection and endowment of a church and schools in a poor district of Westminster, extended her benevolent regards to the settlers in our distant Colonies. Convinced that the most effectual way of providing for their religious wants was to secure the residence of a chief pastor, whose first duty it would be to care for these things, she determined to endow in perpetuity two Bishoprics. Adelaide and Cape Town were selected, and the present and every future generation of settlers in those important Colonies will owe a lasting debt of gratitude to Miss Burdett Coutts. ('The Rise and Progress of the Colonial Episcopate' 1847, p. 10)

During February 1847, Archdeacon Harrison, chaplain to the archbishop of Canterbury and privy to Short's invitation (and probably by that stage, his acceptance), kept his confidences. Coleridge, when writing to Miss Burdett Coutts in February 1847 regarding arrangements for the benefaction, wrote:

> Mr Hawkins has just been here, having seen the Bishop of London, who suggested that the Archbishop might give the authority, in the name of the Trustees, the Episcopal body, for the Treasurers to invest the amount as proposed. The Archbishop has just signed a paper to this effect, and that all is now, I hope, in due course, as desired by [your adviser] Mr Cotton. (LPL, Burdett-Coutts Papers, MSS 1384/5-6)

The announcement of Short's appointment, however, seems to have been made without any immediate contact with Miss Burdett Coutts. A friend, rector of nearby St Martin's, Rev. Sir HR Dunkenfield, wrote to her on 20 March:

> I learn from your note that you have not been informed that Mr Augustus Short has consented to be the first Bishop of Adelaide. I believe it to be an excellent appointment. He was a Student at Christ Church & [following?] a first class examination for his degree he was for some time one of the College Tutors & Bampton Lecturer in this last year. He has latterly been a good parish priest in Northamptonshire. Moreover he is said to be very active & energetic & to be a very amiable person ... I have seen him two or there times lately. He seems full of zest on behalf of his new country at the same time that he is wise and prudent. He is married with a few children & Mrs Short is highly spoken of. His Churchmanship is of a moderate kind & appears wholly [devoid?] of party spirits. If it should be your wish to see him, and you are at home after Easter, I should be very glad to introduce him to you ... I cannot however conclude without expressing my astonishment that the appointment should have been made without any conference with you, and that ... you should not have been informed of it. (MSS 1384/5-6)

Coleridge, as expected, wrote to Burdett Coutts on 26 March 1847 with much enthusiasm:

> I heard yesterday of the certainty of the appointment of Augustus Short and Robert Gray to the two sees ... [F]rom my own knowledge of Augustus Short, who took his degree only the year later I did ... [and] from those most competent to judge, I really believe I may congratulate you on the appointment of two most admirable Bishops to fill these sees ... and you will be glad to hear that it has some encouragement among others ... [T]he Bishop of St Asaph gives his cousin the Bp of Adelaide 100 pounds a year for five years. (MSS 1384/5-6)

Yet there was more to Miss Burdett Coutts's benefaction than simply enthusiasm for the expansion of her Church. The creation of colonial bishoprics was only acceptable insofar as such appointees shared exactly the same entitlements and legal guarantees as episcopal appointees within the British Isles; she was adamant her benefaction must have that understanding and condition. She understood that the consecration of a bishop under the Queen's mandate, or Letters Patent, constituted the individual a bishop of the United Church of England and Ireland, and thus enabled him to act as a bishop in the diocese assigned to him. She saw the public declaration in the Consecration Service of the *Book of Common Prayer* (1662) — that is, to exercise authority 'as ye have by God's Word, and as to you shall be committed by the Ordinance of this Realm' (p. 611-12) — as a public pledge on the part of a bishop that the known principles and practices of the Church of England would be maintained by him. Thus Crown supremacy and episcopal authority were at the core of her ambitions for the Church in the colonies.

Two decades later, writing to the archbishop of Canterbury on 12 July 1865, she expressed these sentiments afresh:

> [A]bout the year 1845 [*sic*] I resolved to offer to the Crown, through the then Archbishop of Canterbury, Dr. Howley, my individual aid towards providing without further delay, for the members of our Church established, in two of its Colonies, the benefit of Episcopal Government ... I had always supposed that, in providing funds for the Endowment of Colonial Sees, I was co-operating with the Archbishops and Bishops of the United Church of England and Ireland, in laying the foundation of a system of efficient Church Government for the members of our National Church resident in the respective Colonies; and that the Crown, by its Letters Patent, had power to give legal effect to an order of things calculated to secure that the doctrine and discipline of the Church of England by law established should be maintained *in their completeness amongst the Congregations of our own Communion in those Colonies. Without this security I should not have guaranteed the Endowment funds.* (NLA, AJCP, Miscellaneous series M1525, emphasis in the original)

By that time Miss Burdett Coutts was reacting to legal findings that the colonial dioceses were on their own and could not be established by law in self-governing colonies.

In the 1840s, however, this future turn of events was unthinkable, at least to Miss Burdett Coutts.[41]

A diocese of Adelaide and an invitation to Augustus Short

News of the creation of new dioceses in Adelaide and in Cape Town became public soon after Miss Burdett Coutts's generous endowment in 1846. In distant South Australia, one of the five Church of England clergy in the Province, Rev. WJ Woodcock (1808-68), noted in his journal in 1846:

> Oct. 30 — A report has reached this colony that South Australia is about to be erected into a separate Bishopric, — an endowment having been most unexpectedly provided by the munificence of a Christian lady. Should this prove true, I shall be disposed to regard it almost as a direct answer to prayer. Judging from recent events in this Colony there was but little hope of any adequate support being obtained from the colonial legislature. Whether the governor will be authorised by the Home Government to make any provisions — by reservations of lands, or otherwise — specially for the South Australian branch of the Establishment, is yet doubtful. The Colonial Bishoprics' Fund is not, I believe, at present in a state materially to aid in the endowment of additional sees. Under these circumstances, our only immediate hope was in the Lord's disposing the hearts of those to whom He has entrusted the silver and the gold, willingly to offer after a princely sort. And this hope is, it appears, about to be realised! Praise be God! (p. 5)

Earlier, on 5 September, the South Australian Church Society, of which Woodcock was the secretary, had issued a Manifesto 'to promote the interests of the Church of England in this colony, by aiding the erection of Churches; the establishment and maintenance of Schools; the formation of Libraries; and the employment of Missionaries and catechists' (South Australian Church Society 1846, p. 1). The document was a call for funds and did not refer to the need for episcopal leadership. If anything, the Manifesto perhaps illustrated the very situation alarming Howley, Blomfield and many others — that is, that the extension of the United Church of England and Ireland (its ministry, its sacramental life, its apostolic succession) would suffer without episcopal leadership and government. South Australia was a strongly Protestant colony; some of the laity and clergy in the Church of England could thus clearly come under the spell of this Protestantism. Woodcock, supported by the SPG, had only been in the colony six months, having previously been a missionary in the West Indies. He would become, under Short's episcopal, and eventually synodical, leadership, a prominent and supportive clergyman in the diocese.

---

41 In 1871, Queen Victoria took the unusual step of creating Burdett Coutts a baroness, and, following Burdett Coutts's death in 1907, she was buried immediately inside the West Door of Westminster Abbey. A simple plaque marks the internment today.

As time passed, Short was clearly seeking greater challenges than Ravensthorpe could provide, and he began to seek, after a decade in his rural parish, preferment elsewhere, as he described in his Reminiscences in 1882:

> Though not discontented with my lot I nevertheless felt at times a want of some wider sphere of action than a country village. An opportunity offering I did, accordingly, apply to the patron of a London church then about to be opened, but the preferment had been destined to another. (In Whitington 1887, p. 42)

The fact that he was overlooked is not surprising; it was a highly competitive environment for clergy seeking preferment, especially in London parishes. His talents, nevertheless, still came to the attention of the appropriate people.

Short had delivered his Bampton Lectures in 1846; in 1845, the Rev. Anthony Grant had had that privilege, his theme being 'The Past and Prospective Extension of the Gospel by Missions to the Heathen'. In this, the focus was the established Church — not this time the pressure for reform within the United Kingdom, but the need for imagination and creativity in the Church's mission as the British Empire took a definite shape. Grant's special concern was the Indigenous populations of the colonies, and ministry to them. Yet the great societies, SPG and SPCK, did not have that as their focus; rather, the emigrant English and their spiritual needs tended to dominate their concerns. Short, although well aware of this debate, was caught up in the more spectacular debates about the future of the established Church within English Christianity. He had reiterated firmly in his Bampton Lectures of 1846 that with obedience to God's will came knowledge of the divine. For the Church of England, this meant fidelity to the apostolic succession through bishops, the three orders of ministry, and the holy sacraments (pp. 9-12, 54-8). This was a reiteration of similar arguments in his ordination sermon in Christ Church Cathedral on Trinity Sunday 1838 (pp. 8-27). A call to be a colonial bishop may have been far from his mind, but he appears to have formed, by the age of forty-four, a clear theology and ecclesiology to underpin his ministry.

Short's recollections are missing regarding how, and by whom, he may have been nominated to Archbishop Howley for one of the colonial sees. A clue is given in Short's first biography. Among the people at Christ Church whom Short recalled in 1882 for the author, Whitington, as colleagues and friends who 'were afterwards distinguished' (p. 11) is the name of Archdeacon Benjamin Harrison (1808-87). Harrison was six years Short's junior, taking his BA in 1830 and achieving distinction as a scholar in classics, theology and Hebrew. Ordained as a priest in 1833, he taught at Oxford for the ensuing decade, including as a teaching colleague with Short for three years; in 1842, he was made one of the six preachers at Canterbury Cathedral. Short and Harrison formed a friendship at Christ Church, and Short recounts in his diary, in late February 1834: 'walked with Harrison' on Christ Church Meadow (SLSA, PRG

160/1). More interestingly, research has revealed that the two were in fact distantly related — Augustus's great-grandfather's sister had married Sir Thomas Harrison, the great-grandfather of Benjamin Harrison, as Augustus's father Charles recorded in his reminiscences (SLSA, PRG 160/32).

Importantly for Short's story, Harrison was in 1843 appointed domestic chaplain to Archbishop Howley, archdeacon of Maidstone two years later and a residentiary canon of Canterbury Cathedral; he remained in these posts until his death in 1887. A prominent figure at the cathedral, and active in community societies, particularly those revolving around cricket, agriculture and archaeology, Harrison was well liked and admired. Given the intimacy and confidences of a chaplain and his archbishop, and his friendship with, and awareness of, Short's intellectual strengths, Harrison was the best-placed person to recommend Short to the archbishop. Harrison would also have been keenly aware that his friend had enjoyed distinction in being elected as the Bampton Lecturer in 1846. At the time, Howley, under some pressure from the SPG and SPCK, had begun earnestly seeking men who could undertake episcopal roles in the colonies.

As a footnote to this speculation, almost six years after Short's consecration, Archdeacon Harrison officiated at the funeral of Bishop Broughton in Canterbury Cathedral, and preached in memory of Broughton 'the day after the burial in the Cathedral', on Sunday 27 February 1853. Some of Harrison's words, by then, applied equally to his friend and colleague, Augustus Short:

> He was sent [having] received the call to go forth, from duty at home, to be a labourer and pioneer ... [He showed] the spirit of true, single-hearted devotedness, disinterested and self-denying, enduring hardness, fixed in steady purpose upon the object set before. (pp. 13-16)

Likewise, Thomas Vowler Short had served as bishop of Sodor and Man from 1841, and on 27 October 1846 had been translated to the Diocese of St Asaph in Wales. His appointment to this diocese had come on the recommendation of the Prime Minister, Lord John Russell, so Archbishop Howley was well acquainted with the Short family and name by the end of 1846. Thomas Vowler Short was as keen a participant in the SPG as Archbishop Howley, and it is more than likely that he may have suggested his young cousin's name to the archbishop. With two such reliable and trusted sources, it is little wonder that Howley wrote to Short in early 1847.

Two further reasons may explain how Short came to Howley's notice. Short, recalling in 1882 his time as a public examiner in classics at Oxford from March 1833, noted that he, 'with my colleagues, had the pleasure of placing in the first class one afterwards known to fame as Archbishop Tait' (in Whitington 1887, p. 11). While Short was residing at Ravensthorpe, AC Tait was his neighbour. Tait had succeeded

Thomas Arnold as headmaster of Rugby School in 1842; Rugby was only twelve miles from Ravensthorpe, which itself was midway between Northampton and Rugby. Short recalled in 1882 that when the controversy regarding Ward's book arose in 1845 and Convocation was summoned, 'I journeyed thither in company with Dr. Tait, then headmaster of Rugby, and the Rev. C. Swainson, of Crick' (in Whitington 1887, p. 18). Already, Tait was seen as a future leader of the established Church; his opinion could easily have been sought by Howley.[42]

It is also noteworthy that Howley had been a canon of Christ Church from 1804 until 1813, and professor of divinity at Oxford from 1809 until 1813. Here was a shared past association between the two men.

Short recollected in retirement, in his reminiscences, the arrival of the invitation:

[A]t length however <u>unsought</u> by me in anyway, a summons came to undertake a higher and more arduous duty than that of a Country Parish Priest. A letter reached me one Saturday in 1847 signed *W. Cantaur* (Archbishop Howley) offering me the newly constituted See of Adelaide — funded by Miss Angela Burdett Coutts (since the Baroness Burdett Coutts) … [A]s the call came unsolicited I felt less difficulty in accepting it; I did not think myself [suitable?] but that I left to the responsibility of those who had picked me out. My chief hesitation was for my wife being separated from her family — on the letter reaching me from the Archbishop [Howley] on Saturday at our breakfast time, I showed it to Mrs Short and asked her to think it over and give me <u>your</u> decision on Monday whether I shall accept or not. On Monday she said she would go to Adelaide with me, and accordingly I wrote to the Archbishop accepting the See. (SLSA, PRG 160/7, emphases in the original)

Short knew his wife would find such a move very difficult, primarily in being so far from her family. For Short, clearly, this move to Adelaide could not be without Millicent's consent.

Howley's letter to Short in early 1847, the precise date of which is unknown, is quoted in full at this chapter's beginning. Howley's comments in the letter presented Short with a difficult choice, given that he knew almost nothing about the Australian colonies. Short recounted many years later that he took Howley's advice and spoke with Hawkins of SPG:

Went to Hawkins and discussed with him the details of the Cape, Adelaide, & Newcastle — Adelaide appeared to be most manageable and most civilised. The other two requiring more of missionary labour & bush life than would suit me or Millicent — went into the city & … obtained some views of Adelaide town & harbour, &

---

42 Tait was to succeed Blomfield as bishop of London in 1856, and was translated to Canterbury in 1868.

industries & scenes of the country. Satisfied by this of <u>the climate</u> and the growing population of the Colony. (SLSA, PRG 160/2, emphasis in the original)

Adelaide probably appealed to him because his ministry would be focused on the settlers, with an opportunity to establish ecclesiastical structures. There was much excitement and anticipation regarding the South Australian colony, and Short probably wanted to be part of that. The same could not be said of Newcastle. While Short understood that his ministry would take him away from Adelaide on many occasions, his primary focus would be on the growing city, whereas providing ministry to an Indigenous population, as was required in some colonial bishoprics, would mean taking a prolonged absence from home. The Adelaide option would therefore be advantageous to his family life.

Here also was an emerging theme of Short's ministry — concern for the welfare of his family. Time and again this concern quite naturally influenced decisions he made. Nevertheless, he was later to show as much enthusiasm for mission ministry to the Indigenous population as for ministry to the settlers.

Howley saw the forty-four-year-old priest and scholar who had been recommended to him as someone eminently qualified for the position, as his letter indicates. Short certainly had 'ability' and 'attainments': his scholarship, teaching and his Bampton Lectures testified to this. Short had shown his 'judgement' publicly in the controversies of Oxford, not least by the fact that he had condemned Ward's book but had not supported the stripping of Ward's degrees. Further, he had chosen to mature his ministry in the more economically deprived location of Ravensthorpe in rural Northamptonshire. In Ravensthorpe's population, the established Church had been clearly in the minority and he had had to develop skills of consensus, consultation and patience — skills not needed at Christ Church. His 'temper' was regarded as considered and hard-working, restrained and cautious.

Communicating on 6 March 1847 with Lord Grey, Colonial Secretary, Howley further ranked Short 'considerably above the level of those who can in general be considered to make the sacrifice required' for the colonial episcopacy (in Brown & Nockles 2012, p. 109). In Short, Howley therefore saw a reliable appointment: a man with ministerial gifts that would enable him to meet the challenges of a colonial episcopate. His judgement proved correct as events testified.

On 1 March 1847, Short entered in his diary:

I wrote to the Archbishop to accept the see of Adelaide — I prayed that I might do right & tho' sorely tried with evil & backsliding I prevailed and have had no misgivings since — on the contrary have felt holy courage and firmness of faith in Christ & trust in God's Providence such as I never felt before. (SLSA, PRG 160/2)

By Saturday 13 March, Short was recording in his diary: 'I received ... the Queen's approval of my appointment. Thus all the preliminary steps are concluded ... I have to pray increasingly for the Spirit of Holiness and Love' (SLSA, PRG 160/2).

Hawkins, secretary of the SPG, had forwarded to Short, on 1 March, the Manifesto from the South Australia Church Society of September 1846. Short lost no time writing to Governor Robe of South Australia on 17 March 1847 (FUL, Short & Coleridge 1847, pp. 1-6). Robe was the President of the Society and Short was keen to make his mark. Acknowledging 'the kindly spirit in which the paper is drawn up', Short declared it 'to be my duty to maintain & endeavour to carry out, in the same spirit, the distinctive principles of our Church' (p. 1). He then referred to building up the Church by 'the authorised means under God's grace' (p. 1). He had scrutinised the official records in the colonial secretary's office already and had a reasonable overview of the state of the United Church of England and Ireland in the colony — all this within one month of accepting appointment. He referred to the need for every locality to have 'a church, churchyard, glebe house and schoolroom' (p. 3). He was also concerned with education:

> My attention has also been directed to the subject of education. There appears to be a want of a good Upper School in North Adelaide combining some classical and Mathematical instruction with the lower branches of education. I cannot but think that one of the clergy who may accompany me, might thus be provided for, giving his Services to the Church on Sundays. The Gentry of the Town & Country will I trust readily support such an Institution which may eventually be enlarged to embrace a Theological Seminary for a Colonial Ministry superseding the necessity of sending Sons for education in this Country. A good National School also for the industrious Classes in South Australia might also, I should think, support itself, & I have it in view if possible to bring out an able School Master and Mistress to take charge of this department. (pp. 4-5)

Indicative of his excitement about his impending arrival and the challenges ahead, he concluded with a flourish: '[S]ingleness of view [will] aid in the building up ... [of] a Spiritual temple to the Lord, wherein founded on the Apostles & Prophets, Jesus Christ himself being the chief corner stone' (p. 6).

Twin considerations for Short became raising funds for his new diocese, and recruiting additional clergy. He wrote to Rev. W Woodcock on 6 April 1847 that he hoped 'that with myself the Church of England ministry will I hope be strengthened by 5 additional labourers' (FUL, Short & Coleridge 1847, p. 21). In early March he wrote to Adelaide, the Queen Dowager (pp.7-8), requesting a donation towards the building of a cathedral; he received £100 within the month. In securing this generous donation, Short was assisted by his friend, Rev. James Anderson, chaplain to Queen Adelaide.

James Anderson himself showed much generosity and insight when he presented to 'The Right Reverend, The Lord Bishop of Adelaide, with kind regards of the Author' two volumes of his own work, *The History of the Church of England in the Colonies and Foreign Dependencies of the British Empire.*[43]

Convinced that the SPCK would be of assistance, he wrote to the executive secretary, Rev. TB Murray, on 26 March 1847, requesting that the committee would 'recommend a Grant proportionate to the Work contemplated, the building namely of Churches and establishment of a Collegiate institution embracing different classes of Schools' (FUL, Short & Coleridge 1847, pp. 8-9). Likewise, Short acknowledged individual supporters such as William Halcomb of Marlborough (pp. 9-10). Communications with the colonial office focused on discussions regarding the boundaries of the new see (31 March) and meeting the Queen's Advocate in London (12 April) regarding this and other matters. He wrote to Earl Grey, the secretary for the colonies, on 1 April concerning the future of the Ravensthorpe living after his departure. On this day, which was Holy Thursday, Short, with his fellow bishops-designate, enjoyed his first episcopal gathering:

> The Bishop had been feasting with great names. The Archbishop of Canterbury gave his annual entertainment to the members of the episcopal bench on Holy Thursday, at Lambeth Palace. Present were the Archbishops of Armagh and Dublin, Bishops of London, Durham, Winchester, Lincoln, Bangor, Rochester, Llandaff, Chester, Gloucester, Exeter, Ripon, Salisbury, Hereford, Worcester, Lichfield, Ely, Oxford, St Asaph, Peterborough, St David's, Cashel, Tasmania. ('English News' 1847, p. 2)

The parishioners of Ravensthorpe shared in the celebrations and honoured their vicar at this time. When returning to Ravensthorpe from London, Short was presented with a testimonial, as he later described in a letter to Miss Powell on 30 April 1851:

> [I was] never more gratified in my life than when I was informed that my Parishioners, whether rich or poor, Churchmen or Dissenters had contributed freely and gladly towards the very handsome Testimonial which I have received. (FUL, Short & Coleridge 1847, n.p.)

Amidst all these matters, there was the search for clergy and schoolmasters for South Australia. As time showed, one of Short's hopeful communications regarded Mr EK Miller of Parkgate School, Rotherdam. The Rev. F Hall obviously testified positively regarding Miller after receiving Short's query of 30 March: Short commented to Rev. Woodcock on 30 March 1847 that 'since writing the above I have had the satisfaction of receiving Mr Miller at [my brother's house in London] and hope to announce in a

---

43   These copies are today in the St Barnabas Collection, Special Collections, at Flinders University.

future letter that he will cast his lot with us and labour in the great cause in which we are engaged' (FUL, Short & Coleridge 1847, pp. 21-3).

Yet it was this intention to recruit Miller which introduced Short to some of the difficulties of episcopal leadership with regards to the recruitment and selection of clergy. Short had been quickly made a vice-president of the Colonial Church Society, the purpose of which was to recruit clergy, catechists and school teachers for the colonies. The society invited applications from clergy and others, with a committee then judging qualifications, first from documentation sent by applicants, then an examination by the 'Clerical Referees of the Society'. Clearly, the secretary of the society was not impressed with Mr Miller, as he communicated to Short on 19 August: 'Mr Miller appeared to me sincere but ignorant of the nature of vital Christianity and like one who had not made up his own mind on any *point*' (FUL, Short & Coleridge 1847, n.p., emphasis in the original). This became an issue for Short — he was obviously interested in recruiting Miller, but the committee was reluctant. As Short put it in a letter to the society on 18 August, Miller 'was backed by high testimonials of his capacity as Schoolmaster' (FUL, Short & Coleridge 1847, n.p.). Short resigned as vice-president, thus removing the conflict, and at the same time asserting his independence as a bishop to recruit, and importantly license, men he thought suitable. To an extent, this was an introduction for him in exercising his diocesan episcopal authority.

Miller, in 1895, recalled these rather exhilarating days:

[At the end of 1846] I wrote the Rev. E. Hawkins, secretary to the S.P.G. ... [A] month or two after this correspondence commenced he wrote to say that through the liberality of Miss Burdet [*sic*] Coutts, funds for the establishment of a Bishopric in South Australia had been provided, and that the Rev. A Short having been designated to the See, he had forwarded our correspondence to him. This was quickly followed by an invitation from Mr. Short to his vicarage at Ravensthorpe, in Northamptonshire, where I spent a few very pleasant days. It was arranged that I should be ordained at once by his cousin, the Bishop of St Asaph, and sail with himself and four others then being selected. Subsequently — probably from a desire to commence episcopal functions soon after reaching his diocese — the Bishop wished me to defer ordination till after arrival in Adelaide, to which I reluctantly consented ... I, not being able to leave quite so soon [with Bishop Short on the *Derwent* in October], the Bishop arranged with his brother, Colonel Short, to select a ship and send me off, which he kindly undertook to do, and from that gentleman and his family I received every kindness and attention during the weeks in London prior to sailing. The S.P.C.K. also kindly made me a grant of sundry valuable works.[44] (p. 4)

---

44 Miller came out as a schoolmaster, became the first headmaster of the Pulteney Street Schools, was ordained, and became later a long-serving parish priest of Magill.

The Rev. AO Budgman of Warrington was unsuccessful in his offer, as Short could not guarantee any stipend beyond what Budgman was already receiving as a curate, a fact he indicated in a letter to Budgman dated 3 April 1847 (FUL, Short & Coleridge 1847, pp.18-9). On 13 April he asked the Rev. Bagshaw to consider whether his health was 'equal to the fatigue of a Missionary life and to the activity required of one who will have to superintend the scattered settlements of a wide district' (FUL, Short & Coleridge, 1847, n.p.). Short declined the offer of the Rev. J Hallifax of Grantham because the clergyman was too strident in demanding aspects of ecclesiological discipline for the clergy which Short was in no place to guarantee, as he advised in a letter to the Reverend on 10 April (FUL, Short & Coleridge 1847, pp. 25-6). That did not deter Hallifax, however, and in further communication with him on 30 April Short moved his argument to reveal his awareness of some of the sensitivities awaiting him in Adelaide:

> [I must] impress upon you that zeal will not stand instead of labour of love, and that next to discretion is especially required in the existing religious state of South Australia. (FUL, Short & Coleridge 1847, p. 30)

Thomas Vowler Short helped in recruiting for the colony by negotiating with the South Australian Company to grant a free passage to the colony for a clergyman. At the same time the company made a 'liberal donation to the Clergy fund of South Australia' for which Augustus was grateful (A Short to SJ Capper 10 April 1847, FUL, Short & Coleridge 1847, p. 26).

The Reverend Mathew Blagden Hale stood out as Short's outstanding recruit. He had been ordained in 1837 and had an interest in evangelising Indigenous populations of the colonies. In 1845, Hale's wife had died, leaving him with two small daughters; he knew that a new future beckoned. In July 1847, he was invited to Pyrton, Oxfordshire, to meet Short. They discussed the colonial Church and especially the welfare of Indigenous people living under British rule. Hale recounted many years later, in 1889, how his recruitment then transpired:

> One day, during one of our conversations [while we were walking] the Bishop, in that peculiar abrupt way, which every one who knew the dear old man will remember, stopped and facing about, and standing opposite to me, said in his peculiar, short, quick manner, 'You must come out and be my Archdeacon'. The thought of going out with him had never entered my mind; but, when I came to seriously consider the matter, I could see that there was really no good and sufficient reason why I should not obey the call which seemed to be thus sent to me.[45] (In Robin 1975, p. 20)

---

45 Hale accompanied Short to Adelaide as the archdeacon and soon became a pioneer in the welfare, education and training of Indigenous people at Poonindie. From 1856, he was the first bishop of Perth.

The excitement of the appointment momentarily disappeared for Short, however, when he received an inappropriate and discouraging letter during March from Colonel George Gawler, a previous governor of South Australia. Gawler had been the second governor of the colony (1838-41); he administered difficult affairs with courage and foresight. The economic difficulties of 1840 had compelled his recall, the reason given being his over-expenditure; however, his legacy was in time acknowledged as beneficial in putting the infant colony on a more self-sufficient basis. Gawler had no hesitation in expressing his views, and wrote to Short in April 1847 requesting that he resign from his position in favour of one of the clergy already in Adelaide, Reverend James Farrell. Gawler had been a parishioner of Farrell's at Holy Trinity Church, North Terrace, and they saw themselves as evangelicals within the Church of England.

Short's shock at receiving this letter did not prevent him replying to Gawler on 10 April with some restraint:

> I have read your letter with the attention it demands and have no doubt of the purity of your motives.
>
> Not having sought the Office to which I have been called, the only question with me was whether I dared refuse the call. I say nothing of the sacrifices it involves, nor of the ability which I have been supposed to possess under God's blessing, for fulfilling its duties. Of that, I left those who in the Providence of God are called to decide, to judge; and even now, if they should deem another more fit to do God's work in South Australia, I would give place; and that I trust without bargain or barter for a full equivalent.
>
> But to resign upon the call of a private individual, however respectable, in favour of one, whom I know not, and concerning whom I have no assurance, that he would be acceptable to the Archbishop and the Government, I am not prepared. And let me add in the same spirit of Christian frankness in which you have addressed me, that amid the pressing cares, Spiritual, Ecclesiastical, Social, and domestic, which are upon me at this time, to receive such a call from one, who, I was led to believe, would afford me his best encouragement and advice, is I confess, a serious disappointment.
>
> I gather from your letter that my good neighbour Mr Cobb declined to concur in the course (no doubt conscientiously) adopted. (FUL, Short & Coleridge 1847, p. 24)

Apart from the affront of his letter, the former governor had ignored the processes utilised by the British government, and the archbishop of Canterbury, in appointing men to the colonial episcopacy. Gawler also seemed not to acknowledge the Church principles much debated during the 1830s and 1840s, so central to the SPG and SPCK endeavours for the colonies. It is likely that as an evangelical Gawler did not share the same views on episcopal authority that Short's appointment represented to others. Nevertheless, he was still requesting his friend be the bishop instead. Quite separately, even if Farrell was respected in Adelaide, a quick perusal of his qualifications for episcopal office showed that they paled when compared with Short's: no theological teaching to be noted, no invitation to publicly lead in Church forums, and intermittent parochial experience. Thus, in this first month of his appointment, Short gained a hint of some of the tougher realities that soon were before him in the colony. Ultimately, however, Short and Farrell became trusted colleagues. Farrell was later appointed dean of Adelaide in 1849 and remained in this ministry until his death in 1869.

In his reply to Gawler, Short mentioned his 'good neighbour', Rev. JF Cobb, vicar of Spratton, the parish adjacent to Ravensthorpe. Amidst all the arrangements for the new life ahead, Short found time on 30 March to continue correspondence with his colleague Cobb on a matter of current theological debate — the sacrament of baptism (FUL, Short & Coleridge 1847, pp. 11-13). The debate about baptism was a key faultline in the established Church at the time: Short, with other clergy of High Church or Tractarian leanings, affirmed the traditional view that infant baptism had been part of the teachings of catholic Christianity since antiquity. The pressure from Protestantism was that divine grace — 'regeneration', as it was referred to — could not be extended to an infant at baptism. Short referred his friend to the twenty-sixth Article appended to the *Book of Common Prayer*, and added: 'Sacraments be effectual because of Christ's institution and promise' (pp. 11-13), and thus, 'Baptism [is] a transaction between Christ and the soul of the Infant' (pp. 11-13). Cobb's concern also had been as much about 'the sins and offences of those who bring (the infants to baptism)'. This exchange was prescient, as this very issue arose as a major controversy for Short in the early 1850s when several evangelical colonists took exception to his views.

Short, with the assistance of friends, quickly organised a committee to inform supporters in England of the needs of his new diocese. On 25 April 1847, the 'Committee of the Society for the Propagation of the Gospel in Foreign Parts for the Diocese of Adelaide', issued a circular entitled 'The (United) Diocese of South and Western Australia'. The colony of South Australia was described as having a population 'believed to exceed 25 000; [due to] the rich Mines of Copper and Lead ... an extraordinary increase by immigration ... may be expected' (A Short 1847, p. 1). It appeared that 'two additional Clergymen are required for North and South Adelaide'; while 'seven other districts' warranted a pastor. Western Australia was referred to as having a 'scattered' population with 'six Clergymen ... and four substantial Churches' (p. 1). However, after seventeen years of colonisation, 'all the Churches are unconsecrated — the youth are unconfirmed' (p. 1).

The circular continued:

[U]ntil local resources can be fully and systematically developed ... the aid of the Mother Country is required', and 'an income of 100 pounds per annum, together with an allowance of 120 pounds for Outfit and Passage, is the lowest remuneration which can be justly offered to any Minister of the Gospel who is willing to give himself to the Lord's service in the Colonial Churches. (p. 2)

Then followed two lists, one describing the 'Existing Church Establishment' (p. 2) in South Australia, the other detailing 'Donations and Subscriptions' (p. 3) from nearly 400 individuals, Church organisations and commercial groups. The circular was signed 'Augustus Short, Bishop-designate of Adelaide'. The eleven members of this committee were listed. It is no surprise that the chairman was the 'Rt. Rev, The Lord Bishop of St Asaph' (TV Short), and that another member was Short's brother, 'Lieut. Col. Short'.

The consecration in Westminster Abbey

On 21 March, the Colonial Bishoprics' Committee (the archbishops and leading bishops) formally recommended to Her Majesty, Queen Victoria, the four bishops-designate. The description of Short was: 'The Rev. Augustus Short, M.A. of Christ Church, Oxford, and Bampton Lecturer for 1846, to the see of Adelaide' ('The English News' 1847, p. 2). Here was confirmation that the distinction of being the Bampton Lecturer had assisted in bringing Short's name to the fore; the bishops were acknowledging it. The London *Government Gazette* of 28 June contained the formal announcement of Short's appointment, which was then reprinted on 9 November in the *Geelong Advertiser*:

> Downing-street, June 28. The Queen has been pleased by letters patent under the Great Seal of the United Kingdom, to reduce the Bishop's see and diocese of Australia, and to divide the same into four several and distinct bishops' sees and dioceses, to be called the bishoprics of Sydney, Newcastle, Adelaide, and Melbourne. Her Majesty has also been pleased to name and appoint the Right Rev. Father in God, William Grant Broughton, heretofore Bishop of Australia, to be Bishop of Sydney, and Metropolitan Bishop in Australasia, subject to the general superintendence and revision of the Archbishop of Canterbury for the time being, and subordinate to the archiepiscopal province of Canterbury. Her Majesty has also been pleased to name and appoint the Rev. William Tyrell, Doctor of Divinity, to be ordained and consecrated Bishop of the said see of Newcastle; the Rev. Augustus Short, Doctor of Divinity, to be ordained and consecrated Bishop of the said see of Adelaide; and, the Rev. C Perry, Doctor of Divinity, to be ordained and consecrated Bishop of the said see of Melbourne … the said Bishops of Newcastle, Adelaide, and Melbourne to be suffragan bishops to the Bishop of Sydney. ('Official Notification of Colonial Bishoprics' 1847, p. 2)

At the time of his consecration Short became one of ninety-seven bishops belonging to the United Church of England and Ireland, or at least deriving their orders from that Church. Of these, twenty-seven were in England and Wales, thirteen in Ireland, six in

Scotland, twenty-one in the colonies, one at Jerusalem, and twenty-nine in the United States ('The Rise and Progress of the Colonial Episcopate' 1847, p. 11).

The ordination and consecration of the four colonial bishops was set for Westminster Abbey. This was a decided break with past practice. After being present at Broughton's consecration in 1836, and then at Selwyn's in 1841, both held in the chapel of Lambeth Palace, Edward Coleridge wrote in protest in October 1841 following Selwyn's consecration service:

> I could not help feeling that we ought to have been thousands rather than tens, gathered together as with one consent in St Paul's or Westminster Abbey to witness the sending out by the Church of the first bishop of her own appointment. (In Whitington 1936, p. 64).

The protest had immediate effect: FR Nixon was ordained and consecrated bishop of Tasmania in Westminster Abbey on St Bartholomew's Day, 1842.

Short's own feelings as he walked into the Collegiate Church of St Peter, Westminster, for his ordination and consecration as a bishop can only be surmised. He left no personal account. This was the 'collegiate church' of his 'collegiate school'; it was the school chapel he had entered for the first time, as a seven-year-old, in 1809, thirty-eight years previously. As a schoolboy he had worshipped continuously in this building from 1811 until 1820. According to his father, he had attended the funeral of his sister, Augusta, there in January 1823 and knew her grave was nearby in the North Cloister (SLSA, PRG 160/32). Charles had, in May 1819, purchased a family home at 35 Great George Street, less than half a mile from the abbey and still retained by the family. How like coming home it must have seemed. Now he had returned to be ordained and consecrated a bishop.

This scene was described in the *Colonial Church Chronicle* ('Consecration of Colonial Bishops' 1847, pp. 41-6) with some enthusiasm (see Appendix C for the full account). The abbey had been selected for this service because it was 'decided that the Consecration should be public, and in the face of the Church'. Sixteen hundred tickets were issued, mainly through the SPG, thus ensuring as grand an ordination service not seen in London for generations. Following Morning Prayers, with the choir singing from the Tallis songbook, 'the venerable Archbishop then began the Communion Service, in which the responses were sung, as set by Tallis; the Bishop of Lichfield reading the Epistle, and the Bishop of Chichester the Gospel' (p. 42, see Appendix C).

Adopting John 21:7 as his scriptural theme (the Lord's commission to St Peter, 'feed my sheep') the preacher, Bishop Blomfield, called on the re-asserted view of the centrality of the episcopate, not only for to the established Church at home, but especially abroad. Blomfield directed his final comments to the challenges of a colonial episcopacy:

> [W]ho are the men whom our Church sends out, to tend and to feed the distant corners of her fold? Are they not those, who are in the actual enjoyment of competency and comfort here, with the prospect, it may be, of a reasonable share of those rewards which the Church has to offer to the learning and piety and diligence of her ministers? And what is there to tempt them to enter the work to which they are called — that of the most arduous and responsible of all offices — invested with no dignity but that which is purely spiritual; clothed with no prerogatives but those which carry with them a preeminence of labour; endowed with no measure of this world's goods but that which may barely suffice for a maintenance? ('The Bishop of London's Sermon' 1847, p. 56)

Then, with the archbishop seated in front of the altar, and the four bishops-designate standing before him, the examination and consecration proceeded, with the Holy Communion concluding the service:

> [I]t is impossible to convey the interest and the heart-stirring felt by those who witnessed it. Our strong feeling was that it was a day worth having lived to see: — to have lived to see four additional Bishops sent out to lands far off, partly by the piety of one member of the Church [Miss Burdett Coutts] — partly by the self-denial of a Prelate, himself for some years labouring in a distant colony [Bishop Broughton] — partly by the devotion and aid of the members of the Church — this was much to be thankful for. But to see these Bishops set apart for their high office in the face of sixteen hundred persons — to witness the devout earnestness and reverent attention of that great congregation, and to partake with nearly eight hundred persons of the Holy Communion — was a comfort, a privilege, and a blessing, which, as we have said, could be fully appreciated only by those who were present. ('Consecration of Colonial Bishops' 1847, p. 46)

The following day, Wednesday 30 June, the newly consecrated Bishop Short attended a meeting of the Parochial Association of the Society for the Propagation of the Gospel in Foreign Parts, the SPG having had its name extended to include 'in Foreign Parts' about this time. This meeting in the Queen's Concert Room, Hanover Square, was on behalf of the Colonial Bishoprics' Fund. The Earl of Eldon was the chair and attending were many of those, ordained and lay, who had been at the service in the abbey the day before. The indefatigable churchman, WE Gladstone, MP, spoke at length, moving a resolution '[t]hat this meeting recognises the duty incumbent upon all who themselves enjoy the blessings of the Gospel, to contribute according to their means towards the strengthening the hands of the new colonial bishops by providing additional clergy to accompany them to their distant dioceses' ('Clergy for the Colonies', 1847, p. 3). With rousing eloquence, Gladstone stirred the audience on behalf of the new colonial bishops, especially his former tutor, Bishop Short:

> But in what sense was it that they were sent to govern the colonies? Not to enjoy civil authority, but to be what our own bishops were, but which they must be more

particularly in the colonies, the chief pastors of vast tracts of country, and of all who did not reject their ministry ... But these bishops to be what they should must be supported by adequate means [hear, hear]. They must be supplied with a faithful and devoted clergy. It might be said that it was difficult to find such clergy ... Why the <u>Bishop of Adelaide</u> said in his presence at a recent meeting, that he had more applications for appointments under him in the colony to which he was going than he could accede to [hear, hear]. If, indeed, they compared the state of the Church at home, enjoying the highest civil and national position, venerated as the greatest of all our national institutions, if, he said, they compared it with the Church in the colonies, which as far as Australia was concerned, possessed none of these advantages, they must see how noble was the devotion of those who were now ready to leave country, home, friends, family, and all, to carry the blessings of the gospel abroad [hear, hear] ...

The Bishop of Adelaide seconded the motion ... [Among others] the Bishop of St Asaph [Thomas Vowler Short] addressed the meeting. (p. 3, emphases in the original)

For the diocese of Adelaide, this meeting was a triumph. Almost a hundred donations were given to the Church Building Fund; in addition to Queen Adelaide's gift of £100 towards a cathedral, Bishop Short gave £100, his friends at Rugby School £32 and Dr Tait, headmaster, £20, his brother-in-law, Rev. W Norris, £20, and his friend Rev. Dr Bull of Lathbury, £50. Among the annual subscriptions promised for five years, Bishop Short pledged £100, his cousin, the bishop of St Asaph, £100, and his former student, Gladstone, £10 ('Home News', *South Australian*, Tuesday 2 November 1847, p. 3).

Departing for South Australia

A new diocese required its own coat of arms. Short saw this as a means of honouring the diocese's benefactor, so he enquired, somewhat quaintly writing in the third person, of Miss Burdett Coutts on 1 July 1847:

> The Bishop of Adelaide presents his compliments to Miss Burdett Coutts and is anxious to make a request that she would permit her arms to be impaled with those of the See on the seal which some kind friends have proposed to the official use. It would be gratifying to the feelings of many of the Members of the Church and on this ground he ventures to hope that she will accede to the request, although the Bishop is well aware how studiously she would avoid all apparent display. (LPL, Burdett-Coutts Papers, MSS 1384/5-6)[46]

---

46 Within a brief period this request materialised in the new coat of arms for the diocese of Adelaide. Miss Burdett Coutts was also presented with a portrait of Augustus Short inscribed with the following words: 'To Miss Burdett Coutts through whose munificence The See of Adelaide was Founded. This Portrait of its first Bishop The Revd. Augustus Short. D.D. is most respectfully dedicated by Her Obedient Servant J Hogarth'. This was a lithograph of a drawing of the forty-five-year-old Short by Sir George Richmond 1847.

His close friend and confidant, Rev. CL Swainson, rector of Crick, joined the appeal, writing to Burdett Coutts on 10 July:

Madam

A few friends of the Bishop of Adelaide are desirous, among other memorials of respect and regard to present him with his Episcopal seal in framing the Coat of Arms for the See, it is very much the wish both of the Bishop and his friends that the arms of the munificent Lady, by whose bounty it has been endowed, should be incorporated ...

But one thing we feel is necessary before any orders are given, and that is, to take the liberty of enquiring how fair such a proposal is agreeable to you.

Will you allow us, Madam, very respectfully to ask your consent to our wishes? And may I beg you to believe me with deep and most sincerely felt respect

Your faithful servant

CL Swainson. (MSS 1384/5-6)

Within a week of his consecration, Short presented also the following Address, signed by thirty-four 'proprietors and merchants' connected with South Australia, to Miss Burdett Coutts:

London, July 3, 1847

Madam, — We the undersigned, connected by various ties with the Province of South Australia, desire to express to you our feelings of respectful gratitude for that act of munificence whereby, with the consent of her gracious Majesty, a Bishopric of the United Church of England and Ireland has been founded in that colony.

We trust that, by God's blessing, it will be instrumental to the spiritual well-being of the colonists, as well as foster their civil & social interests; and we earnestly pray that you may be long spared to know the blessings you have diffused, & to rejoice that you have been led to employ God's gift of wealth to the glory of His name & and the welfare of his people. ('Address to Miss Burdett Coutts' 1847, p. 187)

On 4 August, Short wrote once more to Miss Burdett Coutts and expressed his wish to visit her again: 'The Bishop is also desirous to take leave, as the time of his departure, the 1st of September, is approaching and he will have quitted London for the seacoast by the middle of the month'. He commented:

[A]llow me to also thank you very sincerely for the print of your late father. I could have wished that one also of yourself will hang in the diocesan library at Adelaide. I venture to offer for your acceptance a copy of my Bampton lectures and three other sermons printed by request. If you will give them a place in your Library I will be greatly honoured. (LPL, Burdett-Coutts Papers, MSS 1384/5-6)

In these last two hectic months, Short maintained his appeal in Church circles for support of his new diocese. A Hampshire paper recounted such an event, pointedly personal for Short, on 21 August 1847:

Figure 6.2 Augustus Short. The inscription beneath this artwork reads: 'To Miss Burdett Coutts / through whose munificence / The See of Adelaide was founded. / This portrait of its first Bishop / The Revd. Augustus Short D.D.'.
Source: Lithograph from a drawing by George Richmond.

> A sermon on behalf of the fund for the support of missionaries in the Diocese of Adelaide in South Australia was yesterday morning preached by the Bishop of that Diocese in St James Church ... & a collection was made at the offertory from the whole congregation ... [Afterwards] a meeting of friends and supporters of the Colonial Church in S Australia was held in the National Schoolroom which was presided over by the Rector of Warblington, the Rev W Norris & addressed as well as by the Bishop and the Revs Hatchard, Sumner, Sheppard & Walforde. The rector's wife is His Lordship's sister & their father resided more than 20 years in Warblington, and died there, and the interest of the service & meeting were very much enhanced by the remarks & reflections arising out of these circumstances, & the high estimation in which the family has always been held. (SLSA, PRG160/47)

There were also touching gestures from friends and relations. One was the gift of a splendidly bound edition of the *Book of Common Prayer* inscribed, 'To the Lord Bishop of Adelaide from his affectionate old friend Mary Mayow 14th August 1847. Farewell!'[47]

On the eve of his departure from England, on 1 September, Short wrote to Hawkins at the SPG ('Farewell Letters of the Bishops of Adelaide and Melbourne', pp. 188-9). Short expressed gratitude for 'the deep sympathy which has been shown towards myself and other Bishops ... chief pastors in the Colonial Church'; for 'the unity which has been shown to exist amongst us ... [A]ll were cordially united in maintaining

---

47 The Mayow family had been close to Short's father, Charles, and he had named Short's older brother Mayow in acknowledgement of this friendship. This volume is now held in the St Barnabas Collection, Special Collections, at Flinders University.

Apostolical Episcopacy, and rejoiced in the extension to the Colonial Churches'; and for 'the liberality which has been shown towards the different Churches over which we have been called to preside'. Further, he said he was

> thankful for the earnest missionary spirit which has been called forth by our consecration. Amid numerous offers of Clergymen and Cathechists to go forth with us to the work, we have been enabled to accept the services of those who appear to be animated with singleness of purpose and devotedness to the cause of God ... [S]urely this is a ground for thankfulness to the Church at large.

The notice subsequently appeared:

> On Wednesday, Sept 1, the Right Rev. Augustus Short, D.D. the first appointed and recently consecrated Bishop of Adelaide, set sail from Portsmouth for Adelaide in South Australia. It will be in the recollection of our readers that this Bishopric has been endowed by an individual member of our Church. It remains for others of the laity of England to assist with their cooperation in supplying funds necessary to erect a cathedral and residences for the Bishop and his Clergy at Adelaide. ('Bishops of Adelaide and Newcastle' 1847, p. 156)

Short's diary conveys a final word:

> 1 Sept ... embarked at ½ past one. It was a serious & solemn moment but I was not moved to tears of parting. The ladies had tears in their eyes but the greatness of the cause would not let me cry. I felt even cheerful. The world was all before me & Providence my guide. On board the novelty of the situation drew my thoughts from separation — so passed the first evening at Spithead. (SLSA, PRG 160/2)

So, under Providence, a great adventure was beginning.

Sailing from Portsmouth, as the landscape of southern England faded from sight, Short knew that his family's new home would differ from all with which they were most familiar. Later, a noted Australian author conveyed the emigrant experience:

> If the landscape before them was as lovely as a garden, it also had something of a garden's limitations. There was an air of arrangedness about it; it might have been laid out according to a plan, and on pleasing, but rather finikin lines; it was all exquisite, but just a trifle overdressed ... [H]e was swept up though by a sudden consciousness of England's littleness, her tiny, tight compactness, the narrow compass that allowed of so intensive a cultivation ... these fair fields in miniature! ... these messy hedgerows cutting up good pasture-land into chequerboard squares! ... these diminutive clusters of houses huddled wall to wall ... these narrow, winding lanes and highways that crawled their mile or so from one village to the near next ... these duly preserved morsels of woodland, as often as not guarded, they too, by a leafy wall where songsters trilled. (Richardson 1930, pp. 392-3)

Short was mindful of what lay ahead: he, as the bishop, would be responsible for bringing to a colony of the Empire the form and order of his English Church. In this he was not romantic or even idealistic; his approach was much more utilitarian and pragmatic. These were precisely the attitudes which enabled him to quickly adapt to a landscape so profoundly different, where he would discover

> a love of sunlight and space; of inimitable blue distances and gentian-blue skies … the scanty, ragged foliage; the unearthly stillness of the bush; the long, red roads, running inflexible as ruled lines towards a steadily receding horizon … [He would learn] to descry the colours in the apparent colourlessness: the upturned earth that showed red, white, puce, gamboge; the blue in the grey of the new leafage; the geranium red of young scrub; the purple-blue depths of the shadows … the scent of the aromatic foliage; for the honey fragrance of the wattle; the perfume that rises hot and heavy as steam from vast paddocks of sweet, flowering lucerne — even the sting and tang of countless miles of bush ablaze. (pp. 661-2)

Embracing his new landscape, Short was to live the rest of his working days in it, committed to its people, mostly migrants like him and his family, until in his eighties he returned to England, for the final twenty months of his life.

Postscript

The view and vision from Christ Church Meadow

Strolling and conversing — afternoons for Augustus Short during his university years were often spent ambling, with colleagues, around Christ Church Meadow. The Meadow was the quintessential romantic English landscape — clouds, trees, a water meadow and open fields, cattle drinking from the Isis River's edge, and framed all the while by a mediaeval cathedral and the spires of adjacent colleges. In 1823, the year Short graduated, John Constable was enshrining such a vision in a painting, *Salisbury*

Figure 7.1   Strolling on the Meadow was Short's custom most afternoons.
Source: 'South View of Christ Church. from the Meadows' watercolour by JMW Turner.

Cathedral from the Bishop's Grounds. Sharing the experience of Christ Church Meadow, this painting featured Bishop Fisher and his wife walking and admiring such a view.

Short was not beguiled, however. After almost sixteen years of such settled and romantic views, Short was challenged by the vision of his vocational calling; and this landscape then deferred to another — a village in rural Northamptonshire; poor people, a neglected community, dilapidated church buildings. Not a romantic, Augustus Short held firmly to an orthodox English view of his faith and calling. It was not the natural world that bound people in community; it was the gospel of Jesus that did that. Expressed in its evangelical and scriptural truths, its robust Catholic ecclesiology, the established English Church, for Short, was the kernel of God's kingdom in England. He had chosen to dedicate his life to advancing that kingdom in that Church.

Yet the constant presence in Short's adult life, until he was forty-five, was Christ Church. Since he had attended Westminster School from the age of nine, the reminder was present for him of the intimate and historic link between the school and Christ Church. Resident in Christ Church for almost sixteen years after his schooling, and returning often during his eleven years in a rural parish, he identified as a Christ Church scholar. This nurture influenced his perceptions of the world, the Church and his personal calling; he identified with Christ Church for the remainder of his life, so embracing was its hold on him.

The formation of his character in his Westminster years had always been about behaviour. At school the demands of living, at times, in almost a brutish physical domain meant that his character was influenced then by harshness and competition, and a personal determination to survive, and succeed. This he did. Not until adult life at Christ Church did Short see his character as being formed by more than behaviour; beliefs now moved to the centre. The to and fro of debate and discussion, delving into the great philosophical propositions of the classics, resisting the tugs of wayward behaviours which other undergraduates readily fell for — these would now present him with new questions. These questions regarded his personal beliefs and demanded answers and commitments. The answers presented new aspects in forming his character — as his beliefs in the gospel of Jesus became even more convincing, so his belonging to the established Church of the English firmed. From the age of twenty-five, Augustus Short and his concern for his identity, his character in the eyes of others, his destiny, would be governed by his behaviour in the institution of the established Church to which he belonged and where now his beliefs would be lived out.

A cautious, moving towards prudent, self-assertion had been the foundation of his academic achievements and tutorial teaching, then to be refined to an extent by his experiences as a rural vicar, and as a husband and father. He had effectively governed his self-assertion, preventing it becoming simply self-serving, while being educated at

Westminster and Christ Church. At Ravensthorpe, he experienced self-assertion as a demanding service of his parishioners. It appears that Short approached his ministry at Ravensthorpe as one full of opportunities, including the service of others and tests of his character. Whether it was commencing the first village school, inaugurating a sick club for the workers, or taking private pupils so he could fund repairs to the church and other facilities, all such examples were opportunities for him to realise his calling. He relished, with some impetuosity at times, the continuing contacts with the academic world of Oxford, as there endured a grander stage to which he felt secure in contributing. He learned in these years a certain degree of pragmatism, the advantages of consensus if possible, and first tentative skills of strategic planning. The village landscape was soon enough too small, however.

Constable's painting of Salisbury Cathedral at first distressed its sponsor, Bishop Fisher. Constable saw, looming over the awe-inspiring cathedral, turbulent clouds, as if he were questioning the romantic tranquility the bishop wished conveyed.[48] Constable's view was prescient: the 1830s and 1840s were to be the most tumultuous and exciting period in the life of the established Church for many years. Within his rural ministry, Short found himself drawn to the ecclesiastical debates and controversies. A larger canvas beckoned.

Short often referred to Providence in his life — the grace of God opening his path ahead. No occasion was more unexpected, nor more intriguing, than when the archbishop of Canterbury's invitation to the episcopacy arrived during breakfast on a Saturday morning in winter. Providence again calling him, as he described in 1882 — 'and following the principle I had previously acted on in life, viz., to follow the path opened to me rather than "choose my way"' (in Whitington 1887, p. 18) — he consented because trust in God was fundamental to his faith and its practice.

By early 1847, Short had developed his own ecclesiology. He was not a partisan — not Tractarian, not old-fashioned High Church, not Evangelical. His orthodoxy embraced the established Church's enduring principles of scripture, tradition and reason within an evangelical enthusiasm and an adherence to Catholic ecclesiology. He had reiterated firmly in his Bampton Lectures that with obedience to God's will came knowledge of the divine, expressed for him in the established Church when emphasising its episcopacy and apostolic succession, its three orders of ministry, and the holy sacraments (1846, pp. 9-12, 54-8). Ecclesiastically, Short embraced the reality that his new colonial diocese was greatly dependent on voluntary support from 'home' as well as within the colony itself. This was to be an immediate lesson in the demands awaiting him in administration and leadership.

---

48   In the event, the bishop, a constant friend and supporter of Constable, requested, and received, a second painting minus the looming cloudscape.

Equally, Short had discovered an untiring interest in education, seeing this as central to the work of the established Church in his time. All his advantages in life, realising the opportunities God provided him, were owed to his educational openings and his learning and the joys of assisting others with the same possibilities. His attitudes to education were to mature and flower in the years ahead, seeing it as character forming, a means of social mobility, a personal nurture in response to natural curiosity, even a safeguard to liberty and social order and, thus, a community-enhancing enterprise.

Short had become a devoted family man, enduring with Millicent the sadness of the premature deaths of two of their children while at Ravensthorpe, and tending now to putting the interests of his wife and their children to the fore where possible: this too emerged as central to his sense of belonging.

Yet a certain loneliness hung over Augustus Short. While he had cultivated many friends over the years, they all seem to have been distant ones. He was a somewhat solitary figure as he embarked for Adelaide, yet he was, by his own words, confident, cheerful and determined, having surrounded himself with a handful of able men to assist in the translation of an episcopally governed Church among the settlers in South Australia.

Appendix A

Biographical excerpts from *The Westminster School Register*

Augustus Short

from 'The Westminster School Register from 1764 to 1883'

Brother of Mayow Short (adm 1809); b. June 11,1802 adm. Jan.23,1809; left Christmas 1809; readm. in Nov. 1811; K.S. 1816; elected to Ch.Ch. Oxon.1820 (matric. May 12 1820); 1st class Classics 1823; B.A. 1824; M.A. 1826; D.D. 1847; adm. to the Middle Temple June 5, 1817; ordained 1826; Tutor and Lecturer at Ch.Ch. 1829; Librarian and Censor 1833; Public Examiner 1833-4; Select Preacher 1843; Bampton Lecturer 1846; Curate of Culham, co.Oxon., 1827; Rector of Ravensthorpe, Northants, June 10, 1835-1847; consecrated first Bishop of Adelaide, Australia, June 29, 1847; resigned the see 1882, and returned to England; m. Dec. 10,1835, Millicent, second daughter of John Philips, of Culham; d. Oct. 5, 1883.

Thomas Vowler Short

from 'The Westminster School Register from 1764 to 1883'

Eldest son of the Rev. William Short, D.D., Prebendary of Westminster, by Elizabeth, daughter of the Rev. Tilliman Hodgkinson, Rector of Sarsden, Oxon.; b. Sept 16, 1790; adm 1803 ; KS 1805, elected to Ch Ch Oxon, 1809 (matric May 17 1809); 1st classics and 1st mathematics 1812; BA 1813; MA 1815; BD 1824, DD1837; Tutor of Ch Ch 1819-1829; Proctor 1823; ordained 1813; Curate of Cowley Oxon 1816-1823; Whitehall Preacher 1823; Rector of Stockleigh Pomeroy, Devon, 1823-26, of Kingsworthy Hants., 1826-1834, of St George, Bloomsbury, Middlesex, 1834-41; Deputy Clerk of the Closet to the Queen 1837-41; Bishop of Sodor and Man May 19, 1841, of St Asaph, 1846-70, author; m. Feb 26 1833, May, daughter of Charles Davies, and widow of John Josias Conybeare, d. April 13, 1872

Appendix B

Augustus Short and Henry Bull

Augustus Short formed a lifelong friendship with Henry Bull (1798-1884). They became firm friends at Westminster, continuing at Christ Church where Henry was a few years in advance of Augustus, and remaining 'old sincere friends' throughout life. Every year at the election of scholars to studentships at Christ Church, Oxford, or scholarships at Trinity, Cambridge, Old Westminsters would gather, and Henry Bull was rarely absent.

> The Rev. Henry Bull, who has manifested an untiring devotion to the School, from the day on which he was elected from it to Christchurch, Oxford, in 1815. Before he had taken his degree of M.A. he was appointed one of the Ushers at Westminster School, and in 1821 Under-master. During this time of assiduous labor, and after his retirement, he supplied on several occasions epilogues to the plays, and furnished many epigrams to the Election dinners, and has been ever ready with his counsel to advise, and his presence to animate both masters and scholars. At a time of life, when most men would be courting retirement and repose, he is still vigorous and active; still ready with service of body and mind to benefit the place of his education, as I have lately had reason to experience with feelings of wonder and admiration. (Forshall 1884, p. xii)

Welch, in his book of 1852, recounted the event of the election:

> [T]he days of the election have been changed to the Monday, Tuesday, and Wednesday in Rogation week. On the Tuesday a dinner is given to the Electors, and all persons connected with the School, by the Dean and Chapter, and any old Westminster of sufficient rank or standing is entitled to attend it. After the dinner Epigrams are spoken by a large proportion of the King's Scholars. (p. xv)

Welch noted in particular: 'Mr Bull is a successful writer of Latin epigrams, and very constant in his contributions of Election Tuesday' (p. 479).

Bull was one of the two close confidants whom Short consulted when he was contemplating a public defence of Newman's controversial Tract 90; his friend's advice persuaded Short not to proceed.

In retirement, in 1882, both were keen to resume their relationship:

> [I]n the afternoon [*of the consecration of Short's successor, Bishop Kennion, in the abbey at Westminster*] his old Westminster school and Christ Church college friend, the Rev. Canon Bull, of Lathbury, Bucks, having come to town for the express purpose, called to see how the bishop had got through the fatigues of the day. The visitor — whose own age then reached to four score and four years — was pleased to find the bishop quite capable of enjoying and contributing reminiscences of 'auld lang syne', and the evening passed most happily. (Whitington 1887, p. 274)

Canon Bull (who outlived Short by two years) toured their old school with him, and in the following year was present at the election dinner following Short's death:

> Yet the bishop of Adelaide always regarded Westminster with genuine affection. More than sixty years after he passed out of it he went in his ripe old age once again to the school with one of his Westminster contemporaries, Canon Bull, of Lathbury, Newport Pagnel. (Whitington 1887, pp. 5-6)

Whitington further wrote:

> [A]fter the bishop's visit to the school the election gathering again took place, but the servant of God had meanwhile past (*sic*) to his rest, his old friend, Canon Bull, put an epigram into the mouth of the orator containing amongst others, this happy allusion:-
>
> *"Vita erat illustri felix placidaqua senecta*
> *Finem illis aptum mors nec-opin tulit.*
> *Perfecit cursum, fruiturque quioete parata*
> *Nunc inter Sanctos ac propiore Deo.*
> *Omine nostra bono Schola serum, oramus, in oevum*
> *Usque ferat tales instituatque viros!"* (pp. 5-7)

A detailed account of Canon Bull's further comments appeared in the press:

> (Translation of the Latin Epigram composed by Rev Henry Bull, the Bishop of Adelaide's old sincere friend at Westminster and Christ Church, Oxford. Spoken by M B Bethune, at the Annual Election Dinner of the Queen's Scholars in Westminster Hall 14th June 1884)
>
> The Right Rev Bishop of the South Australian See, one worthy of all our reverenced affection whom we so earnestly welcomed in the Hall has now been taken from us, and we are left to mourn his decease —
>
> > He was rarely present at these festivities; that his appointed path in life compelled but who shall say that we the Queen's Scholars have not a claim to express our true sorrow and indulge in fond regrets for his life? Expatriated as he was & divided from us by this wide world's space, yet his mind ever reverted to the scenes of his youth; he mused upon the familiar spot, the School, these walls, the studies, customs, & associations of Westminster, secretly purposing within himself where the opportunity might offer to reproduce in that distant land the St Peter's College of his boyhood as a bright model

for his new Society in the Antipodes. Nor was the purpose vain, or his hope unfulfilled — At this day in the centre of Adelaide a daughter College of St Peter lifts its fair head conspicuously gracing the City — there the youth of the Colony are trained in the same studies & exercises & modes of thought with those which Queen Elizabeth directed should be cultivated here. (SLSA, PRG 160/81)

Appendix C

Excerpts from the *Colonial Church Chronicle*

An excerpt from the *Colonial Church Chronicle* follows (pp. 41-6). It describes the 'Consecration of Colonial Bishops' in 1847.

THE COLONIAL CHURCH CHRONICLE

AND

𝔐issionary 𝔍ournal.

AUGUST, 1847.

CONSECRATION OF COLONIAL BISHOPS.

THE attached members of the Church and the friends of Missions have never been privileged to witness a more gratifying and interesting ceremony than that which took place on St. Peter's day, in the Collegiate Church of St. Peter, at Westminster. That festival was fixed upon (as many of our readers are aware) for the Consecration of four additional members of the Colonial Episcopate, and it having, happily, been decided that the Consecration should be public, and in the face of the Church, Westminster Abbey was selected as the place in which it should be held.

In consequence of the great and universal interest manifested, the Dean and Chapter of Westminster determined to admit a congregation, not only (as at the usual services) to the choir of the Church, but also to the transepts. For this purpose the close wooden screens, which divided the transepts from the choir, were altogether removed; and to the space thus laid open the public were admitted by tickets. About sixteen hundred tickets were issued, the greater proportion of which were placed in the hands of the Society for the Propagation of the Gospel in Foreign Parts, for distribution among its members, and those interested in the Missionary operations of the Church of England.

The congregation began to assemble considerably before the hour fixed upon for the commencement of the ceremony, on the

42   *Consecration of Colonial Bishops.*

morning of St. Peter's Day; and before the beginning of service not only all those who had tickets of admission, but several persons who arrived at the doors of the church, even from distant parts of the country, unprovided with tickets, and who were specially admitted by the Dean or by the Sub-Dean of Westminster, filled up every available spot in the Church.

Exactly at eleven o'clock the procession began to issue from the entrance to the Jerusalem Chamber, and to move up the nave in the following order:—

Beadle.
Almsmen of St. Peter's, Westminster, two and two.
Choristers, two and two.
Gentlemen of the Choir, two and two.
Minor Canons, two and two.
Canons' Verger.
Canons, two and two.
Dean's Verger.
THE DEAN.
Bishops-Designate, two and two.
Bishops-Assistant.
Archbishop's Verger.
THE ARCHBISHOP OF CANTERBURY.
The Archbishop's Chaplains.
The Secretary and Law Officers.

On the procession arriving in the choir, the Dean and other members of the Church of Westminster entered their stalls, the Bishops-Designate took their places in the sacrarium, the Bishops-Assistant passed on to theirs on the south side, and the Archbishop proceeded to his chair on the north side of the altar. As soon as the various persons who formed the procession were thus in their places, the tones of the organ ceased, and the Morning Prayers were chanted by the Rev. W. H. Cope, the responses being made by the full choir to Tallis's Harmonies, accompanied by the organ. The Psalms of the day were chanted to the first Gregorian tone, fourth termination, as harmonized by Tallis. The First Lesson was read at the eagle by the Rev. H. H. Milman, after which Tallis's *Te Deum* was intoned and sung. The Second Lesson was read by the Sub-Dean, the Rev. Lord John Thynne. Tallis's *Benedictus* was then sung by the choir, and the service proceeded. At the conclusion of the Morning Prayers, the Dean and Canons of Westminster proceeded from their stalls to their places within the rails, on the north side of the altar. The venerable Archbishop then began the Communion Service, in which the responses were sung, as set by Tallis; the Bishop of Lichfield reading the Epistle, and the Bishop of Chichester the Gospel. The Nicene Creed having been intoned by the officiating Minor Canon, and sung as arranged by Tallis, the Bishop of London ascended a pulpit placed on the north side of the Church, at the intersection of the choir and transepts, and delivered the admirable and appropriate sermon, which, by his Lordship's kind permission, we are enabled to present to our readers.

At its conclusion (the preacher having taken his former place at the south of the altar) the Bishops-Designate proceeded to one of the side chapels, on the north of the choir, in order to vest themselves. During their absence, Farrant's exquisite little Anthem, *Lord, for thy tender mercies' sake*, was sung by the choir; and certainly no words more appropriate could have been selected in which to implore God's blessing on the service in which that congregation were about to engage. Surely every heart did very earnestly join with those solemn tones and simple words, " lay not our sins to our charge;" beseeching God not to visit for our former neglects of that very work, in which we were then about to join—the sending forth Bishops and Pastors over Christ's flock in the remote places of the earth, but to " give us grace to amend" this our sinful want of zeal, so that we might, " with a perfect heart," engage in the solemn office then specially about to commence, and " walk before" Him then "and evermore."

At the conclusion of the anthem, the Bishops-Designate returned to the altar-rails, vested in their rochets, and were presented to the Archbishop by the Bishops of Winchester and Gloucester. The Archbishop having then desired the prayers of the congregation, Tallis's Litany was sung by the Precentor of Westminster, and the Rev. J. Lupton, accompanied by the full choir and organ, and the suffrages and concluding prayers by the officiating Minor Canon. The Archbishop then took his place in his chair before the altar, and the four Bishops-Designate standing before him, he proceeded with the examination prescribed in the ordinal. This was a part of the ceremony which had a powerful effect on the congregation; the figure of the venerable Primate sitting in his chair, and those of the four Bishops-Designate, as they stood before him in the simple and severe outline of the rochet, backed by the noble apse of the Church of Westminster, formed a picture (as it was remarked by many who were present) of no common beauty and interest: and the simple, earnest, childlike voice of the venerable Consecrator, as he proposed those solemn questions, and the answers of those who bound themselves to perform those vows, went home in a very real way to the hearts of most persons in that vast congregation. The examination concluded, the Bishops-Designate again retired, and during their absence, Handel's chorus,

The Lord gave the word, with the tenor solo, *How beautiful are the feet*, and the concluding chorus, *Their sound is gone out into all lands*, from the "Messiah," were sung. The Bishops-Designate then returned, robed in the full Episcopal habit, and having knelt down at the altar-rails, the hymn, VENI CREATOR SPIRITUS, was sung over them to the simple tones and grand harmonies of Tallis. The Archbishop then said the Prayer, and the imposition of hands took place; the Bishops of London, Winchester, Gloucester, Chichester, and Lichfield assisting the Archbishop in the laying on of hands. As soon as the Colonial Bishops had been all consecrated, they took their places with the Bishops-Assistant within the rails, on the south-side of the altar, and the Bishop of London proceeded with the offertory. By a very excellent arrangement, a number of the parochial clergy of Westminster had been appointed to receive the offertory basins, and each to collect the offerings of a particular section of the congregation. The time occupied in the gathering of the offertory was, therefore, very short; and when the Precentor and the officiating Minor Canon had collected the offerings of the Clergy within the sacrarium, and had taken their places at the outer rails, the Clergy collecting in the Church brought the offerings gathered by them, and poured them all into two basins, which were then given by the Precentor and Minor Canon to the Sub-Dean, and by him reverently placed upon the altar. The sum thus collected amounted to £550. The Archbishop having then said the prayer for the Church Militant, the non-communicants retired; and the service for the administration of the Holy Communion proceeded, the *Sanctus*, and *Gloria in Excelsis* being sung by the full choir, as set by Tallis. About 760 persons received the Holy Communion, kneeling in rows at the rails of the altar, and between these and the outer rails of the sacrarium; and the Archbishop, the Bishops-Assistant, and the newly consecrated Bishops, all administering the holy Elements. Surely there has not been such a Communion seen in this our day, nor, as we believe, for ages in the Church here in England. The service being concluded, and the Apostolical Benediction pronounced by the Archbishop, the congregation retired. The offertory was handed over to the Rev. Ernest Hawkins, Secretary to the Colonial Bishops Fund.

Such is the bare dry detail of a ceremony of which it is impossible to convey the interest and the heart-stirring felt by those who witnessed it. Our strong feeling was, that it was a day worth having lived to see:—to have lived to see four additional Bishops sent out to lands far off, partly by the piety of one member of the Church—partly by the self-denial of a Prelate, himself for some years labouring in a distant colony—

partly by the devotion and aid of the members of the Church—this was much to be thankful for. But to see these Bishops set apart to their high office in the face of sixteen hundred persons—to witness the devout earnestness and reverent attention of that great congregation, and to partake with nearly eight hundred persons of the Holy Communion—was a comfort, a privilege, and a blessing, which, as we have said, could be fully appreciated only by those who were present.

We ought to have mentioned that, besides the Bishops who assisted in the Consecration in the full Episcopal habit, the Bishops of St. Asaph, Oxford, Madras, Tasmania, and Antigua, were also present in the stalls. We could not help regretting, as we looked upon the three last-named Colonial Prelates, that they were not among those who took part in the imposition of hands, that so the English Church might have presented to the world on St. Peter's day, in St. Peter's Church at Westminster, the great sight of her Bishops from all the quarters of the earth—Europe, Asia, Africa, America and Australasia—officiating in the same service, and ministering at the same altar. It is not many years (if we rightly remember) since we saw an account of the consecration of some Roman Catholic Bishop, we believe in Ireland, in which it was set forth, as a remarkable fact, that among the consecrators and the consecrated were European, Asiatic, African, and American Bishops; and thence an argument was drawn in favour of the Catholicity of the Roman Communion; and this was done, although the Sees of two of the Bishops then present were *in partibus infidelium*—and, though situate in Africa and Asia, yet without Churches, without a diocesan clergy, without a communicating laity, and Sees which the Bishops had never visited, and most probably never would visit. We own that we cannot bear to see another Communion among us arrogating to herself the pretence of that of which the Church of England possesses the reality; and we desire to direct the attention of those who love the Church of England, and desire to recognise in her every feature of the Catholic and Apostolic Church of Christ, to the fact, that among the fourteen Bishops who were present in Westminster Abbey, diocesan Bishops of her Communion, from Europe, Asia, Africa, America, and Australasia, knelt at the same altar, and did eat of that One Bread, and drink of that One Cup, with nearly eight hundred of her faithful children. Did we not then rightly sing on that day, " Their sound is gone out into all lands, and their words unto the ends of the world?" and may we not truly apply to our own beloved Mother the words of St. Augustine: " Vide templum Regis quam late diffusum est. . . . . . Hæc est Catholica Ecclesia: filii ejus constituti sunt principes super omnem terram, filii ejus constituti sunt pro patribus. Agnoscant qui præcisi sunt, veniant ad unitatem, adducantur in templum Regis. Templum suum Deus ubique collocavit, fundamenta Prophetarum et Apostolorum ubique firmavit. Filios genuit Ecclesia, constituit eos pro patribus suis principes super omnem terram."[1]

THE SERMON.[2]

St. John xxi. 17.—"*He saith unto him the third time, Simon, son of Jonas, lovest thou me? Peter was grieved, because he said unto him the third time, Lovest thou me? And he said unto him, Lord, thou knowest all things; thou knowest that I love thee. Jesus saith unto him, Feed my sheep.*"

This remarkable incident in the life of that great Apostle who first opened the door of faith to the Gentiles, seems to present an appropriate subject of meditation, upon the day which the Church has appointed for the especial commemoration of his many excellent gifts, and when we are gathered together to witness the solemnity of ordaining and consecrating certain chosen men of the brethren to the same office with which he was invested, in so far as it is transmissible, in its duties, or its authority, to uninspired men.

It was not without a special meaning that our blessed Lord thrice inquired of the most zealous of his Apostles, *Simon, son of Jonas, lovest thou me?* and thrice enjoined upon him, as a result and proof of the affection which he professed, the duty of feeding his sheep. It was not possible that the warm-hearted and ardent Peter could have seen the countenance or heard the voice of his beloved Master, now risen from the dead, without a painful recollection of that sad and awful night on which he had denied him with imprecations. He could not but be conscious that he had on that occasion displayed no symptom of the depth or strength of his love: and yet that love was both deep and strong; although it gave way for a moment through the weakness of the flesh, and the deceitfulness of a self-trusting spirit. But if it was deep and strong even when he denied his Lord, it surely became deeper and stronger when that denial had been forgiven; and by that degree it may perhaps have exceeded the love of the other Apostles, who, as they had not

---

[1] St. August. in Psalm. xliv. (xlv. 32.)
[2] Preached in Westminster Abbey, on St. Peter's day, 1847, by the Bishop of London, and printed by his Lordship's permission.

References

Books and articles

Ackermann, R 1816a, *The history of Westminster School: Dedicated to the very Rev. the dean and the Rev. the prebendaries of the collegiate church of St Peter's, Westminster*, R Ackermann, London.

___ 1816b, *The history of the colleges of Winchester, Eton, and Westminster: With the charterhouse, the schools of St Paul's, Merchant Taylors, Harrow, and Rugby, and the free-school of Christ's Hospital*, R Ackermann, London.

___ 1816c, *The history of the Westminster School, dedicated to the very Rev. the Dean and the Rev. the Prebendaries of the collegiate church of St Peter's Westminster*, R Ackermann, London.

Arnold, F 1867, *Christ Church days: An Oxford story*, Richard Bentley, London.

___ 1875, *Our bishops and deans*, Hurst and Blackett, London.

Arnold, T 1833a, *Principles of church reform*, B Fellowes, London.

___ 1833b, *Postscript to principles of church reform*, B Fellowes, London.

Aston, TH (ed.), 1984, *The history of the University of Oxford*, Clarendon Press, London.

Avis, P 2002, *Anglicanism and the Christian Church*, T & T Clark, Edinburgh.

Bailey, H 1891, *Bishop Broughton of Australia*, SPCK, London.

Baker, WJ 1981, *Beyond port and prejudice: Charles Lloyd of Oxford, 1784-1829*, Orono Press, Maine.

Barker, GFR & Stenning, AH (eds.) 1927, *The Westminster school register from 1764 to 1883*, Macmillan & Co, London.

___ 1928, *The record of old Westminsters: A biographical list of all those who are known to have been educated at Westminster School from the earliest times to 1927*, Chiswick Press, London.

Best, GFA 1964, *Temporal pillars, Queen Anne's bounty, the ecclesiastical commissioners, and the Church of England*, Cambridge University Press, Cambridge.

Biber, GE 1857, *Bishop Blomfield and his times*, Harrison, London.

Bill, EGW 1973, *University reform in nineteenth-century Oxford: A study of Henry Halford Vaughan 1811-1885*, Clarendon Press, Oxford.

___ 1988, *Education at Christ Church, Oxford, 1660-1800*, Clarendon Press, Oxford.

Bill, EGW & Mason, JFA 1970, *Christ Church and reform 1850-1867*, Clarendon Press, Oxford.

Blomfield, A 1863, *A memoir of Charles James Blomfield, DD Bishop of London, with selections from his correspondence*, John Murray, London.

The Book of Common Prayer and the administration of the sacraments and other rites and ceremonies of the Church according to the use of the Church of England, 1662, Oxford University Press, Oxford, Vivian Ridler, Printer to the University.

Border, R 1962, *Church and state in Australia, 1776-1872: A constitutional study of the Church of England in Australia*, SPCK, London.

Bowen, D 1968, *The idea of the Victorian Church, A study of the Church of England 1833-1889*, McGill University Press, Montreal.

Brilioth, Y 1933, *The Anglican revival: Studies in the Oxford Movement*, Longmans, London.

Britton, J 1821, *The history and antiquities of the Cathedral Church of Oxford*, Longman, Hurst, Rees, Orme and Brown, London.

Brock, MG & Curthoys, MC (eds.) 1997, *The history of the University of Oxford*, vol. 6, *Nineteenth century Oxford, Part 1*, Clarendon Press, Oxford.

Brose, OJ 1959, *Church and Parliament: The reshaping of the Church of England, 1828-1860*, Oxford University Press, London.

Brown, J 1974, *Augustus Short, DD Bishop of Adelaide*, Hodge Publishing House, Adelaide.

Brown, RJ 2014, *Thomas Vowler Short: Bishop of St Asaph 1846-1870*, author's own emailed and unpaginated copy, Tair Eglwys Press, Welshpool.

Brown SJ & Nockles, PB (eds.) 2012, *The Oxford Movement: Europe and the wider world 1830-1930*, Cambridge University Press, Cambridge.

Buckland, W 1820, *Vindiciae geologicae: Or, the connexion of geology with religion explained in an inaugural lecture before the University of Oxford*, Oxford University Press, Oxford.

Burgess, HJ 1958, *Enterprise in education*, SPCK, London.

Butler, C (ed.) 2006, *Christ Church, Oxford: A portrait of the house*, Third Millennium Publishing, London.

Butler, P 1982, *Gladstone: Church, state and Tractarianism*, Clarendon Press, Oxford.

___ (ed.) 1983, *Pusey rediscovered*, SPCK, London.

Carey, H & Gascoigne, J (eds.) 2011, *Church and state in old and new worlds*, Brill, Boston.

Carleton, JD 1965, *Westminster School: A history*, R Hart-Davis, London.

Chadwick, O 1970, *The Victorian Church*, vols. 1 & 2, Adam & Charles Black, London.

Chandos, J 1984, *Boys together, English public schools 1800-1864*, Hutchinson, London.

Church, RW 1892, *The Oxford Movement: Twelve years, 1833-1845*, Macmillan and Co., London.

Churton, E (ed.) 1863, *Memoir of Joshua Watson*, 2nd edn, John Henry and James Parker, Oxford.

Clarke, HL 1918, *The constitutions of the general, provincial and diocesan synods of the Church of England in Australia, together with an introduction to the constitutional history of the Church*, Church of England, Melbourne.

___ 1924, *Constitutional church government: In the dominions beyond the seas and in other parts of the Anglican communion*, SPCK, London.

Clarke, WKL 1959, *A history of the SPCK*, SPCK, London.

Cnattingius, H 1952, *Bishops and societies: A study of Anglican colonial and missionary expansion, 1698-1850*, SPCK, London.

Coleridge, JT 1880, *A memoir of the Rev. John Keble, MA, late vicar of Hursley*, James Parker and Co., London.

Collins, WL 1867, *The public school: Winchester, Westminster, Shrewsbury, Harrow, Rugby, notes on their history and traditions*, W Blackwood and sons, Edinburgh.

Cooper, A 1990, 'Edward Coleridge: Forgotten Australian Anglican', *Pacifica*, vol. 3, no. 3, pp. 257-268.

Cox, GV 1870, *Recollections of Oxford*, Macmillan and Co., London.

Crowther, MA 1970, *Church embattled: Religious controversy in mid-Victorian England*, David & Charles, Devon.

Curthoys, J 2012, *The Cardinal's College: Christ Church, chapter and verse*, Profile Books, London.

Deamer, P 1897, *The Cathedral Church of Oxford: A Description of its fabric and a brief history of the Episcopal see*, George Bell & Sons, London.

Donaldson, AB 1902, *Five Great Oxford leaders: Keble, Newman, Pusey, Liddon and Church*, Rivingtons, London.

Dowland, DA 1997, *Nineteenth-century Anglican theological training: The redbrick challenge*, Oxford University Press, Oxford.

Edwards, D 1978, *Leaders of the Church of England 1828-1978*, Hodder and Stoughton, London.

Engel, AJ 1983, *From clergyman to don: The rise of the academic profession in nineteenth-century Oxford*, Oxford University Press, New York.

Evans, GR 2010, *University of Oxford: A new history*, IB Tauris, London.

Faber, G 1933, *Oxford apostles: A character study of the Oxford Movement*, Faber and Faber, London.

Feiling, K 1960, *In Christ Church Hall*, Macmillan, London.

Ffoulkes, ES 1892, *A history of the Church of St Mary the Virgin, Oxford: The university church, from Domesday to the installation of the late duke of Wellington, chancellor of the university*, Longmans, Green & Co., London.

Field, J 1987, *The King's Nurseries: The story of Westminster School*, James & James, London.

Fletcher, B 2015, *An English church in Australian Soil: Anglicanism, Australian society and the English connection since 1788*, Barton Books, Canberra.

Flindall, RP (ed.) 1972, *The Church of England 1815-1948, A documentary history*, SPCK, London.

Foot, MRD (ed.) 1968, *The Gladstone diaries*, Clarendon Press, Oxford.

Forshall, FH 1884, *Westminster School past and present*, Wyman & Sons, London.

Foster, J 1887 *lumni Oxonienses: The members of the University of Oxford, 1715-1886: Their parentage, birthplace and year of birth, with a record of their degrees. Being the matriculation register of the university*, Parker, London.

Fowler, HW 1926, *A dictionary of modern English usage*, Clarendon Press, Oxford.

France, WF 1941, *The overseas episcopate: Centenary history of the Colonial Bishoprics Fund, 1841-1941*, Colonial Bishoprics Fund, London.

Gash, N 1961, *Mr. Secretary Peel: The life of Sir Robert Peel to 1830*, Longman, London.

Gill, FC (ed.) 1956, *Selected letters of John Wesley*, Epworth Press, London.

Gladstone, WE 1838, *The state in its relations with the Church*, John Murray, London.

___ 1840, *Church principles considered in their results*, John Murray, London.

Gladwin, M 2015, *Anglican clergy in Australia 1788-1850: Building a British world*, Boydell Press, London.

Gourlay, M 2015, *The good bishop: The story of Mathew Hale*, Boolarong Press, Brisbane.

Green, VHH 1974, *A history of Oxford University*, BT Batsford, London.

Harrison, B 1853, *The Church's sons brought back to her from far: A sermon preached in the cathedral church of Canterbury on Sunday, Feb. 27 1853*, Francis & John Rivington, London.

Hawkins, E 1855, *Documents relative to the erection and endowment of additional bishoprics in the colonies 1841-1855*, 5th edn, SPCK, London.

Healey, E 1978, *Lady unknown: The life of Angela Burdett-Coutts*, Sidgwick & Jackson, London.

Henley, R 1832, *A plan of Church reform*, Roake and Varity, London.

Hilliard, D 1986, *Godliness and good order: A history of the Anglican Church in South Australia*, Wakefield Press, Adelaide.

Hobbs, C 1984, *Guide to the papers of Rev. WG Broughton and family (including some papers of Rev. E Coleridge)*, Moore Theological College, Sydney.

Hurd, D 2007, *Robert Peel: A biography*, Wiedenfeld & Nicolson, London.

Hylson-Smith, K 1993, *High Churchmanship in the Church of England: From the sixteenth century to the late twentieth century*, T & T Clark, Edinburgh.

Ince, W 1878, *The past history and present duties of the faculty of theology at Oxford*, James Parker and Co., Oxford.

Ingram, J 1837, *Memorials of Oxford*, vol. 1, JH Parker, H Slatter and W Graham, Oxford.

Jenkins, R 1995, *Gladstone*, Macmillan, London.

Jose, GH 1937, *The Church of England in South Australia 1836-1856*, The Hassell Press, Adelaide.

Kaye, B (ed.) 2002, *Anglicanism in Australia: A history*, Melbourne University Press, Melbourne.

Keble, J 1914, *The Christian year: Lyra Innocentium and other poems*, Oxford University Press, London.

Kenneth, Brother 1983, *From the fathers to the Churches, daily spiritual readings*, Collins, London.

Ker, I & Gornall, T 1961, *The letters and diaries of John Henry Newman*, vol. 1, Clarendon Press, Oxford.

King, RJ 1862, *Handbook to the cathedrals of England*, John Murray, Oxford.

Knight, F 1995, *The nineteenth-century Church and English society*, Cambridge University Press, Cambridge.

___ 2008, *The Church in the nineteenth century*, IB Tauris, London.

Lathbury, DC 1905, *Dean Church*, AR Mowbray & Co., London.

Lee-Warner, J 1868, *A few words on the future of Westminster School*, James Parker & Co., London.

Lewis May, J 1933, *The Oxford Movement: Its history and its future, a layman's estimate*, John Lane the Bodley Head, London.

Liddon, HP 1894, *Life of Edward Bouverie Pusey*, vols. 1-4, Longmans, Green, and Co., London.

Lloyd, C (ed.) 1826, *The formularies of faith put forth by authority during the reign of Henry VIII*, University Press, Oxford.

___ 1838, *A catalogue of books in divinity, ecclesiastical history &c., including a fine collection of the fathers of the Church*, JH Parker, Oxford.

Lobel, M (ed.) 1962, *The Victorian county history of Oxfordshire*, vol. 7, John Hopkins Press, Baltimore.

Maclear, GF 1888, *St Augustine's, Canterbury: Its rise, ruin, and restoration*, Wells, Gardner, Darton & Co., London.

McClatchy, D 1960, *Oxfordshire clergy, 1777-1869: A study of the established Church and of the role of its clergy in local society*, Clarendon Press, Oxford.

McGrath, FJ (ed.) 2006, *The letters and diaries of John Henry Newman*, vol. 9, Oxford University Press, Oxford.

Machin, GIT 1977, *Politics and the churches in Great Britain, 1832-1868*, Clarendon Press, Oxford.

Mallet, C 1924, *A history of the University of Oxford*, Methuen, London.

Marshall, PJ (ed.) 1998, *Oxford history of the British Empire*, vol. 2, *The eighteenth century*, Oxford University Press, Oxford.

Matthew, HCG 1986, *Gladstone, 1809-1874*, Clarendon Press, Oxford.

Miller, EK 1895, *Reminiscences of forty-seven years' clerical life in South Australia*, AH Roberts, Adelaide.

Minchin, JGC 1901, *Our public schools: Their influence on English history*, Swan Sonnenschein & Co., London.

Moberly, CAE 1911, *Dulce Domum, George Moberly, his family and friends*, John Murray, London.

Moberly, G 1834, *A few remarks on the proposed admission of Dissenters into the University of Oxford*, JH Parker, Oxford.

___ 1845, *The proposed degradation and declaration: Considered in a letter to the Rev. the master of Balliol College*, JH Parker, Oxford.

Morley, J 1908, *The life of William Ewart Gladstone*, Edward Lloyd Limited, London.

Mozley, A (ed.) 1890, *Letters and correspondence of John Henry Newman during his life in the English Church*, Longmans, Green, and Co, London.

Mozley, T 1882, *Reminiscences: Chiefly of Oriel College and the Oxford Movement*, Longmans, Green & Co., London.

Naylor, LGR 1962, 'Culham through the looking glass, a peep into the past', *Culham village, Oxfordshire*, viewed 2 November 2015, http://www.culhamvillage.org.uk.

Newman, JH 1841, *Remarks on certain passages in the thirty-nine articles*, JGF and J Rivington, London.

___ 1890, *Tract XC: On certain passages in the XXXIX articles (1841) with a historical preface by EB Pusey (1865), and the case of Catholic subscription to the XXXIX articles considered in reference to Tract XC, by J Keble (1841)*, Walter Smith and Innes, London.

Nockles, P 1994, *The Oxford Movement in context: Anglican High Churchmanship, 1760-1857*, Cambridge University Press, Cambridge.

Norris, W 1852, *Annals of the diocese of Adelaide*, SPCK, London.

Oakeley, F 1855, *Personal reminiscences of the 'Oxford Movement', with illustrations from Dr Newman's 'Loss and Gain'*, Henry Teulon, Islington.

___ 1865, *Historical notes on the Tractarian Movement 1833-1845*, Longman, Green, Longman, Roberts and Green, London.

Ollard, SL 1925, *The Anglo-Catholic revival: Some persons and principles*, AR Mowbray & Co., London.

Orton, D 1980, *Made of gold: A biography of Angela Burdett-Coutts*, Hamish Hamilton, London.

Palmer, W 1845, *Origines Liturgicae or antiquities of the English ritual and dissertation on primitive liturgies*, 4th edn, Francis and John Rivington, London.

Pantin, WA 1972, *Oxford life in Oxford archives*, Clarendon Press, Oxford.

Pattison, M 1885, *Memoirs*, Macmillan and Co., London.

Peel, R & Minchin, HC 1906, *Oxford*, Macmillan, New York.

Prest, J (ed.) 1993, *The Illustrated history of Oxford University*, Oxford University Press, London.

Quiller-Couch, LM 1892, *Reminiscences of Oxford by Oxford men, 1559-1850*, Clarendon Press, Oxford.

Richardson, HH 1930, *The fortunes of Richard Mahoney*, Text Classics, Melbourne.

Robin, A de Q 1976, *Mathew Blagden Hale: The life of an Australian pioneer bishop*, The Hawthorn Press, Melbourne.

Rogers, JET 1861, *Education in Oxford: Its methods, its aids, and its rewards*, Smith, Elder and Co., London.

Sargeaunt, J 1898, *Annals of Westminster School*, Methuen & Co., London.

Shaw, GP 1978, *Patriarch and patriot: William Grant Broughton 1788-1853 Colonial statesman and ecclesiastic*, Melbourne University Press, Melbourne.

Shore, WT 1910, *Public school life: Westminster*, Sir Isaac Pitman & Sons, London.

Short, A 1838, *Sermons intended principally to illustrate the remedial character of the Christian scheme, with reference to man's fallen condition: Preached at Oxford before the university*, J H Parker, Oxford.

___ 1846, *The witness of the Spirit with our spirit, illustrated from the eighth chapter of St Paul's Epistle to the Romans; and the heresies Montanus Pelagius, in eight sermons preached before the University of Oxford in the year MDCCCXLVI*, JH Parker, Oxford.

Short, TV 1822, *A letter addressed to the Very Reverend the dean of Christ Church on the state of the public examinations in the University of Oxford*, J Parker, Oxford.

___ 1829, *Sermons on some of the fundamental truths of Christianity*, J Parker and J Rivington, London.

___ 1832, *A sketch of the history of the Church of England to the revolution of 1688, with a sketch of the life of Bishop Short*, 9th edn, 1875, Longman, Green & Co, London.

___ 1835, *National education and the means of improving it*, John W Parker, London.

___ 1841, *Letters to an aged mother, by a clergyman [i.e. TV Short]*, RB Seeley and W Burnside, London.

___ 1847, *On the management of a parish: Of Sunday Schools: And the method of preparing catechumens for examination*, J Parker, London.

Smith, A 1971, *The established Church and popular religion 1750-1850*, Longman, London.

Smyth, C 1955, *Church and parish: Studies in church problems*, SPCK, London.

Staunton, H 1865, *The great schools of England: An account of the foundation, endowments, and discipline of the chief seminaries of learning in England*, Sampson Low, Son, and Marston, London.

Strong, R 2007, *Anglicanism and the British Empire c.1700-1850*, Oxford University Press, Oxford.

Strong, R 2012, 'The Oxford Movement and the British Empire: Newman, Manning and the 1841 Jerusalem Bishopric', in SJ Brown & PB Nockles (eds.), *The Oxford Movement: Europe and the wider world, 1830-1930*, Cambridge University Press, Cambridge.

Symonds, E 1898, *The story of the Australian Church*, SPCK, London.

Symondson, A (ed.) 1970, *The Victorian crisis of faith*, SPCK, London.

Tait, AC 1845, *A letter to the Rev. the vice-chancellor of the University of Oxford on the measures intended to be proposed to Convocation on the 13th of February*, William Blackwood and Sons, London.

Tanner, LE 1934, *Westminster School: A history*, Country Life Ltd., London.

Thomas, DR 1874, *A history of the diocese of St Asaph: General, cathedral, and parochial*, James Parker & Co., London.

Thompson, HL 1899, *Henry George Liddell: DD Dean of Christ Church, Oxford, a memoir*, John Murray, London.

___ 1900, *Christ Church*, FE Robinson & Co, London.

Thompson, HP 1951, *Into all lands: The history of the Society for the Propagation of the Gospel in Foreign Parts, 1701-1950*, SPCK, London.

Thornbury, W 1892, *Old and New London*, vol. 3, Cassell Limited, London.

Tracey, G 1995, *The letters and diaries of John Henry Newman*, vol. 7, Clarendon Press, Oxford.

Tristram, H (ed.) 1956, *John Henry Newman autobiographical writings*, Sheed and Ward, London.

Tuckwell, W 1908, *Reminiscences of Oxford*, EP Dutton, New York.

Vaiss, P (ed.) 1996, *From Oxford to the people: Reconsidering Newman & the Oxford Movement*, Gracewing, Herefordshire.

Ward, K 2006, *A history of global Anglicanism*, Cambridge University Press, Cambridge.

Ward, WG 1889, *William George Ward and the Oxford Movement*, Macmillan and Co., London.

Ward, WR 1965, *Victorian Oxford*, Frank Cass & Co., London.

Welch, J 1852, *The list of the queen's scholars of St Peter's College, Westminster: Admitted on that foundation since 1633; and of such as have been thence elected to Christ Church Oxford, and Trinity College, Cambridge, from the foundation by Queen Elizabeth, 1561, to the present time*, GW Ginger, London.

Welch, PJ 1961, 'Blomfield and Peel: A study in co-operation between Church and state, 1841-1846', *Journal of Ecclesiastical History*, vol. 12, pp. 71-84.

Westminster School 2016a,'Independent Boarding and Day School', The Registrar, Westminster School, Little Dean's Yard, London

Westminster School 2016b, 'Further information, 2015-2016', Admissions Department, Westminster School, Little Dean's Yard, London.

Whiting, M 2014, *Augustus Short and the founding of the University of Adelaide*, Barr Smith Press, Adelaide.

Whitington, FT 1887, *Augustus Short, first bishop of Adelaide: A chapter of colonial Church history*, Frederick Taylor, Adelaide.

___ 1936, *William Grant Broughton: Bishop of Australia*, Angus & Robertson, Sydney.

Wilson, JM 1870, *The imperial gazetteer of England and Wales, embracing recent changes in counties, diocese, parishes and boroughs: General statistics, postal arrangements, railway systems &c., and forming a complete description of the country*, A Fullarton, Edinburgh.

Wolffe, J 1994, *God and Greater Britain: Religion and national life in Britain and Ireland 1843-1945*, Routledge, London.

___ 2006, *The expansion of Evangelicalism: The age of Wilberforce, More Chalmers and Finney*, Inter-Varsity Press, Nottingham.

South Australian Parliamentary Papers [SAPP] and Debates [SAPD]

SAPP, *Report of The Select Committee of the House of Assembly, Appointed to report upon a System of Education*, Parl. Paper No. 131 (23 August 1861).

Archives

Christ Church Archives [CCA]

___ Dean's Admission Book, DP i.a.6.
___ Censors' Papers, Cen 1.a.4.
___ Collections Book, li.5.b.

Flinders University Library [FUL]

___ Lefroy, E 1832, Letter to Augustus Short, St Barnabas Collection.
___ Short, A & Coleridge, E 1847, Bishop Short's first letter book, microfilm of notebook of copies of letters sent by Bishop Short between 1846-51, State Library of South Australia, Adelaide.

Lambeth Palace Library [LPL]

___ Burdett-Coutts Papers, MSS 1384/1-2, 1846-7.
___ Burdett-Coutts Papers, MSS 1384/5-6, 1846-7.
___ Burdett-Coutts Papers, MSS 1384/33, 1846-7.

National Library of Australia [NLA]

___ Australian Joint Copying Project [AJCP], Miscellaneous M series/1517-1534.
___ Short A 1847, *The (United) diocese of South and Western Australia*, Rex Nan Kivell Collection NK4183.
___ Woodcock, Rev. WJ 1848, 'Journal', *Quarterly Paper No. XLVII*, October 1848, Society for the Propagation of the Gospel in Foreign Parts, Rex Nan Kivell Collection, NK5226.

State Library of South Australia [SLSA]

___ PRG 160/1, Diary of Augustus Short, 5 vols., February-April, July-August 1834, 1852-59, 1867-69 and one undated vol.
___ PRG 160/2, Extracts from Augustus Short's diary and letters, 1847-80.
___ PRG 160/7, Reminiscences of Augustus Short covering the years 1820-47, written in 1882.
___ PRG 160/25, *The Mission field*, a monthly record of the proceedings of the Society

for the Propagation of the Gospel at home and abroad, vol. 22, 1 March 1882.
___ PRG 160/32, Reminiscences of Charles Short (father of Augustus Short).
___ PRG 160/38, Bishop Short's first letter book: A notebook of copies of letters sent by Bishop Short between 1846-51.
___ PRG 160/47, Extract copied from Hampshire paper re support of missionaries in the diocese of Adelaide.
___ PRG 160/81, Copies of letters to, from and about Augustus Short, 1847-77, copies made by Mr KT Borrow in 1965.

Newspapers and periodicals

'Address to Miss Burdett Coutts' 1847, *The Colonial Church Chronicle and Missionary Journal*, 3 July, vol. 1, 1847-48, p. 187.

'The Bishop of London's Sermon' 1847, *The Colonial Church Chronicle, and Missionary Journal*, July, vol. 1, 1847-48, p. 56.

'Bishops of Adelaide and Newcastle' 1847, *The Colonial Church Chronicle and Missionary Journal*, October, vol. 1, 1847-48, p. 156.

'Clergy for the Colonies' 1847, *Sydney Morning Herald*, Saturday 30 October, p. 3.

'Consecration of Colonial Bishops' 1847, *The Colonial Church Chronicle and Missionary Journal*, August, vol. 1, 1847-48, pp. 41-46.

'English News' 1847, *Port Phillip Patriot and Morning Advertiser*, Monday 20 September, p. 3.

'The English News' 1847, *Sydney Morning Herald*, 27 July, p. 2.

'Farewell Letters of the Bishops of Adelaide and Melbourne' 1847, *The Colonial Church Chronicle and Missionary Journal*, September, vol. 1, 1847-48, pp. 188-189.

'Home News' 1847, *South Australian*, Tuesday 2 November, p. 3.

'Official Notification of Colonial Bishoprics', Government Gazette, 28 June 1847, London (reprinted 9 November in the *Geelong Advertiser*, p. 2).

'The Oxford Movement Centenary Prayer' 1933, *Waiapu Church Gazette*, 1 July, p. 2.

'The Report of the Synod of the Diocese of Adelaide' 1869, *South Australian Advertiser*, 27 May, p. 2.

'The Rise and Progress of the Colonial Episcopate' 1847, *The Colonial Church Chronicle, and Missionary Journal*, July, vol. 1, 1847-48, pp. 6-11.

Short, A 1869, 'Letter to the Editor', *South Australian Register*, 11 March, p. 3.

Smith, S 1810, 'Remarks on the System of Education in Public Schools', *Edinburgh Review*, vol. XVI, pp. 326-333.

South Australian Church Society 1846, 'Manifesto', *South Australian Gazette and Register*, 5 September 1846, p. 1.

Legislation

British legislation

Church Building Act 1818 (58 Geo. 3 c. 45).
Church Temporalities Act 1833.
Bishops in Foreign Countries Act 1841 (5 Vict. c. 6).
Corporation Act 1661.
Pluralities Act 1838 (Chapter 106).
Representation of the People Act 1832.
Roman Catholic Relief Act 1829.
Test Act 1673.

Colonial legislation

Church Act 1836 (7 GUI.IV, No.3).

Index of selected terms

A

Adelaide, Diocese of   98, 131-42, 145, 147, 153
Arnold, Thomas (1795-1842)   43, 76, 84-7, 109, 134

B

Blomfield, Bishop Charles (1786-1857)   116-24, 126, 131, 134, 143
Book of Common Prayer   31, 55, 57-8, 69, 87, 94, 105, 127, 130, 141, 147
British and Foreign Schools Society   83, 97
Broughton, Bishop William Grant (1788-1853)   120-3, 125, 128, 133, 142-4
Bull, Reverend Henry (1798-1884)   11, 28, 34, 107, 157-8
Burdett Coutts, Angela (1814-1906)   125-31, 134, 144-7

C

Christ Church Deans
    Gaisford (1779-1855)   46, 65-8, 112
    Hall (1763-1827)   31-2, 34, 39
    Jackson (1746-1819)   21, 30-1, 33, 62-3, 74
    Smith (1765-1841)   39, 62, 65

Coleridge, Reverend Edward (1800-83)   120-3, 125-30, 136-41, 143
Colonial Bishoprics' Fund   117-9, 123-4, 126, 131, 144
Culham   60-2, 68, 155

D

Denison, Archdeacon George (1805-96)   98

E

Evangelicals   75, 81-2, 105

G

Gawler, George   140, 141
Gladstone, William Ewart (1809-98)   XI, 40-1, 52, 64, 98, 102, 110, 116, 118-9, 124, 128, 144-5

H

Hale, Archdeacon Mathew Blagden (1811-95)   139
Harrison, Archdeacon Benjamin (1808-87)   129, 132-3
Hawkins, Reverend Ernest (1802-68)   115, 118, 128-9, 134, 136, 138, 147
Henley, Lord (1789-1841)   69, 83-6, 89

Howley, Archbishop William
(1766-1848)   14, 114-5, 117-8,
123-4, 130-5

K

Keble, Reverend John (1792-1866)   40,
53, 77, 71, 88-91, 102, 104, 121

L

Lloyd, Bishop Charles (1784-1829)   XI,
35-6, 43, 51-62, 74, 76-7, 91, 94,
101, 106, 112-3

M

Methodists   73, 79, 81
Miller, Reverend Edmund King
(1820-1911)   137-8

N

National Society   61, 82, 97
Newman, Reverend John Henry
(1801-90)   XI, 23, 40, 45, 53, 55,
59, 63, 76-7, 81, 89-93, 103-7, 111-3

O

Oakeley, Reverend Frederick
(1802-80)   23, 27-8, 31-2, 34,
38-40, 55, 59
Oxford Movement   XI, 60, 81, 88, 90-1,
94, 99
Library of The Fathers   91-93
Tracts for the Times   90

P

Parliamentary Acts
Church Building Act 1818   82
Roman Catholic Relief Act 1829   52,
77
Representation of the People Act 1832
('*Reform Act*')   98
Church Temporalities Act 1833   86,
89
Pluralities Act 1838   93
Bishops in Foreign Countries Act 1841
('*Colonial Bishoprics Act*')119
Peel, Robert (1788-1850)   21, 52, 74-77,
83, 102, 116, 124
Phillips, Millicent Clara
(1811?-1900)   62, 68
proctor   24, 37, 38-40, 106, 110-1, 155
Pusey, Edward Bouverie (1800-82)   XI,
33-4, 40, 51, 55-6, 59-60, 81, 86,
89-94, 102-4, 110, 113, 120, 122

R

Ravensthorpe   67-8, 92, 95-6, 98-102,
111, 132-5, 137-8, 141, 153-4, 155
Robe, Frederick   136

S

Short, Charles (1764-1837)   3, 7
Short, Thomas Vowler (1790-1872)   XI,
5, 11, 15, 17-8, 21, 33-41, 43, 53,
60-2, 65, 74, 76, 91, 94, 101, 106,
112-3, 118-9, 133, 139, 145, 155
Society for Promoting Christian
Knowledge (SPCK)   116, 118,
132-3, 137, 140
Society for the Propagation of the Gospel
in Foreign Parts   115, 118, 127, 141,
144
South Australian Church Society   131,
136
Swainson, Reverend Charles
(1796-1871)   106, 108-9, 134, 146

T

Tait, Reverend Archibald Campbell
(1811-1882)   66, 108-10, 133-134, 145

Thirty-Nine Articles of Religion   31, 36, 41, 50, 105-6, 108

U

United Church of England and
Ireland   XIII, 1, 21, 51, 54, 78-80, 84, 86, 90, 97-8, 116-7, 120, 122, 127-8, 130-1, 136, 142, 146

University of Oxford
Convocation   39, 41, 67, 74-5, 77, 80, 102, 104, 108, 110-1, 134
The Sheldonian   67, 110

W

Ward, Reverend William George
(1812-82)   53, 108-11, 134-5

Westminster Abbey   3, 7, 9, 11, 45, 131, 142-3

Woodcock, Reverend William James
(1808-68)   131, 136-7

Acknowledgements

I remain most grateful to Dr John Emerson, director, and Rebecca Burton, Zoë Stokes and Julia Keller of the University of Adelaide Press. Their professionalism and interest, and delightful companionship, are the main reason this book has been successfully published.

I am thankful to the Very Reverend Professor Martyn Percy, dean of Christ Church Oxford, whose friendship and encouragement has assisted in one of Christ Church's own being honoured in this way. I am in debt to Judith Curthoys, archivist of Christ Church, who was always so pleasant and ready to seek resources and to inform.

Mr Patrick Derham, headmaster of Westminster School, and Elizabeth Wells, archivist and records manager at Westminster, were enthusiastic and supportive of this project and I appreciated this greatly.

Dr David Hilliard, OAM, willingly shared his exceptional and extensive knowledge of Church history in his review of this publication and I thank him for this.

I acknowledge the interest and support of the former vice-chancellor of the University of Adelaide, Professor Warren Bebbington. He was foremost in recognising the unique contribution Augustus Short made to education in South Australia, especially as the key founder, and the first vice-chancellor, of the University of Adelaide in 1874.

This book is available as a free fully searchable ebook from
www.adelaide.edu.au/press

www.ingramcontent.com/pod-product-compliance
Lightning Source LLC
Chambersburg PA
CBHW042033100526
44587CB00029B/4412